BLACK PERFORMANCE AND CULTURAL CRITICISM
Valerie Lee and E. Patrick Johnson, Series Editors

CONTEMPORARY BLACK WOMEN FILMMAKERS

AND THE

ART OF RESISTANCE

CHRISTINA N. BAKER

THE OHIO STATE UNIVERSITY PRESS

COLUMBUS

Library of Congress Cataloging-in-Publication Data is available online at https://catalog.
loc.gov.

Cover design by Regina Starace
Text design by Juliet Williams
Type set in Adobe Minion Pro

For the women in my family—
especially my mother, Jerri Anne Lovingood,
and in loving memory of my grandmother, Helen Baker.

CONTENTS

ACKNOWLEDGMENTS

I HAVE ALWAYS considered myself to be more of a pragmatist than an artist, so I'm impressed by women who are more imaginative than I am. It is with this fascination that I approached this book about Black women filmmakers. My interest in the magic and power of films started at a very young age, and I have my family to thank for introducing me to a broad range of movies that planted the seed for my growing interest in film as a vehicle to engage and inspire viewers.

Because this is a book about Black women, first and foremost, I want to thank all of the women in my family, who have demonstrated creativity and courage throughout their lives in various ways. Above all, thank you to my mom, Jerri Anne Lovingood. I would not have started or completed this book had you not routinely told me and shown me, by example and through your encouraging words, that I have the ability to do anything that I set my mind to. You have always believed in me, and you always know what to say when my belief in myself begins to waver. To Gloria Baker, my bonus mom—I'm so glad that you are part of our family. Thank you for being there for us all. Thank you also to my grandmothers, Gretchen and Helen, who instilled in all of us a love of learning for its own sake, and to my bonus grandmother, Joann.

To my impressively smart and beautiful sisters, Danielle, Alicia, and Jordan, who I am eternally grateful to also call my best friends. We have all spent countless hours talking about films, family, and everything in between. Danielle, there is perhaps no one else I have watched more movies with (sometimes even attempting to act them out!). You are all among my most important reviewers. I'm thankful that each of you was there to listen to me talk about this book before it actually became a book, and then to read parts of the book once it began to take shape. And, to my niece Makayla—you inspire me with your enthusiasm and persistent search for answers and information.

I am lucky to belong to a family of supportive men. Thank you to my dad, Mitchell Baker, for teaching me the value of resilience. I have learned a lot from your rare blend of strength, kindness, devotion, and fortitude. Thank you to my wonderful grandfathers, Mitchell and Kenneth. To my brothers, Aaron and Samuel, I'm encouraged to see the tremendously talented and caring young men that you have become. And to my thoughtful nephew, Brandon—I'm looking forward to seeing how you continue to positively impact the world.

It was a privilege for me to interview three awe-inspiring Black women filmmakers for this book. Thank you, Tanya Hamilton, Kasi Lemmons, and Gina Prince-Bythewood. You are all skillful storytellers, whose voices are as unique as they are powerful and poignant. I wrote this book not only as a scholar but as a fan, as a tribute to your inspirational work. Thank you, also, to Jake Hollander and Joyce Sherri, who helped coordinate and schedule the interviews that I completed for this book.

Thank you to Sonoma State University (SSU) and the faculty in the American Multicultural Studies (AMCS) department—Mike Ezra, Leny Strobel, and Kim Hester Williams. Thank you, especially, to Kim and Mike for reading parts of this book at various stages in the writing process. Kim, if it were not for your encouragement, it's very possible that I would not have sent this book out for review and publication. There were so many times when you somehow knew what I needed to hear, without me having to say a word. I cannot thank you enough for your straightforward, yet indispensable, advice about writing and publishing. Thank you, not only for rooting for me, but for also providing your invaluable feedback on parts of this book. You are an incredible scholar and artist. Mike, I will always be thankful to you for seeing potential in me several years ago, when being a college professor was still an unrealized goal of mine. I have a great deal of respect for the dedication that you have continuously shown toward your work. I appreciate all that you have done for SSU and AMCS, as well as the crucial feedback that you provided on sections of this book. Your insightful comments influenced a lot of the work that I put into this project and I am extremely grateful to have had your advice.

I have been fortunate to get to know other faculty and staff at SSU who have contributed in different ways to me persisting in the face of challenges. To

Ajay Gehlawat, a true cinephile—your enthusiasm for film is contagious and I greatly appreciate your enormously helpful thoughts on this project. Thank you to Leny Strobel, who was instrumental in helping me move through the tenure process, along with Kim Hester Williams, Patricia Kim Rajal, Charlene Tung, and Elizabeth Martinez. Thank you to Kathy Charmaz, who motivated and guided me and many other faculty through the writing process as the director of the Faculty Writing Program. I also truly value the warm welcome and helpful advice that I have received from the very beginning from Erma Jean Simms, Eli Galvez-Hard, Chuck Rhodes, and Daniel Malpica (and others!). Thank you to Linnea Mullins for all you do for AMCS, and to the amazing librarians and library staff whom I visited repeatedly while writing this book. Thank you to Sonoma State, also, for supporting this project through a sabbatical as well as a research grant that allowed me to devote the necessary time and energy to work on this book.

Thank you to my professors, classmates, and friends in the Sociology Departments at UC Irvine and UCLA. To Belinda Robnett—a kind and inspiring scholar and role model whom I am grateful to have had the opportunity to learn from. Thank you for taking me under your wing as your research assistant and for the numerous ways that you have supported me since then. I also appreciated the friendship and collegiality of Monica, Ting, Makiko, Charlie, Jessica, Kristine, and Sandrine at UC Irvine. Monica Trieu, I really appreciate a useful recommendation that you gave me recently, as I was working on this book. While attending UCLA, I also benefited greatly from the support and guidance of my cousin Donna Armstrong, whose knowledge and experience I continue to benefit from to this day.

A tremendous thanks to everyone I worked with at The Ohio State University Press. Thank you, Kristen Elias Rowley, for your support of this book, for your adept handling of the editing process, and for answering all of the questions that I had. I am also hugely appreciative of the support of the editors of the Black Performance and Cultural Criticism series, Valerie Lee and E. Patrick Johnson. And I am grateful to two anonymous reviewers, who provided very valuable feedback that helped strengthen this book.

I am deeply indebted to Alicia Grey, my unofficial copy editor and my sister (*officially*). Your sharp eye and editing skills were extremely useful in helping me pinpoint some of the details that I missed in my writing and proofreading. I appreciate your thorough and thoughtful comments as well as our enjoyable and productive discussions.

Thank you to my husband, Eric, for being by my side through this all. Thank you also for being the very first person to read this book in its entirety, for offering your very discerning eye for proofreading, for listening to all of my questions and monologues as I thought through each chapter, and for taking all of those father-son trips to the park when I needed just a little more time to write.

And, finally, to Dean. My little artist. My *biggest* inspiration. May you always keep your inquisitiveness, creativity, and passion for life as you grow. Thank you for making me laugh every day and, most of all, for choosing me to be your mom.

Becoming Visible

WHEN I TEACH film courses, I usually find myself in classrooms with students who are, like me, passionate about movies, with strong opinions about the films they have seen. Yet, for most of the last decade, there is one topic of discussion that elicits more questions than answers from my students: Black filmmakers. When I ask students to name and discuss Black filmmakers, many often have difficulty coming up with names other than Spike Lee or Tyler Perry. Every so often John Singleton's name has come up, but Black women filmmakers have generally been overlooked in these discussions. Although the gender imbalance in the number of filmmakers in Hollywood is significant, with males dominating the field,[1] students are actually *not* unfamiliar with the films of Black women. In fact, *Love & Basketball* (2000) has been one of the more popular films that I screen in class. Students often recognize and eagerly anticipate the film when they see it on the course syllabus. Yet, despite their familiarly with *Love & Basketball*, they do not usually know that Gina Prince-Bythewood wrote and directed it. What has always struck me is the sharp contrast between their level of familiarity with the film and the near-invisibility of the woman who is responsible for the film. In a sense, Black women filmmakers have been hiding in plain sight. Their work is visible, but they are not. These women have not received the recognition they deserve.

---

1. Smith, Pieper, and Choueiti, "Inclusion in the Director's Chair? Gender, Race, & Age of Film Directors Across 1,000 Films from 2007–2016."

This marginalization of Black women in Hollywood took center stage on the fourth season of HBO's television show *Project Greenlight,* when Effie Brown, an experienced producer behind the films *Real Women Have Curves* (2002) and *Dear White People* (2014), appeared on the show. *Project Greenlight* was a reality show produced by renowned actors Ben Affleck and Matt Damon, which chronicled the making of an independent film by a novice filmmaker. Each season, Damon and Affleck led a team of professionals responsible for selecting a first-time filmmaker to make a film. During the 2015 season premiere, Brown, Damon, Affleck, and the rest of the selection committee were discussing the individuals they had chosen as finalists to direct a film in which the only Black character is a prostitute who gets hit by her pimp. "I just want to bring up something up . . . I just want to urge people to think about whoever the director is, the way that they're going to treat the character of Harmony. Her being a prostitute. The only Black person being a hooker who gets hit by her White pimp . . ." begins Ms. Brown. However, Ms. Brown, a Black woman and the only person of color in the room, is quickly (and repeatedly) interrupted by Matt Damon, who explains to her that the race of the person chosen to direct the film is insignificant. "When you're talking about diversity, you do it in the casting of the film," he insists, using his position of privilege to silence Ms. Brown, as he ironically suggests that the identity of the people in positions of power on a film is insignificant. At that point, Ms. Brown appears stunned ("Whoo! Wow. Okay," she responds) and attempts to maintain her composure.

Effie Brown's interaction with Matt Damon is a microcosm of the larger battle in which Black women engage in order to be heard. To be truly listened to. Although prior to her appearance on *Project Greenlight* Effie Brown had received a degree in film production and theater and produced several feature films, her credentials and experience did not prevent the devaluation of her contribution. After the episode of *Project Greenlight* aired, Effie Brown explained her thought process during the exchange with Matt Damon in an interview for the *Washington Post*: "Do you possibly get publicly humiliated by your peers or people who you want desperately to be your peers? Or do you turn your back on your mother, your grandmother, your family that brought you up, the women that surround you? My mother won out."[2]

Brown's reference to her mother, grandmother, and other women who played significant roles in her life is her declaration of the importance of these women. By challenging others to consider the way a Black woman character is presented, she is speaking up for generations of Black women. She is giv-

---

2. McDonald, "Effie Brown Challenged Matt Damon. Now She's Ready to Challenge an Entire Industry."

ing them a voice, as she herself is fighting to be heard. This is what feminist scholar and cultural critic bell hooks refers to as an "act of resistance." For Black women, "true speaking is not solely an expression of creative power; it is an act of resistance, a political gesture that challenges politics of domination that would render us nameless and voiceless."[3]

The goal of this book is to make visible the ways that contemporary Black women filmmakers engage in acts of resistance through their filmmaking. To apply bell hooks's language again, these filmmakers are "talking back"[4] to the mainstream representations of Black femaleness. Representation is key in how we understand the world because "we give things meaning by how we *represent* them—the words we use about them, the stories we tell about them, the images of them we produce."[5] Black women filmmakers use film as a creative form of expression to reconstruct meaning and disrupt the unidimensional images that attempt to control their experiences and opportunities. Black women filmmakers are doing what other filmmakers in Hollywood have not. They use the artistic medium of film to resist the objectification and oppression of Black women by "identifying themselves as subjects, by defining their reality, shaping their new identity, naming their history, telling their story."[6]

The use of artistic expression as a form of resistance by Black women is not new. Black women artists have engaged in acts of resistance for decades, through their writing, visual art, and documentary filmmaking, for instance.[7] However, all too often, when the creative written works of Black women are adapted for film, their vision is *re*envisioned by male filmmakers and then presented to audiences as representing Black women's points of view. Ntozake Shange's *for colored girls who have considered suicide / when the rainbow is enuf,* Alice Walker's *The Color Purple,* Terry McMillan's *Waiting to Exhale,* and Sapphire's *Push* (retitled *Precious* for film) were all directed by men when these stories were adapted for the big screen.[8] In an essay, scholar Imani Perry

---

3. hooks, *Talking Back.*

4. Ibid.

5. Hall, Evans, and Nixon, *Representation,* xix.

6. hooks, *Talking Back,* 43.

7. Bambara, *The Black Woman;* Alexander, "Forward: In Search of Kathleen Collins"; Collins, Crawford, and Nelson, *New Thoughts on the Black Arts Movement;* Giddings, *When and Where I Enter;* Guy-Sheftall, *Words of Fire;* Walker, *Anything We Love Can Be Saved.*

8. Tyler Perry directed the 2010 film *For Colored Girls;* Steven Spielberg directed the 1985 film *The Color Purple;* Forest Whitaker directed the 1995 film *Waiting to Exhale;* Lee Daniels directed the 2009 film *Precious: Based on the Novel Push by Sapphire.*

recounts a conversation that she had with filmmaker Julie Dash, which high-lights the potential for a writer's work to be co-opted by a film director:

> She [Dash] warned me that if I wrote a screenplay I'd better direct the movie myself if I wanted the substance to be intact once it was completed. In giving me this warning, she was testifying as to the degrees of ownership of art, the interaction between words and image, and the importance of black female self-articulation in a colonized media.[9]

Once the work of the Black women writers has been adapted by a male film director, it undoubtedly reflects a male perspective of the work, rather than Black female self-articulation.

Although Black women using art as a form of resistance is not new, what *is* relatively new is that contemporary Black women filmmakers engage in cre-ative acts of resistance that are taking the form of commercially released fea-ture films, in which they exercise the vast majority of creative control as writer and director. These filmmakers resist dominant narratives that rely on familiar one-dimensional stereotypes of Black women. Their representations of Black femaleness in theatrically released narrative feature films challenge what film scholar Ed Guerrero describes as "Hollywood's unceasing efforts to frame blackness."[10] In her essay "Language and the Writer," author, social activist, and documentary filmmaker Toni Cade Bambara argued that there are alter-native forms of cinema in the United States that "challenge the notion that there is only one way to make a film: Hollywood style . . . Within that move-ment, there is an alternative wing in this country that is devoted to the notion of socially responsible cinema, that is interested in exploring the potential of cinema for social transformation."[11] Though written decades ago, the senti-ment of her statement is valid today. Contemporary Black women filmmakers challenge Hollywood conventions and explore the potential of film for social transformation; however, the transformative work of several Black women filmmakers is now viewed in theaters across the country.

In *More Beautiful and More Terrible: The Embrace and Transcendence of Racial Inequality in the United States*, Imani Perry offers an innovative approach to thinking about racial inequality, as well as possibilities for social transforma-

---

9. Perry, *Prophets of the Hood*, 189.
10. Guerrero, *Framing Blackness*, 3.
11. Bambara, *Deep Sightings & Rescue Missions*, 141.

tion. Perry calls into question a belief that is all too common, even among those who recognize the fallacy of the perception that we are living in a post-racial society. She challenges the idea that "racism is no longer practiced and that the inequality that we see today can be largely attributed to the legacy of our racist past."[12] While she acknowledges that history has shaped the present, Perry insists that contemporary racial inequality cannot be attributed *solely* to the legacy of our racist past. "The practice of racial inequality is sustained. It is sustained in ways that are important for the maintenance of inequality."[13]

Perry argues that within the continuing and ever-evolving practices that maintain inequality, there also exists the ability to transform this inequality into equality. "Shifting narratives," she explains, is an essential practice of moving toward racial equality. "Narrative shifting is both an internal and external process. It is both about choosing to tell a story different from the one currently dominant about racial groups and about engaging in practices that are expressive of that shifted narrative."[14] She specifies that this shift requires the involvement of those who are the targets of racist practices, as well as those who are not: "From within communities, this is a practice of intentional identity formation. External to communities, it is an acknowledgement of life-worlds outside of the terms of the historic constructions of race."[15]

In this book, I argue that contemporary Black women filmmakers engage in the very practice of narrative shifting that Perry describes as being fundamental to a society in which equality is possible. The filmmakers that are the focus of this book actively choose to create and share stories about Black women that are unlike those that are typically produced by the mainstream. Black women creating films with multidimensional Black women characters at the center are acts of intentional identity formation. That their films are commercially distributed for the general public represents the external acknowledgment of their counter-narratives about Black femaleness.

Why focus on Black women filmmakers? Why not Black women television writers and directors? Put simply, the cultural power and reach of the cinematic narrative and image is unparalleled. There is an unmatched ability for films to draw in and impact the viewer: "In the darkness of the theater most audiences choose to give themselves over, if only for a time, to the images depicted and the imaginations that have created those images."[16] Neverthe-

---

12. Perry, *More Beautiful and More Terrible*, 5.
13. Ibid., 5.
14. Ibid., 188.
15. Ibid.
16. hooks, *Reel to Real*, 4.

less, if you own a television set (perhaps even if you do not), it is difficult to miss the visibility and success of Shonda Rhimes, creator and showrunner of the popular television series *Grey's Anatomy* and *Scandal*. Rhimes has been credited for "diversifying" television through the multiracial ensemble casts of her shows.[17] An important distinction between these television shows and films is that although Rhimes does exercise a considerable amount of power as the showrunner, the range of people involved in a television series is much broader than in a film. In fact, the list of people who have written and directed the numerous episodes of each "ShondaLand" television series is too long to list here. By comparison, the medium of film is one in which the vision of the writer/director plays an especially significant role in shaping the narrative.

In the remaining chapters of this book, I analyze the cinematic constructions of Black womanhood in six feature films that were written *and* directed by Black women filmmakers. Each film included in my analysis is a narrative film, based on an original screenplay, and released theatrically in the United States.[18] Although several talented Black women have written and directed films that did not have a commercial theatrical release,[19] I focus my analysis on theatrically released narrative feature films because of the cultural cachet and ideological significance that these types of films carry. Additionally, some Black women filmmakers have directed feature films that someone else wrote,[20] most notably, Martinique-native Euzhan Palcy was the first Black woman to direct a film for a major film studio (*A Dry White Season,* 1989); however, my goal is to focus on films in which Black women's perspectives informed the majority of the creative process, as director *and* writer of an original screenplay. Referencing a statement made by Toni Morrison, Alice Walker explains, "I write not only what I want to read—understanding fully and indelibly that if I don't do it no one else is so vitally interested, or capable of doing it to my satisfaction—I write all the things *I should have been able to*

---

17. Joseph, "Strategically Ambiguous Shonda Rhimes."

18. Although Black women filmmakers from outside of the United States have made important contributions to film, such as British filmmaker Amma Asante (*A Way of Life,* 2004), I focus my analysis on films that were distributed within the United States. Because race is a socially constructed category, the dominant ideologies associated with "Black womanhood" that are central to my analysis are embedded within the U.S. cultural context.

19. Tina Mabry's *Mississippi Damned* (2009) and Victoria Mahoney's *Yelling to the Sky* (2011), for instance, are recent films that were written and directed by a Black woman that were not distributed theatrically.

20. For example, Maya Angelou directed *Down in the Delta* (1998).

read.[21] I argue that the contemporary Black women filmmakers who are the focus of this book create the stories and images that they want to see and that they should have been able to see, but that no one else in the film industry has been capable of or interested in creating.

Since the revolutionary work of Kathleen Collins (whose 1982 film *Losing Ground* was, unfortunately, not commercially released during her lifetime) and Julie Dash (whose 1991 film *Daughters of the Dust* was the first commercially released feature film written and directed by an African American woman), the narrative films of Black women have gradually gained recognition within the film industry. Surprisingly, relatively little scholarship has been published about their work. The increase in box office earnings of the films written and directed by Black women reflects the increased recognition and popularity of their films. *Daughters of the Dust,* through a grassroots effort, earned $1.6 million when it was released in 1991. In 1997, when Kasi Lemmons released *Eve's Bayou,* it became one of the highest grossing independent films of the year ($14.8 million). A few years later, Gina Prince-Bythewood's *Love & Basketball* (2000) earned over $27 million at the box office. Nevertheless, few scholars have written books that are devoted to the analysis of the cultural and political significance of the work of Black women filmmakers.[22]

When the work of Black filmmakers is the subject of scholarly writing, the intersection of racial and gendered identities is often ignored, making male filmmakers the focus of the analysis.[23] Although a few influential Black women filmmakers may be incorporated into these discussions, their work does not take center stage. This reflects the tendency for scholarship related to Blackness to overlook the "special vantage point"[24] of Black women, as scholars such as Kimberlé Crenshaw, Patricia Hill Collins, Angela Davis, Paula Giddings, bell hooks, Barbara Smith, and Michele Wallace have detailed in their writing.[25]

---

21. Walker, *In Search of Our Mothers' Gardens,* 13.

22. Bobo, *Black Women Film and Video Artists;* Foster, *Women Filmmakers of the African & Asian Diaspora.*

23. Diawara, *Black American Cinema;* Donalson, *Black Directors in Hollywood;* Field, Horak, and Stewart, *L.A. Rebellion;* Gillespie, *Film Blackness;* Guerrero, *Framing Blackness.*

24. Collins, *Black Feminist Thought.*

25. The following seminal texts highlight the importance of examining the intersection of race and gender for women of color: Crenshaw, "Demarginalizing the Intersection of Race and Sex: A Black Feminist Critique of Antidiscrimination Doctrine, Feminist Theory and Antiracist Politics"; Collins, *Black Feminist Thought;* Davis, *Women, Race, & Class;* Giddings, *When and Where I Enter;* Guy-Sheftall, *Words of Fire;* hooks, *Ain't I a Woman: Black Women and Feminism;* Hull, Bell-Scott, and Smith, *All the Women Are White, All the Blacks are Men, But Some of Us Are Brave;* Moraga and Anzaldúa, *This Bridge Called My Back;* Wallace, *Black Macho and the Myth of the Superwoman.*

Jacqueline Bobo's *Black Women Film and Video Artists* is the first and, to date, only book exclusively devoted to the work of Black women filmmakers. Her book is an edited anthology that includes a thorough history of Black female filmmakers that extends as far back as the early 1900s. At the time it was published, there had been only three theatrically released narrative films created by Black women; consequently, the focus of her anthology was on documentary filmmakers, with the exception of Julie Dash. Bobo's book is a pioneering text in its dedication to highlighting Black women's contributions in film. Since the publication of Bobo's anthology, though, a number of Black women filmmakers have made their mark in narrative films that have reached broad audiences. In an essay written by Gloria Gibson ("The Ties That Bind: Cinematic Representations by Black Women Filmmakers"),[26] she applies a Black feminist perspective to her analysis of *Daughters of the Dust* (1991) and three documentary films that were written and directed by Black women: *Sidet: Forced Exile* (1991); *And Still I Rise* (1991); and *Sister in the Struggle* (1991). She proposes that the cinematic representations of Black women by Black women filmmakers are constructed by utilizing aspects of Black women's cultural identity situated within a specific sociohistoric context. Further, she argues that Black women filmmakers incorporate alternative elements of cultural history in their formation of cinematic representations of Black women.

The present study is the first book-length in-depth examination of theatrically released narrative feature films by Black women filmmakers. I focus on their depictions of Black womanhood and address the question: How are contemporary Black women filmmakers using the creative potential of narrative film for storytelling, self-expression, and cultural transformation? I began the research for this book by compiling a list of theatrically released narrative films that were based on *original* (not adapted) screenplays, written *and* directed by a Black woman (see table 1). This book is based on my detailed qualitative analysis of the following sample of six films: Kasi Lemmons's *Eve's Bayou* (1997), Gina Prince-Bythewood's *Love & Basketball* (2000), Tanya Hamilton's *Night Catches Us* (2010), Dee Rees's *Pariah* (2011), Ava DuVernay's *Middle of Nowhere* (2012), and Gina Prince-Bythewood's *Beyond the Lights* (2014). I also completed interviews with filmmakers Kasi Lemmons, Gina Price-Bythewood, and Tanya Hamilton, which I discuss in the remaining chapters.

Rather than attempt to find a "real" or "authentic" representation of Black womanhood in the above-listed films, my analysis stresses the importance of recognizing the multiplicity of representations in the work of Black women

---

26. Gibson's essay is published in *Quarterly Review of Film and Video*, as well as in Bobo's anthology about Black women filmmakers.

filmmakers. I do not make the claim that the specific representations of Black womanhood discussed here apply to all Black women, nor do the filmmakers. In the recent book *Film Blackness,* Michael Gillespie argues that "Black film matters because it offers a critical range of potentialities for understanding blackness as multiaccentual and multidisciplinary."[27] Additionally, in *Technologies of Gender,* Teresa de Lauretis points out that women's cinema seems to "point less to a 'feminine aesthetic' than to a feminine *deaesthetic,*" referring to the ways that women filmmakers deconstruct "femaleness."[28] Although de Lauretis stresses that there are different histories of women and is critical of the fact that Black women have been invisible in White women's films, the analyses of de Lauretis and Gillespie prioritize representations of *White* femaleness or Black *maleness* in film.

The six films analyzed in this book provide a range of possibilities of cinematic representations of Black womanhood. Utilizing E. Patrick Johnson's phrasing in *Appropriating Blackness,* the films of Black women filmmakers illustrate the ways that Black femaleness "defies categorization."[29] The films that I discuss in the remaining chapters were strategically chosen to illustrate the ways that Black women filmmakers resist hegemonic cultural ideology associated with the "controlling images" of Black women and together demonstrate the various perspectives from which they create.[30] Applying an inductive approach, the following thematic issues emerged:

1. Context: Characters are situated within social contexts that highlight the impact of cultural, political, or historical circumstances faced by Black women.
2. Alternative frameworks: Black women filmmakers use the medium of film to express their creative visions of Black womanhood and demonstrate the ways that Black women create meaning and construct their lives independent of the dominant cultural expectations.
3. Validation of Black women's contributions: Using explicit or implicit references, Black women filmmakers pay homage to the cultural and/ or political contributions of other Black women.

---

27. Gillespie, *Film Blackness,* 6.
28. de Lauretis, *Technologies of Gender,* 146.
29. Johnson, *Appropriating Blackness,* 2.
30. According to Antonio Gramsci's theory of ideological hegemony, "mass media are tools that ruling elites use to perpetuate their power, wealth, and status by popularizing their own philosophy, culture and morality" (see Lull, "Hegemony"). In *Black Feminist Thought* (2000), Patricia Hill Collins refers to stereotypical images of Black women, such as "mammy," "matriarch," "welfare queen," and "jezebel," as *controlling images.* Collins explains: "These controlling images are designed to make racism, sexism, poverty, and other forms of social injustice appear to be natural, normal, and inevitable parts of everyday life" (69).

4. Black women's beauty: Characters validate the beauty and aesthetic value of Black women's physical features.

I also draw from the core themes presented in Patricia Hill Collins's formative text *Black Feminist Thought*. Each chapter in the present book focuses on the ways in which Black women filmmakers highlight the afore-mentioned themes (e.g., context, alternative frameworks, validation of Black women's contributions, and beauty) in one of the following areas of Black women's lives: work, motherhood, love, and beauty. The organization of chapters reflects Collins's use of the themes and subthemes of "Work, Family, and Black Women's Oppression," "Black Women and Motherhood," "Black Women's Love Relationships," and "Color, Hair Texture, and Standards of Beauty" as central to Black feminist thought.

In addition to presenting images of Black womanhood that challenge dominant ideology, the films in my sample are also the most recent or the most financially successful of the films from which I drew my sample. Prince-Bythewood's *Beyond the Lights* (2014), DuVernay's *Middle of Nowhere* (2012), Rees's *Pariah* (2011), and Hamilton's *Night Catches Us* (2010) were all released within the last ten years. Lemmons's *Eve's Bayou* (1997) and Prince-Bythewood's *Love & Basketball* (2000), which are the two highest-grossing films that meet my criteria ($14.8 million and $27.5 million, respectively), are also included in my analysis.[31] Based on their contemporary significance and popularity with moviegoing audiences (as indicated by box office earnings), I propose that these films have the greatest potential to contest, challenge, and transform racial and gender ideology.[32]

In the first chapter, "Unicorns: Black Women Filmmakers," I develop a new approach to thinking about the work of contemporary Black women filmmakers, which I refer to as the *womanist artistic standpoint* framework. I apply this framework to my study in order to best capture the unique relationship between race, gender, social context, and creativity involved in the work of Black women filmmakers. This framework is heavily influenced by a womanist approach, first developed by Alice Walker, as well as seminal works of Black women scholar-activists Patricia Hill Collins, bell hooks, and Kimberlé Cren-shaw. I also draw from interviews that I completed with three of the filmmak-ers (Tanya Hamilton, Kasi Lemmons, and Gina Prince-Bythewood), as well

---

31. http://www.boxofficemojo.com/.

32. Hall, Evans, and Nixon, *Representation*; Hall, "The Whites of Their Eyes: Racist Ideolo-gies in the Media."

as published sources (such as news articles) about all five filmmakers who are featured in this book, to provide support for my argument that they intentionally create stories about Black women that resist the one-dimensional images that permeate the commercial film industry. I also briefly discuss the history of Black women filmmakers, highlighting the work of two Black women filmmakers of the narrative genre, Kathleen Collins and Julie Dash, who laid the groundwork for contemporary Black women filmmakers.

The title of the first chapter, "Unicorns," references a statement made by filmmaker Ava DuVernay about filmmakers: "Any film that you see that has any progressive spirit that is made by people of color or a woman is a triumph, in and of itself. Whether you agree with it or not. Something that comes with some point of view and some personal prospective [sic] from a woman or a person of color, is a unicorn."[33] Although unlike unicorns, Black women filmmakers and their work are not mythical, DuVernay's unicorn metaphor underscores the marginalization of women of color in the film industry. Using the words of the filmmakers themselves, I argue that these filmmakers place Black women at the center of their films as a means of challenging the marginalization of Black women's voices.

In chapter 2, "Work as Passion," I analyze two films that were written and directed by Gina Prince-Bythewood: *Love & Basketball* (2000) and *Beyond the Lights* (2014). Both films feature Black women characters who exhibit a high degree of self-determination as they passionately pursue a career-related dream or goal. These films focus on the ways that the Black women characters exercise agency in order to pursue personally meaningful work. One of the most long-standing roles of Black women characters in film has been to support another (usually White and/or male) character, as embodied in the age-old "mammy" controlling image. Although the image that is recognizable to most as "mammy" is mostly (though not totally[34]) absent from mainstream media, it is still common to see Black women characters that are incorporated into a film only as much as they are able to help another character achieve his or her goal, but are otherwise inconsequential. With *Love & Basketball* (2000) and *Beyond the Lights* (2014), Gina Prince-Blythewood asserts the significance and value of Black women in possession of their own goals and agency, while acknowledging the impact of the systematic inequalities faced by Black women in pursuit of their goals. In *Love & Basketball,* the lead character resists gendered cultural expectations and institutional inequality to pursue her goal of playing professional basketball. This film integrates the per-

33. Lee, "Director Ava DuVernay Talks Race, Hollywood and Doing It Her Way."
34. McElya, *Clinging to Mammy.*

sonal experiences of filmmaker Prince-Bythewood, who played basketball for much of her life, with the social significance of the inception of the WNBA. In *Beyond the Lights,* the lead character struggles to gain respect, assert her voice, and resist objectification and exploitation within the music industry. Because of the critique of the treatment of Black women within the music industry that this film provides, in this section, I draw from the work of Black feminist theorists who interrogate the misrepresentation of Black women within hip-hop, such as Tricia Rose and Imani Perry.

Kasi Lemmons's *Eve's Bayou* (1997) and Tanya Hamilton's *Night Catches Us* (2010) are the focus of the third chapter. I discuss how both films feature nuanced portrayals of motherhood and families located within social contexts that are unique to Black communities and rarely portrayed in film. Motherhood is one of the areas in which racial and gender cultural ideology have had the most significant social impact on the lives of Black women.[35] This chapter is titled "Y'all Are My Children," which is a line spoken by one of the characters in the film *Eve's Bayou* as she has a conversation with her niece. This line reflects the ways that motherhood, for Black women, has meant more than bearing and raising children within a nuclear family. In *Eve's Bayou* and *Night Catches Us,* mothering is depicted as "dynamic and dialectical," and consisting of "a series of constantly renegotiated relationships that African American women experience with one another, with Black children, with the larger African American community, and with self."[36] *Eve's Bayou* (1997) focuses on an affluent family that is situated within the context of a Creole community in Louisiana. In Lemmons's film, we see multiple generations of women living together, supporting each other and contributing to raising children, which, unlike dominant portrayals of motherhood, recognizes motherhood as an endeavor that extends beyond the limits of the nuclear family. *Night Catches Us* (2010) features a widowed mother who is involved with the Black Panther Party and whose husband was killed because of his role within the group. She faces the challenge of raising her daughter as a widow, while maintaining her connection to the community of former Black Panther Party members, with whom she has a strong, albeit complicated, kinship.

Lemmons's and Hamilton's films resist the cultural ideology of Black motherhood as deficient, as exhibited through the controlling images of the emasculating "matriarch" or "welfare queen." These films also resist the suggestion that motherhood is a selfless act in which Black women should hap-

---

35. David, "More Than Baby Mamas: Black Mothers and Hip-Hop Feminism"; Collins, *Black Sexual Politics*; David, *Mama's Gun*; Hancock, *The Politics of Disgust*; Roberts, *Shattered Bonds*.

36. Collins, *Black Feminist Thought*, 176.

pily sacrifice their own desires, as is the message behind the "mammy" and "superstrong Black mother" controlling images. Hamilton and Lemmons have created images of Black motherhood that recognize and validate the ways that Black women reframe motherhood and family, often within the context of institutionalized oppression. These filmmakers highlight the ability of Black women to create families that are not restricted by the dominant cultural expectations of motherhood.

Ava DuVernay's *Middle of Nowhere* (2012) and Dee Rees's *Pariah* (2011) are discussed in the fourth chapter, titled "Rebellious Love." DuVernay and Rees provide stories about the relationships and emotional complexity of Black women that resist dominant ideologies that construct Black women as undesirable partners—often depicted through the controlling images of the hypersexual "Jezebel" or emasculating "Sapphire." DuVernay focuses on the challenges faced by a woman whose husband is serving time in prison. In doing so, she uncovers the often-ignored impact that the criminalization and mass incarceration of Black men have on poor and working-class Black women. I draw from the work of scholars who critically analyze the prison industrial complex and mass incarceration of people of color, such as Michelle Alexander, Angela Davis, Beth Richie, and Ruth Wilson Gilmore. Rees's film provides a coming of age story about a teenager's first experiences with love and heartbreak, in which she also deals with sexual identity and homophobia. In this section, I draw from the works of Black feminist, lesbian, activist, and poet Audre Lorde. DuVernay and Rees explore love in its various forms, from romantic to committed and emotional to physical. However, at the center of each story is the process by which each woman begins to appreciate the importance of self-love and learns to define love and partnership for herself, based on her particular situation.

In the fifth and final chapter, "Transformative Beauty," I draw from all six films to argue that one way that the work of Black women filmmakers resists and challenges dominant ideologies is by validating the physical beauty of Black women through their films. In mainstream cinema, Black women's bodies and aesthetic features have been constructed to validate and idealize the physical qualities associated with White womanhood. The physical characteristics that are associated with Black womanhood have been presented in contrast to this ideal, and Black women are presented as beautiful only to the extent that their features approximate those associated with Whiteness, especially in relation to skin coloring and hair texture. By contrast, the films in my analysis highlight the physical beauty of Black women of various skin tones and hair textures. In this chapter, I draw from scholarship related to the social impact of colorism and the cultural, political, and aesthetic significance of hair for Black women.

Film producer Effie Brown's experience on *Project Greenlight,* described at the beginning of the introduction, highlights the need for more women of color in positions of power in the film industry if we are to see images of Black women that begin to explore the complexities of their experiences. By standing up for herself, Brown demonstrated her resistance to oppressive images of Black women and to the silencing of Black women's perspectives. Contemporary Black women filmmakers assert their willingness to stand up and fight for Black women to be heard, as many other Black women filmmakers and artists have done before them. They use their voices, pens, and cameras to create and share stories from their standpoint. Black women filmmakers bring to light the necessity for Black women to create meaning independent of dominant cultural expectations.

Recently, I have actually noticed a slight transformation in student responses when I ask them to identify Black filmmakers. In the past few semesters, every so often, I hear students somewhat hesitantly respond to my question about Black filmmakers with "the person who directed *Selma.*" And I confirm that Ava DuVernay, a Black woman filmmaker, did in fact direct the 2015 Oscar-nominated film *Selma.* She may be somewhat of a "unicorn," but, I argue, she is one of the so-called unicorns who has the potential to alter our sense of reality as she and her work continue to become more visible. Although an incomplete process, Black women filmmakers transform narratives about Black women through the medium of film as a form of artistic resistance, which I detail in my film analyses in the remaining chapters of this book.

CHAPTER 1

Unicorns

Black Women Filmmakers

> If I didn't define myself for myself, I would be crunched
> into other people's fantasies for me and eaten alive.
>
> —AUDRE LORDE[1]

"Beyoncé's 'Lemonade' Is What Happens When Black Women Control Their Art" announces a 2016 article.[2] With *Lemonade,* Beyoncé created and successfully distributed an album that has been described by many as a contemporary Black feminist statement[3] (although it was not without criticism[4]). Beyoncé is an artist whose work has become increasingly political as she has risen in popularity, moving from telling men to "put a ring on it" in her 2008 hit "Single Ladies," to addressing highly politicized issues such as police brutality and Hurricane Katrina in the video for "Formation."[5] The way in which Beyoncé took control of the creative process, through the content and dissemination of her visual album, was bold. This album was as popular[6] as it was unapologetically Black: "Beyoncé publicly embraced explicitly feminist blackness at a

---

1. Lorde, *Sister Outsider,* 137.
2. King, "Beyoncé's 'Lemonade' Is What Happens When Black Women Control Their Art."
3. Harris-Perry, "A Call and Response with Melissa Harris-Perry: The Pain and the Power of 'Lemonade'"; Kang, "Beyoncé's Lemonade Didn't Win That Grammy Because It Wasn't Made for Everyone—and Adele Knows That"; Bale, "Beyoncé's 'Lemonade' Is a Revolutionary Work of Black Feminism: Critic's Notebook"; Robinson, "How Beyoncé's 'Lemonade' Exposes Inner Lives of Black Women"; Harris-Perry, "Beyoncé: Her Creative Opus Turned the Pop Star into a Political Force."
4. hooks, "Beyoncé's Lemonade Is Capitalist Money-Making at Its Best."
5. The song "Formation" was the lead single for the *Lemonade* album.
6. *Lemonade* earned Beyoncé album of the year from *Rolling Stone,* several Grammy nominations, and a runner-up spot for *Time* magazine's person of the year.

politically risky moment."[7] In case there was any doubt that she is fully aware of the resistant statement of her music, she ends her song "Formation" by declaring, "You know you that bitch when you cause all this conversation."[8]

Not only did Beyoncé publicly embrace feminist Blackness, with *Lemonade,* she also embraced the work of pioneering Black woman filmmaker Julie Dash. Beyoncé's visual album *Lemonade* was partly inspired by the imagery in Dash's film *Daughters of the Dust.*[9] Although less visible than Beyoncé, contemporary Black women filmmakers create films that explicitly embrace feminist Blackness. The filmmakers discussed in the present study place the voices of Black women at the center of their stories. I argue that because of their focus on telling nuanced stories about Black women, in which they draw from their personal experiences, their work reflects my articulation of a *womanist artistic standpoint,* which I describe below (whether or not these filmmakers have referred to their work as "feminist" or "womanist"). For Black women filmmakers, the creative process of filmmaking is, at least partly, an act of self-definition that resists the hegemonic cultural narratives that, as Audre Lorde states, crunch them into other people's fantasies.

WOMANIST ARTISTIC STANDPOINT

The creative work of Black women filmmakers reflects their unique standpoint as Black women artists, which I refer to as a *womanist artistic standpoint.* The womanist artistic standpoint framework that I apply throughout this book primarily draws from the works of Alice Walker, Patricia Hill Collins, bell hooks, and Kimberlé Crenshaw. This framework theorizes that Black women filmmakers create from a position of being uniquely situated within the social structure, based partly on their shared history and experiences of ideological and structural oppression.[10] In order to resist this oppression and exclusion, Black women filmmakers have forged new paths in the film industry. Whereas dominant cultural ideologies historically and presently represent Black women as hypersexual Jezebels, emasculating Sapphires and matriarchs,

---

7. Harris-Perry, "TIME Person of the Year Runner Up."

8. Beyoncé's use of the word "bitch" reflects the attempts of many women to "reclaim" the word as a symbol of power and resistance to the gendered expectations of women. See Patricia Hill Collins, *Black Sexual Politics.*

9. Anderson, "25 Years Later, Writer-Director Julie Dash Looks Back on the Seminal 'Daughters of the Dust'"; Julious, "Julie Dash's Work Is More Important Than Ever"; Grierson, "'Daughters of the Dust.'"

10. Collins, *Black Feminist Thought.*

welfare queens, or subservient mammies,[11] Black women filmmakers create nuanced images and narratives that draw from their histories, experiences, and perspectives. By applying this framework, I emphasize the importance of applying an intersectional perspective[12] that centers on the shared experiences of Black women, and the role of film as a form of artistic expression and a tool of social resistance.

The womanist artistic standpoint stems from the womanist and Black feminist standpoint theoretical perspectives, which both highlight the importance of moving the voices of Black women from margin to center.[13] Alice Walker originated the term "womanist" to refer to a Black feminist or feminist of color. In her collection of essays, *In Search of Our Mothers' Gardens: Womanist Prose,* Walker defines "womanist" as stemming from the Southern colloquial term "womanish," which is the opposite of "girlish" (meaning frivolous, irresponsible, or not serious). She further explains that the term is usually used to refer to behavior that is "outrageous, audacious, courageous or willful,"[14] which suggests that to be a womanist is to deliberately resist social expectations. Additionally, a "womanist," according to Walker, is "a woman who loves other women, sexually and/or nonsexually, appreciates and prefers women's culture, women's emotional flexibility, and women's strength."[15] The merging of these various definitions suggests an appreciation of both femaleness and Blackness, as well as the inherent resistance to hegemonic cultural expectations that have been placed on Black women.

Since Walker coined the term, womanism has evolved into an intersectional framework for thinking about race and gender that privileges the experiences and voices of Black women. Essential to a womanist perspective is a resistance to the dominant culture's dehumanization and exclusion of Black women. Womanism challenges the tendency of mainstream feminism to prioritize the voices and needs of White women and marginalize those of Black women. As bell hooks explains, "White women who dominate feminist discourse today rarely question whether or not their perspective on women's reality is true to the lived experiences of women as a collective group. Nor are they aware of the extent to which their perspectives reflect race and class biases."[16] For instance, in 1980, when poet and activist Audre Lorde spoke to White feminists about the interests of Black women, she explained, "You fear

11. Ibid.; Harris-Perry, *Sister Citizen.*
12. Crenshaw, "Demarginalizing the Intersection of Race and Sex."
13. hooks, *Feminist Theory.*
14. Walker, *In Search of Our Mothers' Gardens,* xi.
15. Ibid.
16. hooks, *Feminist Theory,* 3.

your children will grow up to join the patriarchy and testify against you, we fear our children will be dragged from a car and shot down in the street, and you will turn your backs upon the reasons they are dying."[17] Unfortunately, this sentiment is as true today as it was when Lorde gave this speech.[18] The womanist approach resists the silencing of Black women by bringing the realities of their experiences to the forefront. In doing so, it provides a broader perspective than was previously incorporated into feminist discourse. Likewise, the intersectional approach of legal scholar and activist Kimberlé Crenshaw highlights the ongoing need to fight the (often overlooked) injustices that Black women face within the criminal justice system.[19]

The womanist artistic standpoint is also informed by Black feminist standpoint theory. Black feminist standpoint theory stems from standpoint theory, which is a theoretical perspective that argues that knowledge stems from one's social position. Standpoint theory emerged from the Marxist argument that people from an oppressed class have special access to knowledge that is not available to those from a privileged class. In *Black Feminist Thought*, Patricia Hill Collins theorizes that Black women have distinctive ways of viewing and experiencing the world in response to a highly effective system of economic, political, and ideological control used against them. Specifically, the exploitation of Black women's labor, the denial of rights and privileges afforded to men and White women, and the use of controlling images of Black women have systematically worked together to suppress the voices and interests of Black women.

This is not to suggest that there is one standpoint that represents an authentic truth for all Black women. In fact, a central element of Black feminist standpoint theory is the recognition that "no homogenous Black *woman's* standpoint exists. There is no essential or archetypal Black woman whose experiences stand as normal, normative, and thereby authentic . . . [I]t may be more accurate to say that a Black *women's* collective standpoint does exist."[20] Acknowledging differences in age, social class, and sexual orientation, as well as the various ways that Black women can and do react to common challenges, is one way to resist the dominant cultural practice of simplifying and homogenizing the experiences of Black women. Nonetheless, Black women are impacted by similar challenges that result from living in a society that historically and routinely denigrates women of African descent, which means that it is "essential for continued feminist struggle that black women recog-

17. Lorde, *Sister Outsider*.
18. Khaleeli, "#SayHerName: Why Kimberlé Crenshaw Is Fighting for Forgotten Women."
19. Ibid.; Crenshaw, "Demarginalizing the Intersection of Race and Sex"; Crenshaw, "Why Intersectionality Can't Wait."
20. Collins, *Black Feminist Thought*, 28.

nize the special vantage point our marginality gives us and make use of this perspective to criticize the dominant racist, classist, sexist hegemony as well as to envision and create a counter hegemony."[21]

By applying the womanist artistic standpoint as a framework to my analyses of the work of Black women filmmakers, my goal is to highlight the specific and varied contributions of Black women's creative work as an instrument of ideological change and resistance. The work of Black women filmmakers reflects more than a desire to simply replace the negative stereotypes of Black women with more positive images. They are not interested in engaging in "politics of respectability."[22] The Black women filmmakers who are discussed in this study are part of a tradition of artists such as Alice Walker, Audre Lorde, Lorraine Hansberry, Nina Simone, June Jordan, and Ntozake Shange (to name a few), who have all used their creative work as a tool of social resistance to problematize dominant ideologies about Black women. As poets, playwrights, and singer-songwriters, these Black women artists have used artistic expression as a means of creating narratives that challenge the racial and gender oppression experienced by Black women. I argue that contemporary Black women filmmakers also work to challenge oppression by creating images and narratives that resist the marginalization of Black women's perspectives by drawing from their experiences and perspectives as Black women. Black women filmmakers call into question the stereotypes of Black womanhood that, as Patricia Hill Collins explains, "permeate the social structure to such a degree that they become hegemonic" and are used to justify oppression.[23]

In the following section I provide a brief history of the work of a selection of Black women filmmakers who, like the contemporary filmmakers who are the focus of this book, defied social expectations in order to exercise their creative voices through film. Rather than providing an exhaustive history of Black women filmmakers, my goal is to highlight the relationship between the recent work of Black women filmmakers and that of the women who have come before them, as well as recognize the work of several Black women filmmakers who have been overlooked by many film historians. I devote special attention to Kathleen Collins and Julie Dash, who are pioneers of narrative feature film for Black women.[24]

21. hooks, *Feminist Theory*, 16.
22. Higginbotham, *Righteous Discontent*.
23. Collins, *Black Feminist Thought*, 5.
24. Also see Jacqueline Bobo, *Black Women Film and Video Artists* for more information about the history of Black women filmmakers. Additionally, the webpage titled "African-Amer-

BLACK WOMEN FILMMAKERS' ENTRANCE INTO FILM

Lorraine Hansberry proclaims, "It is probably the most fulfilling experience a human being can have—to try and create something and to have it received with any measure of recognition for the effort. So that I can only say it in personal terms: I get an enormous sense of personal fulfillment and—a slight sense of justification for being."[25] One distinguishing feature of the work of the contemporary Black women filmmakers who are the focus of this book is that their work has achieved relatively wide recognition through theatrical distribution. However, Black women filmmakers have not always received recognition for their work, which is often unconventional in images, narratives, and storytelling techniques. This often-unconventional approach reflects a womanist approach of *courageously* resisting social expectations. Despite the fact that far too many Black women filmmakers have been overlooked by film critics and scholars, there are accounts of Black women creating films since the beginning of the twentieth century.[26]

Several notable and pioneering Black women filmmakers have made significant contributions in the genre of documentary film, including acclaimed novelist Zora Neale Hurston.[27] It is not well known that Hurston shot ten rolls of motion pictures between 1927 and 1929 to document various activities, such as children's games and dances, which, according to film scholar Gloria Gibson, may represent the earliest film footage shot by an African American woman.[28] Hurston's 1940 documentary film, titled *Commandment Keeper Church, Beaufort South Carolina, May 1940,* in which she captures the religious services of a South Carolina Gullah community, was selected for the National Film Registry by the Library of Congress as being culturally, historically, or aesthetically significant.[29]

The *courageous* and *audacious* behavior that is central to womanism is reflected in the work of Zora Neale Hurston, as well as that of Eloyce King Patrick Gist, both of whom Gloria Gibson refers to as "risk-takers" who "realized the power of the camera as a way to capture, preserve, and critique

---

ican Women in the Silent Film Industry," which is part of the *Women Film Pioneers Project* at Columbia University, is a useful resource for the early work of Black women filmmakers. And the website http://www.sistersincinema.com/, which is created by Black woman filmmaker Yvonne Welbon, includes recent information about Black women filmmakers.

25. Hansberry, *To Be Young, Gifted and Black: Lorraine Hansberry in Her Own Words,* 111.

26. Bobo, *Black Women Film and Video Artists.*

27. Ibid.; Gibson, "Cinematic Foremothers: Zora Neale Hurston and Eloyce King Patrick Gist."

28. Gibson, "Cinematic Foremothers: Zora Neale Hurston and Eloyce King Patrick Gist," 206.

29. "Preservation."

African-American culture."[30] Eloyce Gist worked with her husband, James, to create films that were based on religious beliefs and African American folk culture. Within Gist's films, a primary goal was encouraging racial progress, which reflects a desire to resist and challenge the status quo. Gist enjoyed a fair amount of recognition for her depictions of African American culture, as evidenced by the fact that she and her husband caught the attention of the NAACP when they toured with their two films *Hell Bound Train* (1930) and *Verdict Not Guilty* (1933).[31]

During the second half of the twentieth century, several Black women narrative and documentary filmmakers, whose work was not available for commercial theatrical release, made bold statements about personal and political issues that were relevant for Black women: these included Jacqueline Shearer, Madeline Anderson, Camille Billops, Michelle Parkerson, Carroll Parrott Blue, Alile Sharon Larkin, O.Funmilayo Makarah, Barbara McCullough, Zeinabu Irene Davis, Jessie Maple, and Kathleen Collins, to name just a few. These filmmakers have challenged the marginalization of Black women and laid the groundwork for many contemporary narrative and documentary filmmakers. Notably, in 1974 Jessie Maple became the first Black woman to join the International Photographers of Motion Picture and Television Union.[32] Maple is also considered to be one of the first African American women to direct an independent feature-length film (*Will*, 1981); however, like the work of Kathleen Collins, it did not receive theatrical distribution.[33]

Although the focus of the present book is on theatrically released narrative films, a genre that Black women have more recently entered and gained recognition in, the work of Black women filmmakers in documentary film is exceptional. Madeline Anderson's *I Am Somebody* (1970) is a documentary about four hundred Black women workers who went on strike in Charleston to fight for equal wages and humane working conditions. In a 2013 interview, Anderson highlighted the importance of her standpoint as a Black woman artist: as a Black woman, she felt that she could identify with the struggles of the Charleston workers, after having faced similar obstacles based on gender, racial discrimination, and marginalization in her work as a filmmaker.[34]

---

30. Gibson, "Cinematic Foremothers: Zora Neale Hurston and Eloyce King Patrick Gist," 197.

31. Ibid., 200.

32. Oxendine, "Remembering Jessie Maple and Her Landmark 1981 Feature-Length Film, 'Will.'"

33. Black Film Center/Archive, "Into the Archive"; Oxendine, "Remembering Jessie Maple and Her Landmark 1981 Feature-Length Film, 'Will.'"

34. Martin, "Madeline Anderson in Conversation: Pioneering an African American Documentary Tradition."

Similarly, Camille Billops and Michelle Parkerson draw from their own identities and experiences in their documentary films. For instance, Billops's film *Finding Christa* (1991), which documents her reunion with the daughter that she put up for adoption, places her personal narrative and identity as a Black woman artist at the center of the film, as it challenges dominant ideologies about family and motherhood. This film received the Grand Jury Prize at the 1992 Sundance Film Festival. Parkerson also often draws from her personal identity and experiences, specifically her identity as a Black lesbian filmmaker. Her films often focus on issues related to sexual identity, such as *A Litany for Survival: The Life and Work of Audre Lorde* (1995), which profiles the work and activism of Black lesbian feminist Audre Lorde.

Alile Sharon Larkin, Barbara McCullough, and Zeinabu Irene Davis were a few of the Black women who were part of a revolutionary group of Black film students who attended UCLA in the 1970s and 1980s, who have been dubbed the "L.A. Rebellion."[35] The themes that were incorporated into much of the work of the L.A. Rebellion were influenced by the social activism and the emphasis on Black pride of the 1960s. This period of filmmaking at UCLA has been referred to as a modern Harlem Renaissance for film.[36] Julie Dash (discussed in detail below) and Charles Burnett (whose critically celebrated 1977 film *Killer of Sheep* is included in the National Film Registry and was selected as one of the 100 Essential Films of all time by the National Society of Film Critics), were among the L.A. Rebellion filmmakers.[37]

L.A. Rebellion filmmakers McCullough, Larkin, and Davis used their work to rebel against the film industry's one-dimensional depictions of Black women. Barbara McCullough explains that the filmmakers of the L.A. Rebellion were interested in "having another image out there" besides the one produced by Hollywood.[38] McCullough's *Water Ritual #1: An Urban Rite of Purification* (1979), which has been recognized as a pioneering work in Black feminist and experimental filmmaking, celebrates the beauty of Black women and the female body.[39] Alile Sharon Larkin's first film, *The Kitchen* (1975), is a narrative short that centers on Black women's experiences within a dominant "beauty culture that values straight hair over 'natural' African Ameri-

35. Other women of the L.A. Rebellion include Carroll Parrott Blue, Shirikiana Aina, Julie Dash, Jacqueline Frazier, and Stormé Sweet. See https://www.cinema.ucla.edu/la-rebellion/filmmakers.

36. Bobo, *Black Women Film and Video Artists.*

37. "Killer of Sheep—A Film by Charles Burnett."

38. Field, Horak, and Stewart, *L.A. Rebellion,* 3.

39. Masilela, "Women Directors of the Los Angeles School"; "Water Ritual #1: An Urban Rite of Purification."

can hair."[40] Like McCullough and Larkin, Zeinabu Irene Davis also centralizes Black women's bodies as a source of self-reflection and self-determination. Her film *Cycles* (1989) creatively demonstrates a woman performing African-based rituals as she awaits her overdue period, and *A Powerful Thang* (1991) dramatizes a woman's decisions about love, celibacy, and sexual intimacy.

Kathleen Collins was one of the first Black women filmmakers to dive into the unchartered waters of narrative feature film. Her social position as a Black woman and her avant-garde approach to film changed the "face and content of black womanist film."[41] In 1979, while on the faculty of City College at the City University of New York, she became the first African American woman to write, direct, and produce a full-length feature film (*The Cruz Brothers and Miss Malloy*). This was no small feat, considering that she was repeatedly told that there was no such thing as a Black woman filmmaker after she wrote her first script.[42] Additionally, Collins had very limited financial resources for her film. In a lecture, she jokingly refers to herself as the "lowest budget independent filmmaker around."[43] Amazingly, she was able to complete production of *The Cruz Brothers* on a budget of only $5,000.[44] Although the film was never theatrically released, the film did well enough that Collins was able to secure funds for her next film project, *Losing Ground* (1982), which she wrote, directed, and coproduced.

Losing Ground was the first feature-length narrative film created by a Black woman designed to tell a story intended for popular consumption.[45] The film focuses on an area of the Black experience rarely examined in film: that of a middle-class Black female intellectual. As a member of the faculty at City College, this was an experience with which Collins identified. Collins's film centers the intersecting identities of race, gender, and class in its intimate look at the emotional life of a middle-class Black woman. Although the film was not described as autobiographical, her role as a Black female professor mirrors that of the lead character in the film. Collins also has explained that she relates

---

40. Field, "Rebellious Unlearning: UCLA Project One Films (1967–1978)," 105.
41. Page, *Encyclopedia of African American Women Writers*.
42. *Kathleen Collins Interview, 1984*.
43. Ibid.
44. Foster, *Women Filmmakers of the African & Asian Diaspora*. As a comparison, when Ava DuVernay directed the Disney film *A Wrinkle in Time* (released in March 2018), her production budget was over $100 million (see http://www.latimes.com/entertainment/movies/la-et -mn-wrinkle-budget-20160803-snap-story.html).
45. Bobo, *Black Women Film and Video Artists*.

to the main character's emotional journey of self-exploration.[46] The female protagonist in the film, Sara, embarks on a path toward self-discovery and liberation that calls into question dominant expectations of marriage. Rather than providing stock images of Black female identity, Collins's film indicates that "the life of a black person—in particular, of a black woman—is a perilous existential adventure."[47] In addition to its unconventional narrative, the film applies other unique cinematic techniques, such as nonlinear storytelling and the use of jazz, salsa dance, and theater reenactments through which the characters express themselves.[48]

Losing Ground was not released commercially in the United States during Collins's lifetime. Because of the avant-garde approach to the film and non-stereotypical characters, she was told by studio executives that Black people would not identify with the characters.[49] Film scholar Clyde Taylor remarks that the refusal to accept non-stereotypical, humanized images of Black people often reaches a level of absurdity, as was the case in Collins's film. Taylor references Collins's neighbor's refusal to allow Collins to use her mansion for shooting *Losing Ground* because, after reading the script, she decided, "These are not anything like the Black people that I know."[50] Despite resistance, Collins never faltered from her artistic vision. The film received broad international acclaim and won first prize at the Figueroa de Foz Film Festival in Portugal.[51] Before she was able to complete another film, her life was tragically cut short when she passed away at the age of forty-six. According to a lecture that she gave after the completion of *Losing Ground,* she was working on a film script that would provide an introspective look at the life and motivations of the first Black woman aviator.[52] Kathleen Collins's interest in telling complex stories about African American women characters was not limited to film. She wrote two plays, *In the Midnight Hour* and *The Brothers,* which both detail the internal struggles of African American characters in the midst of the social changes of the civil rights era.[53] Nonetheless, it's "one of the great tragedies of

---

46. *Kathleen Collins Interview, 1984.*

47. Brody, "Lost and Found: Kathleen Collins's Feature Gets Its First Release at Film Society of Lincoln Center."

48. Williams, "Re-Creating Their Media Image: Two Generations of Black Women Filmmakers."

49. *Kathleen Collins Interview, 1984.*

50. Field, Horak, and Stewart, *L.A. Rebellion,* xxii.

51. "Collins, Kathleen, 1941–1988."

52. *Kathleen Collins Interview, 1984.*

53. "Collins, Kathleen, 1941–1988."

the modern cinema that Collins didn't make any subsequent movies in which to pursue her powerful art and her powerful ideas."[54]

Kathleen Collins may not have openly referred to herself as a Black feminist or womanist, but existing sources indicate that Kathleen Collins's desire to express her identity as a Black woman and challenge dominant ideologies about Black women was at the forefront of her life and filmmaking, reflecting the womanist artistic standpoint. Poet and scholar Elizabeth Alexander says of Collins, "She does not strive to simplify nor does she fear the complexity of the black female interiority. Her vision is clear."[55] Collins has been described as a pioneer of "post black cinematic aesthetics" due to the way her films complicate how viewers see and process race.[56] Similar to the Black feminist standpoint described by Patricia Hill Collins,[57] Kathleen Collins felt that it was important to avoid falling into the trap of writing a story to explain *the* Black experience, which can lead to attempts to cater to White audiences and present stories that are not authentically human.[58] She has also been lauded for her "pioneering feminist vision" and for creating narratives that feature Black characters who are struggling to find meaning in their lives.[59] In an interview for *Heresies* magazine, she highlighted her intersectional perspective: "Black women are not white women by any means; we have different pasts, different approaches to life, and different attitudes. Historically, we come out of a different tradition; sociologically, our preoccupations are different."[60] She often spoke about the need for Black women to tell their stories through film as part of a "redemptive process" necessary to achieve change.[61] Also, in 1977 Collins wrote about the sexism in Hollywood films, which relegates Black women to the periphery, in a piece entitled "A Place in Time and Killer of Sheep: Two Radical Definitions of Adventure Minus Women." In this piece, she argues that films like *Shaft* and *Superfly* reproduced, in a different hue, the misogynistic conventions of White Hollywood cinema.[62] In addition to challenging cultural conventions with her films, she challenged social conven-

54. Brody, "The Front Row."
55. Alexander, "Forward: In Search of Kathleen Collins," xv.
56. Beverly, "Phenomenal Bodies: The Metaphysical Possibilities of Post-Black Film and Visual Culture."
57. Collins, *Black Feminist Thought.*
58. *Kathleen Collins Interview, 1984.*
59. "Collins, Kathleen, 1941–1988."
60. Campbell, "Reinventing Our Image: Eleven Black Women Filmmakers."
61. Foster, *Women Filmmakers of the African & Asian Diaspora.*
62. Williams, "Re-Creating Their Media Image: Two Generations of Black Women Filmmakers."

tions through political activism: she was involved with the Student Nonviolent Coordinating Committee's push to help register voters in the South.[63]

Following the work of Kathleen Collins, Julie Dash's *Daughters of the Dust* (1991) became the first feature-length narrative film created (written and directed) by an African American woman to receive a general theatrical release. Because of this achievement, Dash's film has often been included in scholarly research that analyzes the work of Black filmmakers.[64] In 2004 *Daughters of the Dust* was placed in the National Film Registry by the Library of Congress. Because only twenty-five films are chosen each year by the National Film Registry in order to "ensure the survival, conservation and increased public availability of America's film heritage,"[65] the inclusion of *Daughters of the Dust* reflects its historical and cultural significance.

Julie Dash's involvement with the progressive group of film students at UCLA, the L.A. Rebellion (mentioned above),[66] is indicative of the revolutionary structure and content of her films. Dash began making documentary films while she lived in New York, but she moved to Los Angeles in the 1970s to attend film school at UCLA and make narrative films.[67] Dash's creative goals as a filmmaker were clearly womanist in intent: she aimed to increase the visibility of the images and stories of Black women.[68] While in Los Angeles, Dash created three short films that were the precursors for *Daughters of the Dust* (1991): *Four Women* (1975) explores the preservation of African American stories through dance; *The Diary of an African Nun* (1977) was based on a short story by Alice Walker, and won a student award from the Directors Guild of America; *Illusions* (1982) won the Jury Prize for Best Film of the Decade awarded by the Black Filmmakers Foundation. Diawara notes four characteristics of these films, which are shared with *Daughters of the Dust*: women's perspective, women's validation of women, shared space rather than dominated space, and attention to female iconography.[69] The centrality of women characters and the emphasis on shared community, which is illustrated in Dash's

63. Page, *Encyclopedia of African American Women Writers.*

64. Bobo, *Black Women as Cultural Readers*; Bobo, *Black Women Film and Video Artists*; Diawara, *Black American Cinema*; Donalson, *Black Directors in Hollywood*; Foster, *Women Filmmakers of the African & Asian Diaspora*; Guerrero, *Framing Blackness*; Yearwood, *Black Film as a Signifying Practice.*

65. "National Film Preservation Board."

66. Field, Horak, and Stewart, *L.A. Rebellion.*

67. Dash, *Daughters of the Dust.*

68. Ibid.

69. Diawara, *Black American Cinema.*

films, are integral to the films of the Black women filmmakers discussed in the remainder of this book.

In Dash's narrative short film *Illusions,* she provides a window into the film industry and the challenges that Black women face within it. This film offers a "complex vision and theoretical analysis of Black women's cinema, of the responsibilities and challenges confronting Black women in the contemporary filmmaking industry, and of strategies for negotiating these."[70] Dash "asks her audience to consider what might happen if women of color were in a position to create images of themselves. Would this result in a more multidimensional depiction of black women or would economic pressures force the usual cultural compromises?"[71] The film is set during the 1940s and explores the experiences of Black women in Hollywood from the perspectives of two Black women characters: Mignon Dupree, a Black studio executive passing for White within an environment where Blacks are denied access, and Esther Jeeter, an aspiring jazz singer who is hired to covertly dub the voice of a White actress. Dupree navigates a setting in which other studio executives play out their racist and sexist suppositions about Black women,[72] while Jeeter is made invisible because of the racist and sexist assumptions made about Black women. In *Illusions,* Dash imagines how a Black woman within this context subversively exercises power and, unbeknownst to others, helps create space for other Black women within the film industry.

Dash's first feature film, *Daughters of the Dust,* was groundbreaking in the way it centralized several complex African American women characters and in its application of unique narrative devices. Dash states that her goal was to do what is rarely done: privilege Black women above all others, above Black men and White women.[73] This counter-hegemonic approach to the portrayal of Black women was not initially met with support from film studios. Dash was repeatedly told that there was no market for the film. However, as she explains, she challenged the idea that the predominantly White male studio executives should dictate what African American women want to see and should be allowed to see.[74] The unwillingness of studio executives to appreciate the value of Dash's story led her to seek support for the film outside of Hollywood, and it was through grassroots organizing and support from groups

70. Ryan, "Outing the Black Feminist Filmmaker in Julie Dash's Illusions," 1320.
71. Williams, "Re-Creating Their Media Image: Two Generations of Black Women Filmmakers," 48.
72. Ibid.
73. Dash, *Daughters of the Dust.*
74. Ibid.

such as the feminist media organization Women Make Movies that she was able to distribute the film.[75]

Daughters of the Dust tells the story of three generations of women living on South Carolina's St. Helena Island in 1902. Dash completed ten years of research for the film, with the goal of taking factual information and infusing it with an "imaginative construction," which led film scholar Ed Guerrero to compare the narrative structure of the film to the Latin American literary concept of magic realism.[76] In addition to its innovative narrative structure, the film also breaks new ground in its celebration of dark-skinned Black women and of Black women as complex beings who possess physical and spiritual beauty.[77] Film scholar Jacqueline Bobo explains that Dash was able to reach Black female viewers through her film in a way that no other film had: ninety percent of the audience of *Daughters of the Dust* was composed of Black women who specifically sought out the film's showings, and most women said they left the theater with a feeling of empowerment, rejuvenation, and connection to other Black women.[78]

Since the release of *Daughters of the Dust,* the number of films created (written and directed) by Black women filmmakers that have been supported by mainstream and independent film studios has slowly increased, as has the critical recognition of their work. Within a few years of the release of *Daughters of the Dust,* Leslie Harris's *Just Another Girl on the I.R.T.* (1992), and Darnell Martin's *I Like It Like That* (1994) were released in theaters. In 1997 Kasi Lemmons's first feature film, *Eve's Bayou,* became one of the highest-grossing independent films and was referred to as "one of the very best films of the year" by film critic Roger Ebert.[79] Gina Prince-Bythewood's breakout feature film *Love & Basketball* became the top-grossing film written and directed by an African American woman when it was released in 2000. Recently, Ava DuVernay, who has written and directed multiple films, became one of the most sought after and recognizable filmmakers after directing the 2014 Academy Award–nominated film *Selma.* In 2017, DuVernay became the first Black woman to be nominated for an Academy Award in the Documentary Feature category, for directing *13th.*[80]

---

75. Ibid.
76. Ibid.; Guerrero, *Framing Blackness.*
77. Dash, *Daughters of the Dust*; Donalson, *Black Directors in Hollywood.*
78. Bobo, *Black Women as Cultural Readers.*
79. Ebert, "'Eve's Bayou' a Remarkable Directing Debut."
80. *Selma* and *13th* are socially significant films; however, I do not discuss them in depth in this book because they do not meet the criteria for inclusion in my chosen sample of films

In the remainder of this chapter, I detail the experiences of the five contemporary Black women filmmakers who created the films that are analyzed in the chapters that follow (Ava DuVernay, Tanya Hamilton, Kasi Lemmons, Gina Prince-Bythewood, and Dee Rees), focusing on how their approaches to filmmaking reflect the womanist artistic standpoint (described above). I reference interviews with Tanya Hamilton, Kasi Lemmons, and Gina Prince-Bythewood that I completed as part of my research for this book, as well as published news articles and interviews with all five filmmakers. This information highlights (1) the centrality of their standpoints as Black women to their filmmaking process, (2) their desire to resist dominant ideologies related to Black femaleness through their films, and (3) the challenges of finding the necessary support for their creative vision from a film industry that has often marginalized the voices of Black women. Another key theme that emerged from my data collection was their practice of supporting other women of color filmmakers, which reflects their collective identity as Black women and an embrace of the idea of "lifting as we climb."[81]

TRANSFORMING THE MYTH OF BLACK WOMANHOOD IN FILM

"We are Black women who seek our own definitions, recognizing diversity among ourselves with respect," proclaims Audre Lorde.[82] Placing Black womanhood at the center of the creative process is an integral part of the womanist artistic standpoint, and something that each of the five filmmakers discussed in the remaining chapters of this book prioritizes. They transform the controlling images, or myths, about Black women and emphasize the importance of "finding a voice to express a collective, self-defined Black women's standpoint," which is a core tenet of a Black feminist perspective.[83]

(theatrically released narrative films, written and directed by a Black woman). Although *Selma* was directed by DuVernay, she was not the screenwriter. Also, *13th* is not a theatrically released narrative film (it is a Netflix-released documentary).

81. Cooper, *Beyond Respectability*. "Lifting as we climb" was the motto of the National Association of Colored Women, which was founded in 1896 and whose founders included activists such as Ida B. Wells-Barnett and Mary Church Terrell. This motto signified a desire to promote autonomy among a collective of Black women as well as promote racial "uplift." Although historically expressions of racial uplift may have partly reflected class divisions among African Americans, I use this phrase to emphasize a sense of shared experiences that have led to self-support among Black women.

82. Lorde, *Sister Outsider*, 144.

83. Collins, *Black Feminist Thought*, 99.

Ava DuVernay (*Middle of Nowhere*, 2012) describes anything that comes from the point of view of a woman or person of color in Hollywood as a "unicorn."[84] Her statement underscores the scarcity of films being created from these points of view, to the point that a film made by a woman of color is almost unheard of—a myth. DuVernay's goal is to challenge this marginalization. Film scholar Michael T. Martin compares DuVernay's work to that of Julie Dash because of her sustained engagement with Black women's agency and subjectivity.[85] This emphasis on agency and subjectivity for Black women illustrates the womanist artistic standpoint. Foregrounding the perspectives of Black women is a priority for DuVernay, which she made clear in a 2015 interview: "I will never make a film without Black women in it. I can say that very clearly. There is no world in which I am interested in telling stories where we are not there."[86] She is determined that Black women will move beyond the level of myth in Hollywood. Her first two narrative feature films, *I Will Follow* (2010) and *Middle of Nowhere* (2012), illustrate this through the nuanced African American female lead characters.

When DuVernay directed the Oscar-nominated Martin Luther King biopic *Selma* (2014), she creatively gave a more significant voice to several Black women characters, whose involvement in the civil rights movement has often been minimized:

> When I tackled the film and came on board with the film, I brought in about 27 new characters and insisted that the women of the movement be portrayed, so I expanded the character of Coretta Scott King. I added the character of Diane Nash, added the character of Amelia Boynton, added the character of Richie Jean Jackson, and expanded the character of Annie Lee Cooper. So there are women throughout that have major work to do in the film.[87]

Additionally, although DuVernay's *13th* primarily documents the impact of mass incarceration on Black men, she features several Black women in the film as experts on the problem of mass incarceration, such as scholar-activists Angela Davis and Michelle Alexander. Their input and presence are integral to the film's critique of the prison industrial complex. DuVernay's focus on transforming images of women and girls of color in film continued with her

---

84. Lee, "Director Ava DuVernay Talks Race, Hollywood and Doing It Her Way."

85. Martin, "Conversations with Ava DuVernay—'A Call to Action': Organizing Principles of an Activist Cinematic Practice."

86. Kovan, "Interview with Ava DuVernay on 'Selma' and Telling the Stories of Black Women."

87. Ibid.

casting of the Disney film *A Wrinkle in Time* (released in 2018). One article that exemplifies this is aptly titled "Ava DuVernay Thinks Little Brown Girls Should Be Space Travelers, Too."[88]

Kasi Lemmons (*Eve's Bayou*, 1997) has experienced the challenges of being a Black woman in Hollywood behind as well as in front of the camera—unlike other filmmakers discussed in this book, Lemmons began her film career as an actress.[89] The challenges that she encountered when looking for work as a Black actress inspired her to pursue filmmaking and change the narratives being told in Hollywood about Black women. Lemmons explained that her attending film school was a result of this frustration and the limited roles for Black women: "The New School came at a time when I began to realize how much time I had on my hands. You know, being a Black actress . . . I wanted to do something more meaningful than going to auditions, waiting for auditions or waiting for the phone to ring. I thought that I should really learn to make films."[90] Attending film school and creating narrative films was Lemmons's way to insert her voice into the narratives of American cinema.

In *Eve's Bayou* (1997), Lemmons created a world, which she explains was based partly on her own experience growing up, where being Black was an unquestioned and unproblematic part of one's existence. Being a Black woman in a culture and industry that has not valued Blackness, Lemmons was inspired to create a film that focused on Black people, and, as she described in an interview, she made a decision that there would be no White people and no mention of White people in *Eve's Bayou*. Lemmons explained: "There was one mention of White people in an earlier draft, but as people started to tell me, 'Well can't you have a White character even if it's a White racist character?' I said, 'No.' Then finally I said, 'Ain't no White people in Eve's Bayou' . . . It became a statement of mine."[91] As a reflection of the womanist artistic standpoint, Lemmons's film makes a statement that Blackness is significant in and of itself, rejecting the social expectation of representing the characters in relation to the dominant culture.

Gina Prince-Bythewood has achieved commercial success with films like *Love & Basketball* (2000), *The Secret Life of Bees* (2008), and *Beyond the Lights* (2014). In all of her films, Prince-Bythewood prioritizes placing Black characters—Black women in particular—at the center of the narrative. One of her goals as a Black woman filmmaker is to transform the perceptions that film

---

88. Kahn, "Ava DuVernay Thinks Little Brown Girls Should Be Space Travelers, Too."

89. A few of Lemmons's acting roles include *School Daze* (1988), *Silence of the Lambs* (1991), and *Fear of a Black Hat* (1994).

90. Alexander, *Why We Make Movies*, 255.

91. Ibid., 260.

executives and audiences have about films that center on Black characters. In my interview with Prince-Bythewood, she explained: "That's the issue that I have and many of us have with Hollywood. It's the boxes that we're put in, and as soon as there are people of color in a film, it loses its genre." Her statement reflects the tendency for Hollywood to rely on limiting cultural ideologies associated with Blackness, which does not provide the space for a film with Black characters to be viewed beyond dominant cultural assumptions about Blackness. She creates films that center on Black women characters in a variety of social contexts in order to resist this marginalization and compartmentalization of Blackness in Hollywood.

Tanya Hamilton (*Night Catches Us,* 2010) makes it clear that her goal is to create stories and characters that focus on Blackness in unconventional ways. She expresses the "courageousness" of a womanist by intentionally resisting the unidimensional characters and familiar narratives that are all too common in mainstream media. In my interview with Hamilton, she explained: "It's important for me to do my best to illustrate the Black experience in the most complicated and layered way possible. I do not believe that that is something the Black experience is often afforded." Critical of the tendency for the film industry to capitalize on extremely narrow representations of Blackness, she added:

> What I don't love is the Black experience as one thing: we are struggling in one way or another. Well, how about struggling just as ordinary people? How about struggling because you love somebody and they don't love you back? Or you've got to raise your kid and your kid's a problem and you don't know how to deal with it? So I think I didn't want any more struggling porn . . . I'll take this much of it, but I feel like the Black experience extends so far beyond that.

Her first feature film, *Night Catches Us* (2010), moves beyond the dominant ideologies about Black womanhood by focusing on a Black woman who has lost her husband as a result of his involvement with the Black Panthers. Her film transforms dominant narratives by centering the experience of a Black woman within a social movement that has largely focused on the role of men.

Dee Rees (*Pariah,* 2011) was inspired to make *Pariah* because of the near-absence of Black lesbian characters on-screen when she was growing up.[92]

---

92. Filmmaker Cheryl Dunye, the first openly gay Black woman to write and direct a theatrically released feature film (*The Watermelon Woman,* 1996), has also emphasized the invisibility of Black queer women as an impetus in her filmmaking. See Anderson, "Director Cheryl Dunye on Her Groundbreaking LGBTQ Film 'The Watermelon Woman,' 20 Years Later."

Making *Pariah* was based on a desire to create a film with a character that she could have identified with: "Growing up, I rarely saw my image reflected on screen. *The Color Purple* and *Women of Brewster Place* are the few films I was allowed to watch when I was younger that touched on sexuality. I made *Pariah* to portray images on screen that we hadn't seen before, and to bring to light the experiences of gay youth of color because those stories hadn't been fully told."[93] Rees describes the script for *Pariah* as "cathartic." "Going into a room and saying, 'I'm a Black lesbian'—it's a strike against you,"[94] she acknowledges. But embracing her sexuality and identity as a Black woman is essential to her filmmaking: "I can't put anything out that's not me."[95]

Because of Rees's courage to put herself out there, *Ebony* magazine identified her as one of "America's Black LGBT pioneers."[96] The success of *Pariah* was just the beginning of Rees's focus on increasing the visibility of Black women LGBTQ characters in media. Following *Pariah*, Rees wrote and directed the 2015 HBO film *Bessie*, which explores the life of blues singer Bessie Smith and centers issues of race, gender, and sexual identity. Rees smoothly weaves Smith's sexual relationships with women *and* men into the film. Rees's depiction of Smith's sexuality and her multifaceted relationships is one of the film's "most striking contributions."[97] Rather than simplifying Smith's relationships, Rees transgresses dominant cultural expectations by highlighting Black women's sexual agency and self-determination.[98] By drawing from her perspective as a Black lesbian filmmaker, Rees centralizes and normalizes Smith's relationships with women. This reflects the womanist artistic standpoint of creating films that resist the limited representations of Black women in film.

OVERCOMING RESISTANCE AND MAINTAINING ARTISTIC VISION

The filmmakers that are the focus of this book fight resistance from the commercial film industry—which is a by-product of the larger social, political, and economic context—as they strive to maintain their artistic vision. In her essay "Back to the Avant-Garde," bell hooks describes the difficulty of navigat-

---

93. Swadhin, "GLAAD Interviews 'Pariah' Director Dee Rees."

94. Littleton, "'Bessie' Director Dee Rees on Bessie Smith's Ferocity and Facing Prejudice."

95. Ibid.

96. Baron, "Not Just Indie: A Look at Films by Dee Rees, Ava DuVernay and Kasi Lemmons," 209.

97. Smith, "Bessie."

98. Ibid.

ing this environment, from her perspective as an artist doing unconventional work: "I am acutely aware of the way in which our longing to experiment, to create from a multiplicity of standpoints, meets with resistance from those whose interest in that work is primarily commercial, from audiences and from critics."[99] Hooks argues that "black artistic production will be severely damaged if the values of the marketplace overdetermine what we create."[100] Each filmmaker in the present study is also aware of the potential for her art to be co-opted by those who are primarily interested in the financial profitability of her films. The filmmakers discuss the challenges they have faced and strategies they apply in the process of maintaining and finding support for their creative vision within this context. Rather than letting the commercial film industry control their art, they prioritize their artistic vision, even in the face of resistance.

Ava DuVernay has faced this tension between her artistic vision and the expectations of the commercial film industry, which she discussed in an interview with film scholar Michael T. Martin: "Just to be able to continue to make films is success for me personally and may inspire others. So, if you're looking to be an artist, sustain your craft."[101] She wrote the script for what she hoped would be her first narrative feature film, *Middle of Nowhere,* in 2003 (which I discuss in detail in chapter 4 of this book), but the process of bringing the project to fruition took nine years. The film centers on the personal journey of a Black woman who puts her life, including medical school, on hold when her husband is unexpectedly arrested and incarcerated. Filmmaker Gina Prince-Bythewood, who had already achieved success with her breakout film *Love & Basketball,* was supportive of the film and was interested in producing it. Hollywood studios, on the other hand, were not. DuVernay explains:

> Gina Prince-Bythewood and Reggie Bythewood were good friends and clients at the time and said, "We really love this. We want to produce it." So we went out and we attached Sanaa Lathan and Idris Elba and shopped it in the traditional way that you did in 2003 when you were in Black Hollywood. You'd go to the studios and it was, "Oh, wow, great script, but we don't make movies about the interior life of Black women."[102]

---

99. hooks, *Reel to Real,* 129.

100. Ibid., 107.

101. Martin, "Conversations with Ava DuVernay—'A Call to Action': Organizing Principles of an Activist Cinematic Practice."

102. Cooper, "Love on the Outside."

Faced with rejection and the devaluation of her creative voice from the commercial film industry, which is an all too common experience for Black women filmmakers, she put *Middle of Nowhere* on hold and made her first documentary (a project that required fewer financial resources). DuVernay's directorial debut was the 2008 hip-hop documentary *This Is the Life,* which was self-distributed and produced. Following *This Is the Life,* she directed a documentary for television, titled *My Mic Sounds Nice: The Truth about Women in Hip Hop* (2010). She was then able to make her first full-length narrative feature film, *I Will Follow* (2010), which she wrote, directed, and produced. *I Will Follow* won Best Screenplay from the African-American Film Critics Association and was nominated for an NAACP Image Award for Outstanding Independent Motion Picture. After *I Will Follow,* DuVernay was, finally, able to garner enough support to direct the first narrative screenplay she had written, *Middle of Nowhere,* which was released in 2012. The process of sustaining her artistic vision required persistence and creativity, as well as a focus on prioritizing that vision over the expectations of the commercial film industry.

As a filmmaker, Kasi Lemmons has been able to find the artistic fulfillment that eluded her as an actress. "The most artistically fulfilling experiences I've had, have been directing. Definitely directing. Writing-directing, is a beautiful thing when you come at a project from zero, and try and capture it . . . there is a lot of creative control, as a director," declared Lemmons during my conversation with her. With *Eve's Bayou* (1997), Lemmons's first feature film, she was able to fully realize her artistic vision. However, finding support for the film, which focuses on a well-to-do Black family living in Louisiana in the 1960s, did not come easy. One article reports that it took several years and over one hundred meetings before she was able to find support for the film.[103] When discussing resistance to finding support for her first feature film, Lemmons explained, "There was a deep feeling of, 'What is the audience for this movie?' and that African-American art films do not perform well."[104] She was also told that the film was "impossible to produce."[105] In my conversation with Kasi Lemmons, she emphasized the necessity to be persistent in the face of the resistance: "I think, so much of the key is, just, not being squashed. Like, getting up. Like, you just get up. And, really, it's part of the journey, and part of the trick to it; like, 'last man standing wins.' You just keep going. If this is what you do, then, just keep going." Her intense devotion to her art provided her with the necessary drive to face this resistance: "I had a big dream that I was very

103. Galloway, "Capitalizing on Success."
104. Ibid.
105. Ascher-Walsh, "Lemmons and Lines."

intent on vigorously fulfilling . . . That's the way I lived it: I'm an artist. I know my history, I know my roots, I know I can be an artist,"[106] explains Lemmons.

In a 2002 interview, Lemmons discussed the obstacles that Black women filmmakers face as they attempt to sustain their artistic vision: "There is still a culture and belief system in Hollywood that glorifies young White men . . . A lot of them are making fabulous films, but so are (a lot of Black filmmakers). It's not as if they are looking to celebrate us."[107] She further illustrates the racial and gendered biases in Hollywood when describing the preconceived ideas about filmmakers: "He's 25 to 45 and has that kind of scruffy, slightly rumpled look . . . And he's a White man. I do not fit that aesthetic."[108] With *Eve's Bayou,* Lemmons not only gained the personal sense of fulfillment that came from expressing her artistic vision, she also achieved validation for that vision when it became one of the highest-grossing independent films of 1997.[109] The film's success perhaps provided her with, in the words of Lorraine Hansberry, "a slight sense of justification for being."[110]

Tanya Hamilton's desire to tell her unconventional story about Blackness was not initially embraced by Hollywood studios, and it took ten years to find enough financial support to make *Night Catches Us.* She began working on the film in 2000, and by the time the film premiered ten years later, she explains that she felt as though she had gone through a "small war."[111] In my interview with Hamilton, she explained:

> I think back then people were sort of like "why do you want to make this story? And who really cares?" And by that I mean, not the people that were our supporters, who are very ardent, but the people who we were looking for money from. It took us a really long time to get financing, and I think in part because socially it made no sense to them.

Although Hamilton found support from places such as Sundance, when it came down to finding someone to invest money into the film, she ran into roadblocks: "I think as far as 'I can help you make this movie, for real. I can help you go find money. I can give you money,' we couldn't find anybody. And that was hard for a long time."

106. "Third Act."
107. Galloway, "Capitalizing on Success."
108. Kuhn, "Distaff and Distinguished."
109. Mask, "Eve's Bayou: Too Good to Be a 'Black' Film?"
110. Hansberry, *To Be Young, Gifted and Black: Lorraine Hansberry in Her Own Words.*
111. Adams, "Simmering in the City."

Although financing *Night Catches Us* was challenging, Tanya Hamilton approaches filmmaking from an artist-activist perspective. When I asked Hamilton if she considers herself an artist, she replied, "I think it's in my genes. I was a painter for a long time. It's how I learned to express myself early on and I don't think I could ever be disentangled from that." She studied painting at the Duke Ellington School of the Arts in Washington, DC, and made a transition to film after she attended Cooper Union for the Advancement of Science and Art and Columbia University's Film School. She recognizes the potential for film to act as a form of self-expression *and* a vehicle to move people, emotionally and intellectually. "I want to make movies that are respectful of the notion of art as a way to communicate. And art as a way to educate and to uplift and to make us self-reflective," said Hamilton in my interview with her. She achieved this goal with her first feature film, *Night Catches Us* (2010), in which she reenvisions a social movement that is often oversimplified in the country's historical memory and creatively presents a part of that movement that has been overlooked.

Gina Prince-Bythewood had incomparable educational and professional achievements prior to making her first film, *Love & Basketball* (2000). She walked in the footsteps of Julie Dash and other L.A. Rebellion filmmakers by attending film school at UCLA. She worked as a writer on several television shows, including *A Different World* (1992–1993), *South Central* (1994), *Sweet Justice* (1994), *Courthouse* (1995), and *Felicity* (1998). She also wrote and directed the CBS Schoolbreak Special *What about Your Friends* (1995), for which she won an NAACP Image Award for Best Children's special and Emmy nominations for writing and directing. Despite Prince-Bythewood's impressive resume and the social capital that she developed early on in her career, she was not immune to the resistance that other Black women filmmakers faced. Of *Love & Basketball*, Prince-Bythewood says, "I worked on the script for about a year and a half and completed about fifteen drafts of the script before I finally went out and tried to sell it, and everybody turned it down. The biggest note I got from most people was that it was too soft . . . We still get the same argument that Black dramas don't sell."[112] Similar to Kasi Lemmons's emphasis on the importance of persistence, Prince-Bythewood attributes her success as a filmmaker to her ability to fight and overcome the inevitable "No": "Every project is a fight but what I learned very early on with *Love & Basketball* is overcome 'No.'" However, while filming *Love & Basketball*, her legitimacy as a director was often called into question by "older White men" who wondered what she was doing on the set and some who regularly questioned her deci-

---

112. Alexander, *Why We Make Movies.*

sions.[113] Prince-Bythewood says, "You wonder, 'Is it because I'm a first-time filmmaker—or a Black woman?'"[114] *Love & Basketball* went on to win a long list of awards, including the Independent Spirit Award and Humanitas Prize at Sundance. It also became the highest-grossing film written and directed by a Black woman filmmaker.

After writing and directing a film that was popular with critics and audiences, one might expect that Prince-Bythewood had proven her ability to take control of her art. *Love & Basketball*'s success did make Gina Prince-Bythewood a highly sought-after filmmaker. However, she has continued to face resistance to her vision and voice, especially when it comes to telling non-stereotypical stories with women of color at the center. In our conversation, she observed,

> I'm in the fortunate position where when I write something, still banging on the door—I am in the fortunate position of being able to be in the room with the people who can say "yes"—So every time I do, more opportunities open up and the reality is if I wanted to do a film a year, I could. I do get offered a lot of films and have to turn down a lot of films . . . [but] the hard thing is the ones that I want to write and direct right now focus on women of color, and those are the harder things to get made.

She has continued to tell stories that focus on Black women, which is her goal as an artist. Prince-Bythewood's focus on centering Black women's stories takes audaciousness within a context that marginalizes Black women's perspectives, and reflects the womanist artistic standpoint.

Dee Rees made the courageous move of explicitly placing her personal narrative front and center for her first creative cinematic endeavor. She refers to *Pariah* (2011) as "semi-autobiographical."[115] Self-definition is an essential part of Black feminism, and the other Black women filmmakers discussed in this book draw from their personal experiences for their creative process, as their films illustrate; however, none has placed her personal identity exploration so directly at the center of her films as has Rees. Similar to Ava DuVernay and Kasi Lemmons, Dee Rees did not begin her career as a filmmaker. She earned a master's degree in business administration from Florida A&M University and worked in marketing for Proctor & Gamble. She made the deci-

---

113. Wiltz, "'Love and Basketball's' Champion Director Gina Prince-Bythewood Takes a (Successful) Shot at the Hollywood Game."

114. Ibid.

115. Hardy, "Interview with Dee Rees, Director of Pariah"; Zack, "'Pariah' Director Dee Rees Confronts Disapproval"; NPR Staff, "A Gay Black Teen Learns How to Be in 'Pariah.'"

sion to attend film school and tell stories on her own terms, rather than take the financially safe route of telling stories about products to which she felt no personal connection.[116] Rees explains the relationship between her personal experiences and her creative depiction of these experiences in *Pariah*: "When I came out, I had a struggle with my parents accepting who I was, and I also had the internal struggle of realizing that my spirituality and my sexuality were not mutually exclusive . . . Those are things I dealt with in my own coming out experience, and I placed them on to this 17-year-old character."[117] Filmmaking, then, merged artistic expression and self-definition for Rees.

Rees's story about a young Black lesbian's personal identity exploration was not an easy sell. Rees refers to the fund-raising efforts for the film as "incredibly difficult," which I believe to be an *incredible understatement*: "People loved the script but would call it 'too small' and 'too specific,' which was basically code for 'too black' and 'too gay,'" says Rees.[118] In the end, Rees received financial support for *Pariah* from donors who believed in the story and felt that it had to be told, regardless of the expected commercial success.[119] The film premiered at Sundance in 2011 and had the support of renowned filmmaker Spike Lee, who served as an executive producer. Although Rees's artistic vision was not initially fully appreciated by many studio executives, it ultimately won several awards, such as the John Cassavetes Award, the GLAAD Media Award, an Image Award, and the award for Best Independent Film from the African-American Film Critics Association.

LIFTING AS THEY CLIMB

Alice Walker writes that a womanist is "committed to survival and wholeness of an entire people."[120] In *Black Feminist Thought*, Patricia Hill Collins echoes this sense of shared community, in which Black women support and affirm one another—there is a shared recognition among Black women, who may not know each other, but "who see the need to value Black womanhood."[121] The Black women filmmakers who are the focus of this book embrace a commitment to the survival of other Black women in the film industry and affirm the value of the work of other Black women filmmakers.

116. Zack, "'Pariah' Director Dee Rees Confronts Disapproval."
117. Swadhin, "GLAAD Interviews 'Pariah' Director Dee Rees."
118. Zack, "'Pariah' Director Dee Rees Confronts Disapproval."
119. Ibid.
120. Walker, *In Search of Our Mothers' Gardens*, xi.
121. Collins, *Black Feminist Thought*, 103.

Ava DuVernay affirms and celebrates the work of other Black women through her films, television series, and distribution company. In 2010 DuVernay founded the African-American Film Festival Releasing Movement (AFFRM), whose name has since been changed to ARRAY. ARRAY is described as "a community-based distribution collective dedicated to the amplification of films by people of color and women filmmakers."[122] "It's not about knocking on closed doors," said DuVernay in a 2012 interview. "It's about building our own house and having our own door."[123] DuVernay also emphasizes that there is an activist spirit that drives her company: "We are by definition on a mission to further and foster the Black cinematic image in an organized and consistent way, and to not have to defer and ask permission to traffic our films: to be self-determining."[124] DuVernay's first two narrative films, *I Will Follow* (2010) and *Middle of Nowhere* (2012), were distributed through ARRAY. ARRAY also distributed the work of another Black woman filmmaker, Tina Mabry, whose 2009 film, *Mississippi Damned,* was released on Netflix.

DuVernay's amplification of the work of Black women has also been demonstrated through her work within episodic television, which is a format that has the option to be inclusive of multiple voices throughout various episodes and seasons. In the television series *Queen Sugar* (2016–), which DuVernay created and executive produced, she made a decision to hire only female directors for the first season because she was aware of the difficulties that talented women directors face in Hollywood.[125] DuVernay explains, "We are hiring an all women directorial team. A lot of women that we know from the Black independent space . . . [I]t's an exciting time to invite women into the show and really try to tell the story of this family of really strong women."[126] In fact, in 2016 Tanya Hamilton directed an episode of *Queen Sugar*.[127] Notably, it was another Black woman, Shonda Rhimes, who hired DuVernay to direct an episode of her popular television show *Scandal,* giving DuVernay her first shot at directing episodic television. Through her creative work and distribution company, DuVernay has facilitated the artistic expression of numerous other Black women.

122. http://www.avaDuVernay.com/#/array/.

123. Rickey, "She's a Graduate of an Unusual Film School: Ava DuVernay and 'Middle of Nowhere.'"

124. Martin, "Conversations with Ava DuVernay—'A Call to Action': Organizing Principles of an Activist Cinematic Practice."

125. Butler, "Why Ava DuVernay Hired Only Female Directors for Her New TV Show 'Queen Sugar.'"

126. "Tanya Hamilton Joins the 'Queen Sugar' All-Female Directorial Team."

127. Ibid.

The challenges that Kasi Lemmons has faced as a Black woman filmmaker have inspired her to support other women filmmakers and filmmakers of color. For example, when I interviewed Gina Prince-Bythewood, she spoke very highly of the support that she received from Lemmons when she was in the process of making *Love & Basketball*.[128] When I interviewed Lemmons, she was an associate arts professor at New York University's Tisch School of the Arts. She expressed the fulfillment that she now gets from mentoring aspiring filmmakers, especially filmmakers from underrepresented backgrounds:

> The kids that gravitate to me are not, necessarily, the straight, White men. But, I get them, too. But, I do feel that the students of color and the women need me. They need me, by example. And, they also need me, specifically. And so, that's been very important to me; and, also incredibly fulfilling for me, in terms of the artists that I'm helping to support. It's gratifying, because, you feel like you're changing the world. You're changing the landscape.

This sentiment reflects Lemmons's desire to change the narrative through her own filmmaking, as well as supporting the work of other marginalized groups.

Tanya Hamilton expresses a sense of connection to other filmmakers who have struggled to find support for their films, particularly other women of color. "A lot of the people I've talked with over the years have been women, which I think is interesting. Certainly, more Black women than women who are not Black or Latina," she shared during our conversation. Because she has achieved the goal of having her film distributed theatrically, she feels a responsibility to help others do the same:

> What I feel compelled by is when someone doesn't have resources or their resources are small. In that way, I feel a greater responsibility to share what I have. Because I know exactly what it feels like to not have any resources and to really need even just one tiny thing. Something easy that someone can do but that can really mean a lot . . . I remember so clearly not having enough money or not feeling like I had enough access to a world that could help me.

This shared recognition of the struggle that she and other women of color face is integral to her work and to her supporting other Black women.

Gina Prince-Bythewood, like the other filmmakers discussed in this chapter, is aware of the importance of supporting other women of color who are attempting to share their stories through film. This is demonstrated by Prince-Bythewood's early support of Ava DuVernay's 2012 film *Middle of Nowhere*

---

128. See appendix D.

(discussed above). Prince-Bythewood also fondly discusses the support that she received from filmmaker Kasi Lemmons and her admiration for Lemmons's *Eve's Bayou*: "Kasi Lemmons has been a huge support, and I talked to her before I started *Love & Basketball*. *Eve's Bayou* I loved so much. Sitting in the theater watching that film—it just filled me. It was just such a beautiful film and I was just so enamored with the film and with her. I had the opportunity to talk with her right before I was going to shoot *Love & Basketball* and she was incredibly supportive, and that was really a gift." She adds, "The way that Kasi was supportive of me is how I've tried to be for filmmakers that I identify that have talent."[129] In 2015, Prince-Bythewood received formal recognition for her support of other filmmakers when she received a woman of the year award, in which she was honored for her ability to show the "goodness in people, the complexity of humanity and the ability to overcome," and for making it her mission to "introduce young people into the industry."[130] During my interview with Prince-Bythewood, she also mentioned a few emerging Black women artists in film and television whom she admires,[131] indicating her continuing efforts to *lift as she climbs*.

•

"Though it be a wonderful thrilling and marvelous thing to be merely young and gifted in such times, it is doubly so, doubly dynamic—to be young, gifted *and black*. Write if you will, but write about the world as it is and as you think it ought to be and must be—if there is to be a world. Write about *our people*: tell their story. You have something glorious to draw on begging for attention. Don't pass it up. *Use* it."[132] The work of the Black women filmmakers who are discussed in this chapter are the embodiment of these words, spoken by Lorraine Hansberry.

DuVernay, Hamilton, Lemmons, Prince-Bythewood, and Rees have all declared their intention of creating stories that reflect their experiences as Black women. Their careers reflect the core elements of the womanist artistic standpoint: they assert their identities as Black women, rebel against the dominant narratives and marginalization of Black women in film, and prioritize

---

129. See appendix D.

130. Sentinel News Service, "Gina Prince-Bythewood Selected Woman of the Year."

131. During my interview with Gina Prince-Bythewood, she lauded the work of Lena Waithe (who, in 2017, became the first Black woman to win an "Outstanding Writing for a Comedy Series" Emmy Award) and Tina Mabry (whose film *Mississippi Damned* was released on Netflix through Ava DuVernay's distribution company, ARRAY).

132. Hansberry, *To Be Young, Gifted and Black: Lorraine Hansberry in Her Own Words*, 256–57.

their creative vision over commercial success. Within their candid discussions about their experiences making films in Hollywood is their desire to fight and resist the practice of suppressing or homogenizing the stories of women of color. They are taking control of the creative process and fighting for their stories to be recognized within the film industry. These filmmakers "have something glorious to draw on begging for attention," to apply Lorraine Hansberry's words, and they are *using* it for social transformation through film.

CHAPTER 2

Work as Passion

Love & Basketball and *Beyond the Lights*

> You will be beautiful when you do not try to be something you are
> not: when you are true to yourself then you will become like a swan:
> released in the grace of natural and spontaneous purpose.
>
> —JUNE JORDAN[1]

> Within the celebration of the erotic in all our endeavors, my
> work becomes a conscious decision—a longed-for bed which
> I enter gratefully and from which I rise up empowered.
> Of course, women so empowered are dangerous.
>
> —AUDRE LORDE[2]

PASSION CAN BE all-consuming. It is an intense, pleasurable feeling. It can inspire and motivate. But, for whom and toward what end? What if this feeling of intensity is applied to activities that are expressions of one's self? What does passion look like when it is attached to purpose? In this chapter, I discuss two of Gina Prince-Bythewood's films that show how passion can be applied toward work that allows women to fully embrace their talents and, as June Jordan writes, be "released into the grace of natural and spontaneous purpose." *Love & Basketball* (2000) and *Beyond the Lights* (2014) illustrate the potential for work to be an avenue of personal fulfillment for Black women. Both films take a look at the lead characters' pursuits within two high-profile, male-dominated fields (basketball and hip-hop). Through in-depth explorations of two women's journeys, Prince-Bythewood calls into question the roles in which women are typically presented within these fields.

Audre Lorde urges women to view work as a celebration of the power of the erotic—something one longs for. She points out the fallacy in the cultural

---

1. Jordan, "The Creative Spirit."
2. Lorde, *Sister Outsider,* 55.

perception that the value of work is determined by its external rewards. Lorde explains, "The principal horror of any system which defines the good in terms of profit rather than in terms of human need, or which defines human need to the exclusion of the psychic and emotional components of that need . . . is that it robs our work of its erotic value, its erotic power and life appeal and fulfillment."[3] The erotic is not only sexual and it is not to be confused with pornographic depictions, which are the denial of power and the opposite of the erotic: "Pornography emphasizes sensation without feeling."[4] Lorde explains, "When I speak of the erotic, then, I speak of it as an assertion of the lifeforce of women; of that creative energy empowered, the knowledge and use of which we are now reclaiming in our language, our history, our dancing, our loving, our work, our lives."[5]

In *Love & Basketball* and *Beyond the Lights*, Prince-Bythewood creatively depicts Patricia Hill Collins's declaration in *Black Feminist Thought*: work can be fulfilling, empowering, and creative.[6] Work can be an expression of one's passion and purpose. It is no coincidence that Prince-Bythewood is the artist behind the two films that are the focus of this chapter. *Love & Basketball* and *Beyond the Lights* portray Black women passionately and determinedly pursuing a career that is a significant part of their life and identity, which is something that Prince-Bythewood embraces in her own professional life. She credits her determination and drive to succeed to her background as an athlete. "I absolutely attribute my ability to fight and my stamina to growing up playing sports, because that's what you're taught . . . [W]anting to be the best is good. And those are absolutely things little girls are not taught outside of sports. So, have swagger. When you walk in that court, own that court," she explained during my interview with her. This passion, persistence, and "swagger" have certainly worked for her. Prince-Bythewood has been successful in maintaining her artistic vision and getting others to believe in that vision, as well. The results of her passion and persistence can also be seen in the audience reception of her films: Price-Bythewood's films, which she both wrote and directed, have been the most financially successful of any Black woman to date.[7]

---

3. Ibid.

4. Ibid., 54.

5. Ibid., 55.

6. Collins, *Black Feminist Thought*, 48.

7. This refers to films that were written *and* directed by a Black woman filmmaker, as of 2017. The domestic box office gross for *Love & Basketball* was $27,459,615, and her film adaptation of the book *The Secret Life of Bees* earned $37,770,162 (www.boxofficemojo.com), which are higher earnings than for any other film that was written and directed by a Black woman. *The Secret Life of Bees* (2008) is Prince-Bythewood's highest-grossing film so far; however, I do

CONTROLLING IMAGES OF BLACK WOMEN AS LABORERS

Zora Neale Hurston's reference to Black women as the "mules" of the world in her 1937 novel *Their Eyes Were Watching God* has often been cited as a metaphor for the ways that Black women are dehumanized and expected to carry the load of others.[8] The specific image of the mythical "mammy" is one of the most enduring images of Black womanhood as existing to carry the load of others.[9] This controlling image envisions Black women as self-sacrificing caregivers with no personal qualities that signal that their personhood exists outside of that which is needed to fulfill the desires of others. I propose that the qualities of the mammy controlling image continue to permeate the cultural ideology surrounding Black womanhood. However, Gina Prince-Bythewood's films challenge these expectations that deny or disparage Black women's ability to pursue passionate, purposeful, and even erotic self-definition through vocation.

Cinematic depictions of Black womanhood have often been constructed to help define the purpose of *other* characters. The first time a Black woman was considered for an Academy Award, she played a character without a name. In 1939 Hattie McDaniel became the first person of African descent to be nominated for and win an Academy Award, for her role in *Gone with the Wind,* in which she is known only as "Mammy." Her character was not given an identity or purpose other than that which involved serving others. It was ten years after McDaniel's win that another Black actress was nominated for an Academy Award, and it took fifty years for another Black actress to win,[10] but McDaniel's portrayal of "Mammy" resonated with mainstream America. As Melissa Harris-Perry explains, although McDaniel's life was a "complex mixture of ambition, compromise, resistance, rejection, and success . . . it was her embodiment of mammy that won her national acclaim, praise, and validation."[11] The complexity of McDaniel's story was reduced to that of a one-dimensional misrepresentation of Black womanhood.

The mammy image is the antithesis of self-determination: a "faithful, obedient domestic servant," whose primary or sole interest is in caring for

---

not include that particular film in my analysis because my focus is on films in which a Black woman wrote the original (not adapted) screenplay.

8. Collins, *Black Feminist Thought*; Harris-Perry, *Sister Citizen*.

9. Bogle, *Toms, Coons, Mulattoes, Mammies, and Bucks*; McElya, *Clinging to Mammy*.

10. In 1949 Ethel Waters was nominated for Best Actress in a Supporting Role for *Pinky*, and in 1990 Whoopi Goldberg became the second Black actress to win a Supporting Actress Academy Award for her role in *Ghost*.

11. Harris-Perry, *Sister Citizen*, 76.

the White family that she serves.[12] With the mammy image, Black women who worked in White homes during and immediately after slavery were reimagined as willing participants in the system that exploited their labor. That mammy always cared for and nurtured the White family that she served better than her own symbolized the dominant group's perceptions of the ideal position of Black women within the power structure. "She was a trusted advisor and confidante whose skills were used exclusively in service of the white families to which she was attached."[13] Mammy was stripped of any desires, interests, or needs of her own.

African American women *and* men were frequently limited to servant roles in films during the early twentieth century;[14] however, "the mammy image is central to intersecting oppressions of race, gender, sexuality, and class."[15] The mammy myth was created to "justify the economic exploitation of house slaves and sustained to explain Black women's long-standing restriction to domestic service."[16] The lack of options available to Black women outside of domestic work and the economic and psychological exploitation that Black women who worked within White homes experienced was easily disregarded with the invention of the mammy image. Instead of recognizing Black women as laborers, mammy was represented as "enjoying her servitude."[17]

The mammy image also served to maintain the sexual oppression of Black women. Whereas the myth of Black women's lasciviousness and fertility (embodied in the "Jezebel" stereotype) was initially meant to justify the sexual abuse of enslaved women, "after slavery's demise, the specter of racial intermixing in the context of (nominal) legal equality became a national anxiety. Black women who labored in white homes had to be reimagined . . . [and] an asexual, omnicompetent, devoted servant was ideal."[18] Consequently, this image did not allow Black women the possibility of interpersonal relationships that may involve a family or partnership based on their own desires.

Although the mammy was presented as having a deep "love for white folk who she willingly and passively served," the reality for domestic servants was, of course, strikingly different.[19] Domestic servants who worked in Southern plantations were usually teenagers or very young women who were taken

---

12. Collins, *Black Feminist Thought*, 72.
13. Harris-Perry, *Sister Citizen*, 72.
14. Bogle, *Toms, Coons, Mulattoes, Mammies, and Bucks.*
15. Collins, *Black Feminist Thought*, 73.
16. Ibid., 72.
17. Harris-Perry, *Sister Citizen*, 77.
18. Ibid., 71.
19. hooks, *Ain't I a Woman: Black Women and Feminism*, 84.

from their own families and coerced into nursing and otherwise caring for the children of White families. "It was white supremacist imaginations that remembered these powerless, coerced slave girls as soothing, comfortable, consenting women."[20]

It has been nearly a century since Hattie McDaniel portrayed "Mammy" in *Gone with the Wind*. Black women are no longer limited to the role of domestic servant, and the majority of employed Black women do not perform paid domestic work.[21] You may wonder: Has the mammy image become obsolete in contemporary society? In *Clinging to Mammy: The Faithful Slave in Twentieth-Century America*, Micki McElya argues that "mammy"

> remains dear to the hearts of many . . . The myth of the faithful slave lingers because so many white Americans have wished to live in a world in which African Americans are not angry over past and present injustices, a world in which white people were and are not complicit, in which the injustices themselves—of slavery, Jim Crow, and ongoing structural racism—seem not to exist at all. The mammy figure affirmed their wishes.[22]

Additionally, like racism, the mammy image has repeatedly reinvented itself in ways that have allowed the image and ideology to continue. This is reflected in the mammy-like image of "Aunt Jemima" that has persisted, but in more modernized forms, since its first appearance in the late 1800s.[23]

Moreover, Melissa Harris-Perry points to the Emmy Award–winning HBO series *Sex and the City* (1998–2004), as well as the film version of the show (2008), as illustrations of the ways Black women seem to magically appear as "modern mammies" in television and film, with the sole purpose of helping solve the problems of White women.[24] Although Black women characters rarely appeared on *Sex and the City*, a few that did make a brief appearance did so only to make the lives of the White women characters better. In these roles, the Black women characters are not working as maids or servants, but their devotion to helping others is strikingly similar to the mammy controlling image. As the mammy image and its modernized versions exemplify, when

20. Harris-Perry, *Sister Citizen*, 72.

21. DuMonthier, Childers, and Milli, "The Status of Black Women in the United States."

22. McElya, *Clinging to Mammy*, 3.

23. Ibid.

24. Harris-Perry, *Sister Citizen*. In one episode of the series, a nameless Black woman chauffeur comforts Carrie and treats her to a meal after Carrie has had a stressful night. In the film, Jennifer Hudson plays the role of "Louise," a personal assistant to Carrie. Louise is in Carrie's life for a short time, but she is able to quickly fix Carrie's computer and love life before moving back home to St. Louis.

Black women are shown in film, they are often secondary and there to support another (usually White and/or male) character.[25]

In the two films that are analyzed in this chapter, *Love & Basketball* (2000) and *Beyond the Lights* (2014), Gina Prince-Bythewood created two Black women characters whose passionate devotion to their vocations is at the center of the story. In *Love & Basketball*, Monica (Sanaa Lathan) devotes her energy toward the goal of being the first woman to play in the NBA (most of the film takes place prior to the formation of the WNBA), and challenges any and all protests that suggest she will not be successful in this endeavor. *Beyond the Lights* focuses on Noni (Gugu Mbatha-Raw), who is passionate about music, and who learns to stand up to others who attempt to control the direction of her music career. Monica and Noni both regularly come up against people and situations that are representative of the ideologies that are meant to limit the options and success of Black women. Monica is constantly told that there is no place for women in professional sports, and Noni is told that the music she wants to perform has no place in the music industry. In their own way, Monica and Noni each find their path toward personal expression and fulfillment through their chosen vocation.

Work is not all that Monica and Noni are passionate about. Prince-Bythewood also created a romantic relationship for each character. The lead characters in both films are passionately dedicated to their work, but this dedication does not preclude them from a romantic partnership. *Love & Basketball* and *Beyond the Lights* have each been referred to as a "love story" by film critics.[26] While Prince-Bythewood does incorporate romantic love into the lives of Monica and Noni, defining these films as a love story simplifies the films' narratives. It overlooks the more complex interrogation and imagining of success for Black women. It also risks the films being interpreted as fitting into the dominant narrative that a woman "needs a man" to be happy.

By applying the womanist artistic standpoint framework, the inclusion of a love story for these characters can be read as an act of resistance by Prince-Bythewood. I argue that adding a love story to these films challenges domi-

---

25. With notable exceptions, such as the recent Academy Award–nominated *Hidden Figures* (2016). Though this film was exceptional in its focus on Black women's intellectual contributions to the space program, it was also critiqued for the White male writer/director incorporating the "white savior" trope.

26. "All's Fair in Love & Basketball: Childhood Adversaries Turned Sweethearts Are the Subjects of Romantic Love Story"; "A Story about Friendship, Rivalry and Ultimately . . . Love: Epps, Lathan, Woodard Star in Romantic Drama 'Love and Basketball'"; Grant, "'Beyond' Director Ponders Perception of Black Love"; Greenstein, "Black Love."

nant ideologies that construct Black women as undesirable romantic partners. In an interview for *Beyond the Lights,* Prince-Bythewood said the following, related to resisting dominant cultural ideologies about love between two Black lead characters: "We never see it, but it is imperative . . . Imaging is so important and there's so many negative images of us out there in the world every single day on TV and in film and there's nothing contradicting that."[27]

By providing the lead characters in *Love & Basketball* and *Beyond the Lights* with a Black male romantic partner, Prince-Bythewood is embracing a womanist perspective. Womanism emphasizes the need to prioritize and give a voice to Black women, while *also* providing an avenue to foster stronger relationships between Black women and Black men.[28] Alice Walker's definition asserts that womanists are "committed to survival and wholeness of entire people, male *and* female."[29] Several Black women writers and scholars who express the need to address the exploitation and sexism faced by Black women (which occurs within and across racial lines) also recognize the value of forming cross-gender relationships with Black men.[30] In each of Prince-Bythewood's films, the lead character is dedicated to achieving career success on her own terms but also has a Black male partner who learns to understand, embrace, and support her professional goals. Monica and Noni do not sacrifice professional success for a romantic relationship, nor are they portrayed as dismissing the possibility of a partnership because of that success.

By providing a romantic relationship for Monica and Noni, Gina Prince-Bythewood is also resisting a characteristic that all of the controlling images of Black women have in common: that Black women are undesirable partners and are not capable of romantic love. "Mammy" is asexual, with no personal relationships, let alone any hint of potential for a love life. "Sapphire" is emasculating. "Jezebel" is sexually promiscuous or predatory.[31] Another controlling image that often goes unnoticed, but that also reinforces the ideology that Black women are undesirable romantic partners, is that of the middle-class "black lady."[32]

The "black lady" represents a middle-class version of Black womanhood, in which Black women are portrayed as educated and hardworking profes-

27. Grant, "'Beyond' Director Ponders Perception of Black Love."

28. Collins, "What's in a Name? Womanism, Black Feminism, and Beyond."

29. Walker, *In Search of Our Mothers' Gardens,* xi.

30. Morgan, *When Chickenheads Come Home to Roost*; Perry, *Prophets of the Hood*; Rose, *Black Noise.*

31. See chapter 4 for a detailed description of the "Sapphire" and "Jezebel" stereotypes.

32. Collins, *Black Feminist Thought*; Lubiano, "Black Ladies, Welfare Queens, and State Minstrels: Ideological War by Narrative Means"; Thompson, *Beyond the Black Lady.*

sionals, which may not appear to be a controlling image at first glance. But, like other controlling images, it has also been used to criticize and justify the exploitation of Black women. This controlling image is comparable to the promotion of a "politics of respectability," a term coined by Evelyn Brooks Higginbotham to describe the efforts of middle-class Black women to counter stereotypes of their immorality during the turn of the nineteenth century.[33] Wahneema Lubiano explains the ideology behind the "black lady" that allows for the recent success of middle-class professional Black women to be disparaged, rather than celebrated: the black lady's "disproportionate overachievement stands for black cultural strangeness" and "ensures the underachievement of the black male in the lower classes."[34] Successful Black women are "strange" because they are disrupting the "normal" patriarchal hierarchy. Within this perspective, their success is constructed as preventing the success of Black men. Because of the assumption that the economic prosperity of men is required for a family or community to thrive, the success of the "black lady" is viewed as being at the root of the problems that impoverished segregated Black communities have faced.

This myth of the "black lady" serves to marginalize Black women who have achieved professional success; she is regarded as "cold, ambitious, sexually repressed, and therefore racially inauthentic."[35] Scholar Lisa B. Thompson points to the public scrutiny of the private and professional lives of two high-profile Black women political figures as examples of the ways that middle-class Black women have been depicted through the lens of this image: Anita Hill, during the 1991 Clarence Thomas hearings, and Condoleezza Rice, during her tenure as secretary of state (2005–2009).[36] Additionally, Patricia Hill Collins refers to the "black lady" as a modern middle-class version of the mammy: it suggests that it is expected and acceptable that middle-class professional Black women selflessly work twice as hard as everyone else.[37] Similar to the mammy, this devotion to her job suggests that a personal life of any kind is not a possibility for a middle-class Black woman.

In *Love & Basketball* and *Beyond the Lights*, Prince-Bythewood imagines how Black women can be true to themselves in their work, independent of social expectations and boundaries. *Love & Basketball* illustrates how a Black woman basketball player manages to play professional basketball despite the

---

33. Higginbotham, *Righteous Discontent*.

34. Lubiano, "Black Ladies, Welfare Queens, and State Minstrels: Ideological War by Narrative Means," 335.

35. Thompson, *Beyond the Black Lady*, 26.

36. Ibid.

37. Collins, *Black Feminist Thought*.

fact that athletics, specifically professional basketball, is ideologically and structurally a male-dominated field. Similarly, *Beyond the Lights* imagines how a Black woman expresses her voice within a culture and music industry that often treats Black women as silent objects. Unlike the dominant ideologies of Black womanhood, the characters in Prince-Bythewood's films reveal the beauty of being true to themselves through passionate devotion to their vocations.

LOVE & BASKETBALL

Prince-Bythewood has done something that may seem familiar, yet is actually unusual in film: she envisions what it is like for Black women to "have it all." With her first film, Gina Prince-Bythewood's goal was to transform the narrative surrounding Black female success—to challenge the ideologies that place limits on women and deny those women who are driven and passionate in their careers their full humanity. In my interview with Prince-Bythewood, she emphasized the desire to problematize the perception of "strangeness" (to use Wahneema Lubiano's phrasing, in her analysis of the "black lady" controlling image) that is applied to successful Black women. She explained that in addition to *Love & Basketball* being a story about a woman who is determined to play professional basketball, it

> was also about ultimately a woman who wants to have it all; she wants love and she wants a career. Girls are often told you can't do both, so I just wanted to normalize the belief that you can have both. I wanted to normalize girls like Monica, who were girls like me, who grew up playing sports and were told often that we were a tomboy, or that you're not like other girls and you know, made to feel different.

The challenges that Monica faces in *Love & Basketball* cannot be separated from her identity as a Black woman.[38] One film reviewer noted: "In its own unassuming way, Prince-Bythewood's film tackles a number of issues that other film-makers don't care to touch . . . Perhaps most significantly, it plainly acknowledges sexism among black men without either defending or crucifying them."[39] Prince-Bythewood's ability to frame these social issues in relatable

---

38. Comparisons have been drawn between *Love & Basketball* and *Bend It Like Beckham* (Gurinder Chadha, 2002). Both are woman of color–directed films that focus on a woman of color character in sports. However, the two films have very different racial and social contexts that are central to the films' narratives. See O'Reilly, "The Women's Sports Film as the New Melodrama."

39. Zacharack, "Love & Basketball."

and meaningful ways won her critical and commercial success. The film was nominated for an Independent Spirit Award for Best First Feature, and Prince-Bythewood won the Independent Spirit Award for Best First Screenplay. Additionally, when *Love & Basketball* premiered at the Sundance Film Festival in 2000, it won the Humanitas prize, for its depiction of "the human condition in a nuanced, meaningful way which, ultimately, inspires compassion, hope and understanding in the human family."[40]

Seeking Inclusion in Basketball

By choosing basketball as the centerpiece for her film, Gina Prince-Bythewood highlights the historical and cultural context in which Black women have been included within the institution of sports. She also places front and center the ongoing sexism that has prevented women basketball players from reaching parity with men, in terms of economic rewards and social status. No other sport is presently associated with Blackness more than basketball.[41] In addition, basketball, like sports in general, is gendered as male. If basketball is currently constructed as a Black male sport, where do Black women basketball players fit in to this picture?

Women began playing basketball at the end of the 1800s, around the same time period as men, and it was played by more American women than any other sport.[42] Although Black women were initially excluded from basketball leagues, the sport became one of the activities in which they were able to exhibit a sense of purpose and accomplishment. As the sport gained momentum among women in the United States during the early 1930s, it was "met with particular enthusiasm within African American communities . . . Basketball also spread to historically black colleges, where women were forging an expansive sense of womanhood suited to the broad range of challenges faced by African American communities during the Jim Crow Era."[43]

Ideologies of Black womanhood have diverged from those associated with dominant social expectations for women: Black women's bodies have been used for labor since the antebellum period, and they have consistently worked outside of the home at higher rates than White women.[44] Most of the work that

40. The Humanitas Prize: http://humanitasprize.info/welcome/?page_id=28.
41. hooks, "Neo-Colonial Fantasies of Conquest: Hoop Dreams."
42. Grundy and Shackelford, *Shattering the Glass*.
43. Ibid., 62.
44. https://www.dol.gov/wb/media/Black_Women_in_the_Labor_Force.pdf.

has been open to Black women has been alienating or exploitive.[45] As a result, Black women have sought opportunities and meaning through alternative routes. Sports was one of the spaces where Black women have had opportunities for self-definition, separate from the dominant social expectations for women. "Black women's own conception of womanhood, while it may not have actively encouraged sport, did not preclude it. A heritage of resistance to racial and sexual oppression found African American women occupying multiple roles as wageworkers, homemakers, mothers, and community leaders."[46] The success of Black women athletes during the middle of the twentieth century—such as professional tennis player and golfer Althea Gibson and track and field athlete Wilma Rudolph—served as important symbols of racial pride for many African Americans during a time of legalized racial segregation in the United States.[47]

Black women's participation in basketball has steadily increased, and Black women are represented in college and professional basketball at higher rates than other groups of women. When the 1996 U.S. Olympic women's basketball team took home the gold, nine of the twelve players were African American.[48] Unlike the small portion of Black women in most other college sports,[49] recent NCAA statistics show that more African American women play for Division I college basketball teams than women from any other racial category (similar to the disproportionate participation of African American players in men's basketball).[50]

As *Love & Basketball* begins, we hear the soulful voice of Al Green singing "Love and Happiness," expressing the powerful and multifaceted emotion that is love. This film is about love—that much is clear from the film's title and opening song. But, love of what? We soon learn that basketball is the object of Monica's affection. It is something she unwaveringly gives her whole self over to. Filmmaker and basketball player Gina Prince-Bythewood fully embraces her love for basketball as well, structuring the film like a basketball game: in quarters.

45. Collins, *Black Feminist Thought.*

46. Cahn, *Coming on Strong,* 117.

47. Grundy and Shackelford, *Shattering the Glass;* Wiggins and Miller, *The Unlevel Playing Field.*

48. Members of the team included soon-to-be WNBA players Sheryl Swoopes, Lisa Leslie, and Dawn Staley.

49. DeFrantz, "Overcoming Obstacles"; Washington, "Black Women in Sports: Can We Get off the Track?"

50. "Sport Sponsorship, Participation, and Demographics Search."

When the "first quarter" begins, the year is 1981. Monica is introduced as a passionate, skilled, and competitive ball player who does not back down from opposition. We first see Monica as an eleven-year-old girl dressed in a baggy T-shirt and jeans, her hair covered in a Lakers baseball cap, and it is immediately evident that her character rebels against dominant gendered expectations. She confidently walks up to a group of similar-in-age boys play-ing basketball in their upper-middle-class Los Angeles neighborhood; they assume she, too, is a boy. Monica's family has just moved to the neighbor-hood from Atlanta. She wastes no time asking to join the boys. When Monica removes her hat to reveal her hair, the boys realize they were wrong in their initial assumption—that he was a "she." Her new next-door neighbor Quincy says, "Girls can't play no ball," but she quickly retorts that she can play better than him, and then proceeds to school him further on the court. During this first exchange between Monica and Quincy, Monica declares that she is going to be the first girl in the NBA. Through her "courageous" and "willful" behav-ior, Monica embodies the definition of a womanist.[51]

Quincy, struggling to restore the gender hierarchy after being caught off guard by Monica's athletic ability, makes the comment that Monica can be his cheerleader when he plays in the NBA. Author and former basketball player Mariah Burton Nelson argues that "manly" sports like basketball, in which the only visible women are cheerleaders, create an environment that sustains the illusion of male supremacy in a society where women are gaining more power.[52] When Monica demonstrates her exceptional skill on the basketball court, Quincy attempts to regain his sense of power by placing her in the supportive, cheerleader role. Monica refuses to be Quincy's "cheerleader," of course, which represents a refusal to have her life revolve around supporting someone else. Like the mythical "mammy," the dominant understanding of cheerleaders is that they work to ensure the success of someone other than themselves. Monica is no cheerleader. She does not exert her energy and tal-ents for anything other than that which she is passionate about. And for her, it's playing basketball.

Quincy's difficulty with the idea that a girl might beat him at basket-ball comes to a head when Monica is close to winning the game—she has the ball and Quincy shoves her to the ground. Monica scrapes her cheek on the ground during her fall, which she perceives as a badge of honor. Quincy appears shocked and apologetic (he later makes her a handmade "I'm sorry" card when he gets home). This game would be the first of many power strug-

51. Walker, *In Search of Our Mothers' Gardens*, xi.
52. Nelson, *The Stronger Women Get, the More Men Love Football*, 7.

gles between the two of them, some of them on the basketball court and others during their verbal exchanges, as Monica attempts to prove that she deserves respect as a ball player and Quincy attempts to maintain the rigid boundaries of masculinity and his privileged status. When Monica and her mother come over to Quincy's house after their first game of basketball, he continues to express disbelief in Monica's basketball skills: he asks her how she can play basketball and says he has never known a girl who could play ball.

With Monica and Quincy's first interactions, Gina Prince-Bythewood has cleverly set up the interpersonal and institutional sexism that Monica faces as an aspiring basketball player. Quincy's remark that "Girls can't play no ball," followed by his astonishment when he realizes that she really *can* play ball, illustrate the sexist ideology that he has learned at a very young age. Quincy's macho and competitive attitude is a product of his social environment: at one point, we see eleven-year-old Quincy being scolded by his father for saying, "I can't do this shit"—because *"can't* should never be in a man's vocabulary." Sports is especially powerful in shaping the gender ideology of children. It essentializes athletic ability as a male trait and places limits on the opportunities for women and girls in sports. Sports sociologist Michael Messner explains that "sport provides a context in which the fiction of separate, categorically different, and unequal sexes can be constructed and made to appear natural, even in this allegedly 'postfeminist' era."[53] Mariah Burton Nelson echoes this idea: "Even if the best athlete in the neighborhood was a girl, we learned from newspapers, television, and from our own parents' prejudices that batting, catching, throwing, and jumping are not neutral, human activities, but somehow more naturally a male domain."[54] Quincy's aggressive physical reaction to Monica's competitive spirit and her adeptness at basketball illustrates his discomfort with Monica challenging this ideology.

Prince-Bythewood sets the historical context with eleven-year-old Monica's declaration that she will play in the NBA and that she wants to be like Magic Johnson. Monica dreams of playing in the exclusively male National Basketball Association, viewed as the pinnacle of professional basketball, and her idol is Magic Johnson, the point guard for the Los Angeles Lakers. She is envisioning a future for herself playing professional basketball, but there are no female professional basketball players or teams for her to incorporate into her vision. It was not until 1996 that the American Basketball League (ABL) began, which focused solely on women's basketball, and was organized by a group of independent owners based in California.[55] The next year (1997), the

53. Messner, *Taking the Field*, 2.
54. Nelson, *The Stronger Women Get, the More Men Love Football*, 2.
55. This league was dissolved after two seasons, due to the success of the WNBA.

NBA-sponsored women's basketball organization (WNBA) had its first season.[56] But in 1981, when Monica and Quincy meet on the court for the first time, institutional constraints only allowed women to climb so far before they had nowhere to go—there are no opportunities for women to play basketball professionally in the United States that are comparable to the NBA. Despite this, Monica's passion for basketball and sense of purpose make it feel achievable to her.

Monica's passion for basketball seems to elicit more than a competitive rivalry from Quincy—it also sparks a personal interest, and he soon asks Monica to be his "girl" when they ride their bikes to school, each with a basketball in hand. She agrees, after he offers Twinkies as part of the arrangement. They seal the deal with a short and sweet kiss, which they mutually decide will last five seconds, exactly. But, their egalitarian romantic relationship during the "first quarter" is short-lived. Quincy immediately demands that Monica ride on his bike with him to school and Monica refuses. She is perfectly capable of riding her own bike to school. Monica exhibits many qualities of a womanist, after all, which means that she is "traditionally capable."[57] Quincy's idea of a girlfriend is someone who lets him take control as she goes along for the ride—his dad drives the car, while his mom sits in the passenger seat, he tells Monica. Similar to her refusal to be seen as Quincy's "cheerleader," Monica refuses to remain on the sidelines of someone else's actions or accomplishments. As one reviewer puts it, Monica "finds his eleven-year-old machismo out of control."[58] Monica can accept a relationship with Quincy only if she can interact with him on a level playing field. The basketball court is the closest the two of them come to relating to each other as equals.

Monica continues to directly challenge Quincy's perceptions of sports, gender, and relationships through their friendship and her steadfast commitment to being a ball player. When Monica is a senior in high school (in the "second quarter"), Gina Prince-Bythewood demonstrates the institutional sexism in basketball in a subtle, yet effective way. There is a sharp contrast between the experiences of Monica and Quincy during their time as high school basketball players. It is evident that Quincy and the men's team are favored and receive more support from the community; everyone is on pins and needles waiting to find out where Quincy will play college ball. He makes the announcement that he will attend University of Southern California (USC) during a press conference, as fans watch and eagerly await his decision.

56. Grundy and Shackelford, *Shattering the Glass*, 224.

57. Walker, *In Search of Our Mothers' Gardens*, xi.

58. "All's Fair in Love & Basketball: Childhood Adversaries Turned Sweethearts Are the Subjects of Romantic Love Story."

On the other hand, when Monica finds out that she was also offered a spot on USC's basketball team, Quincy is the only other person to hear her news. In contrast to the press conference that is held for Quincy, Monica's revelation comes when she opens the envelope with USC's offer letter late at night in the yard next to her house in virtual solitude. Although Title IX increased opportunities for women in sports after its inception in the 1970s,[59] it did not immediately dismantle the cultural ideology that genders sports as masculine.

This construction of sports as an expression of hegemonic masculinity also causes differences in the public perception and personal relationships of Monica and Quincy. Quincy is shown surrounded by friends, fans, and females who long to be with him. He hears occasional warnings that he should be on guard against women being interested in a sexual relationship with him solely for his success and fame. As hip-hop scholar Tricia Rose points out, within hypermasculine spaces, for some women, the only option available for social mobility or success is their (sometimes sexual and/or exploitative) relationships with men.[60] Monica, on the other hand, gets relatively little positive attention for her athleticism. Whereas Quincy's aggressiveness and physical strength on the court are viewed as ideal and attractive masculine traits, Monica's display of similar qualities causes her to be perceived as an unfeminine "tomboy." When there is a school dance, Monica would stay home alone were it not for the fact that her sister finds a date for her.

This depiction of the exclusion that Monica feels from her peers is based on the personal experiences of filmmaker Gina Prince-Bythewood. That Prince-Bythewood drew from her perspective and experience in her portrayal of "Monica" reflects the womanist artistic standpoint. Prince-Bythewood, who grew up playing sports, expressed that she could relate to Monica's difficulty fitting in because of her own love of sports. ("I wanted to normalize girls like Monica who were girls like me who grew up playing sports and were told often that we were a tomboy, or that you're not like other girls and you know, made to feel different," said Prince-Bythewood during our interview).

Women athletes face challenges based on gender ideology, in general, but Black women have confronted a specific set of social challenges: a "historical legacy of disrespect, distortion, and stereotyping of black womanhood and black female sexuality demands that contemporary African American athletes navigate a complex set of currents."[61] The media's frequent disparaging com-

59. Grundy and Shackelford, *Shattering the Glass*; Cahn, *Coming on Strong*. An important caveat to this is that Title IX has resulted in very few opportunities in sports *other than basketball* for Black women. See Suggs, "'Left Behind': Title IX and Black Women Athletes."

60. Rose, *The Hip Hop Wars*.

61. Cahn, *Coming on Strong*, 269.

ments about the body of professional tennis player Serena Williams[62] and the racist and sexist remarks made about the Rutgers women's basketball team[63] are recent examples of the racialized sexism that Black women athletes face. In *Black Sexual Politics,* Patricia Hill Collins discusses the ways that representations of Black women athletes replicate and contest power relations of race, class, gender, and sexuality.[64] The combination of the stereotype of Black women being less feminine than White women along with the stereotype of female athletes being more masculine than other women means that Black women athletes are particularly vulnerable to being stigmatized. Stereotypes related to sexuality often come into play, as well. For example, although the homophobic stereotype that all women athletes are lesbians is meant to marginalize women athletes,[65] Collins points out that Black women athletes are more likely than other women to be stereotyped as lesbians, which affects the public discourse surrounding Black women athletes.[66] In an effort to counter these cultural perceptions, the predominantly Black WNBA's initial media campaign attempted to femininize the players.[67]

By the end of the "second quarter" of the film, Monica and Quincy have found their way back into each other's arms through their shared passion for basketball—and after Quincy experiences the pangs of jealousy when he sees Monica with another man at the school dance. After the dance, they talk about their respective dates—Monica tells Quincy that while she was with her date after the dance, she was distracted because she couldn't remember how many offensive rebounds she had during her last game. Monica is surprised when Quincy replies "four." She's impressed and touched that he remembers this detail about something that is so important to her. When Monica gets the letter from USC, her last opportunity to play college basketball, she knows that Quincy is the one person who will understand the significance of this opportunity for her. Paradoxically, Quincy embodies the cultural ideologies that reinforce basketball as a male-dominated space, while their shared devotion to the game makes it possible for Monica to find in him a relationship in which she can embrace her own passion for basketball—something that she views as integral to her sense of self.

62. Cepeda, "Courting Destiny"; McKay and Johnson, "Pornographic Eroticism and Sexual Grotesquerie in Representations of African American Sportswomen."

63. Radio host Don Imus referred to the women on the predominantly African American Rutgers basketball team as "nappy-headed hos" during a 2007 broadcast. See "Rutgers Players Describe How Imus' Remarks Hurt."

64. Collins, *Black Sexual Politics.*

65. Griffin, "Changing the Game: Homophobia, Sexism, and Lesbians in Sport."

66. Collins, *Black Sexual Politics,* 135.

67. Heywood and Dworkin, *Built to Win*; Collins, *Black Sexual Politics.*

This paradox between their shared devotion to basketball and the male supremacy that divides them follows Monica and Quincy to college (in the film's "third quarter"). "Quincy resents the time Monica devotes to her sport when there are so many more attentive women he could date."[68] As Monica struggles to prove herself to her coach and teammates at USC, Quincy asks her to risk it all for him. One film reviewer very bluntly says, "Quincy, who was a self-centered male chauvinist pig even as a little boy, slowly turns into a bona fide jerk."[69] Quincy asks Monica to stay out late with him to talk and keep him company after he finds out that his basketball-star father, whom he idolizes, has been cheating on his mother. Monica comforts Quincy and is sympathetic, but she would risk her position on the team if she stays out with him. She asks that he come to her room to talk; if she's not in her dorm by curfew, she won't suit up for the game. Quincy tells her not to "sweat it" and says that she should go. She reluctantly leaves for her dorm and he grudgingly stays out alone. After that night, he ignores her, flaunts other women in front of her, and then breaks up with her—accusing her of not being there for him. Quincy had put Monica in the position of choosing between her passion for basketball and her love for him that night. And she did not allow someone else to decide what her priorities would be. In doing so, she exhibited an essential element of Black feminism: self-definition.[70]

Monica graduates from USC (in the "fourth quarter") before there is a WNBA or ABL for her to join. Whereas Quincy is drafted into the NBA during college, institutional factors leave Monica no options for playing professional basketball in the United States. But this is not the end of basketball for Monica. Instead of letting go of the activity in which she feels most like herself, she seeks alternative ways to continue to devote herself to basketball. One avenue open to women basketball players after college was playing outside of the United States. This had not been part of Monica's vision when she was eleven years old, but faced with the reality that she was not drafted into the NBA, she adjusts her path and moves to Spain in order to continue to play basketball.

By the end of the film, Prince-Bythewood places the ball back in Monica's court, so to speak. Although playing ball overseas had allowed her to continue playing basketball after college, being separated from family and friends and living within a place that did not feel like home did not allow her to fully express herself. Within this context, she was not able to wholeheartedly embrace her passion for the game. As a result, Monica chooses to move back home, despite

68. O'Reilly, "The Women's Sports Film as the New Melodrama," 293.
69. Roberts, "Playing the Game of 'Love and Basketball.'"
70. Collins, *Black Feminist Thought.*

the lack of opportunities for women to play basketball in the United States at the time. She reconnects with Quincy, who is hospitalized after having recently suffered from a knee injury while playing for the NBA. He is slightly humbler than his younger self. He is also engaged to be married to a flight attendant (played by supermodel Tyra Banks). Nonetheless, Monica audaciously declares her love for Quincy and reveals that part of why she stopped playing basketball overseas was because she missed sharing her passion for basketball with him. This is her version of wanting "it all." She is making the conscious decision to seek the feeling of empowerment by reclaiming what Audre Lorde calls the "erotic" in love, work, and life. Monica challenges Quincy to a game of one-on-one for his "heart," through which they both rediscover their passion for the game and for bringing out the athlete in one another.

The film ends when we see Monica running up to the starting line in the Great Western Forum; "Wright-McCall" (presumably Monica's married name) is written on her Los Angeles Sparks jersey. The WNBA has been established. One of the structural barriers that had previously limited her basketball career has been eliminated, opening up an opportunity for Monica and many other Black women. And Quincy is in a position that runs counter to hegemonic expectations of men, sitting on the sidelines with their daughter, cheering for Monica. Gina Prince-Bythewood presents a counter-narrative to the one found in many popular women's sports films: that a woman who wants to "find a place of her own in sports must be willing to sacrifice things that are dear to her, such as romance."[71] True to the definition of a womanist, Monica is front and center, resisting social expectations, and pursuing her passion.

Throughout the film, the relationship between Monica and her mother, Camille, also demonstrates a central tenet of the womanist artistic standpoint—that there is not *one* Black woman's standpoint; rather, there are a variety of standpoints. Camille chose to devote her life to taking care of her two children and husband, rather than opening the catering business that she had planned to start before she had children.[72] Monica and Camille constantly clash because Monica thinks that her mother does not fight for herself, whereas Camille thinks Monica should be more "ladylike." When Monica returns from Spain, she has a conversation with her mother, where they both reveal their feelings about the roles that they have chosen. Just as Camille does not understand Monica's commitment to basketball, Monica does not understand why Camille chose to stay home and raise her children instead of

---

71. O'Reilly, "The Women's Sports Film as the New Melodrama," 296.

72. This portrayal of Monica's mother as a middle-class, married, stay-at-home mom challenges the media image of Black motherhood. See chapter 3 for a detailed description of controlling images of Black motherhood.

starting her catering business. These two characters seem to be at odds with each other, but together they represent the possibilities for Black womanhood to take on multiple meanings. Camille chose to stay at home and raise her children. This is no less valid a choice than the one Monica makes to pursue a basketball career. By the end of the film, Camille says that she may be "prissy," but she has always admired the "fight" in Monica. Depicting these differing viewpoints reflects the womanist artistic standpoint: specifically, it acknowledges the heterogeneity of Black women as well as the various ways that Black women react to common challenges, which is one way to resist the dominant cultural practice of simplifying Black womanhood.

BEYOND THE LIGHTS

Similar to Monica in *Love & Basketball,* Gina Prince-Bythewood felt a connection to Noni (the lead in *Beyond the Lights*) and her emotional and professional journey: "A woman fighting to find her voice and her place in the world absolutely connected to me as an artist and who I want to be as an artist, and being able to speak my mind and speak my truth to the world, and to be authentic," said Prince-Bythewood in my interview with her. Finding one's voice is tantamount to the self-definition that a Black feminist perspective stresses.[73] *Beyond the Lights* (2014) not only portrays the goals and challenges of a Black woman who is working to achieve success on her own terms in a high-stress and high-profile profession, it also confronts the objectification and hypersexualization of Black women in the music industry. Notably, *Beyond the Lights* draws from themes similar to those in Julie Dash's short film *Illusions* (1982). Both films provide critiques of the artifice, based on racist and sexist ideology, that goes into the media construction of Black womanhood, and explore how Black women manage to carve out their own spaces in the media.

Beyond the Lights is Prince-Bythewood's third theatrically released feature film as writer/director. She began working on *Beyond the Lights* in 2007, but took a break to work on *The Secret Life of Bees* (2008), a film that was based on the best-selling book of the same name. Even with the success of *Love & Basketball* (2000) and *The Secret Life of Bees* (2008) under her belt, Prince-Bythewood still faced resistance when she was seeking support for her third feature film.[74] "I never heard the word no used in so many ways and as often as I did while shopping *Beyond the Lights* around. I was really shocked that every-

---

73. Collins, *Black Feminist Thought.*

74. Ford, "Gina Prince-Bythewood"; Henderson, "Beyond the Lights Movie Review"; Robertson, "Behind 'Beyond the Lights.'"

body turned us down,"[75] says Prince-Bythewood. But, she was determined to stay true to her vision and was steadfast in that determination. The film premiered at the Toronto International Film Festival and was released theatrically in the United States in 2014. *Beyond the Lights* was nominated for four NAACP Image awards, including Outstanding Motion Picture and Directing, and seven Black Reel Awards, including Best Film, Director, and Screenplay.

From Objectification to Empowerment in the Music Industry

Of *Beyond the Lights,* Prince-Bythewood says,

> While I wanted it to be entertaining, I also wanted to shine a spotlight on the dark side of the music industry and how pop music promotes a hypersexual image of young girls to sell records. Through this movie, I wanted to show that maybe there's another way. Gugu's character Noni goes through a real transformative period. She learns to love and respect herself on her terms and soon understands her worth and power.[76]

This "dark side of the music industry" pushes "Noni" to consider jumping off a balcony and ending her life at the height of her music career.

Prince-Bythewood's inclusion of an attempted suicide toward the beginning of the film has parallels to Ntozake Shange's award-winning play *for colored girls who have considered suicide / when the rainbow is enuf,* which presents the struggles of several Black women characters who ultimately embrace self-love.[77] In the opening monologue of Shange's play, the "lady in brown" testifies to "never havin been a girl." She continues: "somebody / anybody / sing a black girl's song / bring her out / to know herself . . . she doesn't know the sound of her own voice / her infinite beauty." When the lady in brown declares that she has never "been a girl" and that she "doesn't know the sound of her own voice," the implication is that she did not have the privilege of experiencing the kind of carefree girlhood that fosters self-exploration and self-discovery. This sentiment also reflects Noni's feeling of disconnection from her own body, voice, and experiences, which began at a very young age. This sense of disconnection from herself (depicted through her objectification

75. Wilson-Combs, "'Beyond the Lights' Is a Box Office Hit."

76. Ibid.

77. Although Noni's attempted suicide parallels Shange's play, Prince-Bythewood explained that she was motivated to include this in the film for personal reasons—there was an experience with a family member that influenced her decision to include the attempted suicide in her film. See interview in the appendix.

within the music industry) leads Noni to consider ending her life. However, by the end of the film, she has learned to express herself in a way that feels authentic to her—she has begun to move toward the end of her own rainbow.

Long straight blond hair. Skin-tight revealing clothing. Legs spread for the camera. Seductive movement for the enjoyment of others. This is the image of "Noni" that is being projected on the big screen at the Billboard Music Awards show, as she performs in a duet with rapper Kid Culprit (Machine Gun Kelly) in the film. For this performance, Noni wins her first Billboard Music Award. But this experience does not enhance Noni's feelings of personal empowerment or pleasure. This award is the result of her trying to be something she is not. This is why her smile fades as soon as she walks away from the crowd of fans after the awards show. And, instead of leaving the awards show feeling fulfilled, she attempts to end her life.

Black feminist discussions of women in hip-hop provide a useful framework for the discussion of Noni's objectification and other experiences within the music industry. Although Noni is not a rap artist herself, she is embedded within that context: the song for which she wins a Billboard Music Award is a duet with rapper Kid Culprit, with whom she also has a relationship (a relationship that appears to have little substance and was initiated for publicity). Commercial hip-hop music is by no means the sole contributor to the objectification and hypersexualization of Black women—it would not be as successful at selling music if it did not reflect dominant social ideologies about Black womanhood[78]—but it has been the subject of more public discourse and criticism for its treatment of women than any other form of music.[79] Black women writers such as Tricia Rose, Imani Perry, Gwendolyn Pough, Marlo David, and self-declared hip-hop feminist Joan Morgan explore the complex relationship between hip-hop and feminism, while engaging with the possibilities for it to be a space of personal empowerment for Black women.

"Hip hop is in a terrible crisis," declares Tricia Rose in her 2008 book *The Hip Hop Wars*.[80] Rose further explains, "The most commercially promoted and financially successful hip hop—what has dominated mass-media outlets such as television, radio, and recording industries for a dozen years or so—has increasingly become a playground for caricatures of black gangstas, pimps, and hoes. Hypersexism has increased dramatically."[81] Melissa Harris-

---

78. I discuss the hypersexualization of Black women and the "Jezebel" controlling image in depth in the fourth chapter.

79. Perry, *Prophets of the Hood*; Rose, *The Hip Hop Wars*.

80. Rose, *The Hip Hop Wars*, 1.

81. Ibid.

Perry compares the presentation of women's bodies in hip-hop to the exploitation and exhibition of Saartjie Baartman (referred to as "Hottentot Venus").[82] Beginning in the late 1990s, Black women became increasingly portrayed as "hoochies" and "hoes" through the corporate-controlled music of male hip-hop artists.[83]

Referring to hip-hop as being "in crisis" is a dramatic shift from Rose's earlier work, in which she discusses hip-hop as a reflection of the complexities of Black urban cultures, from its origins in the 1970s to the increase in its popularity over the next two decades. She begins her first book, *Black Noise,* by referring to hip-hop as "a confusing and noisy element of contemporary American popular culture"[84] that brings together "a tangle of some of the most complex social, cultural, and political issues in contemporary American society" and "prioritizes black voices from the margins of urban America."[85] Imani Perry similarly expresses a mix of praise for hip-hop as an art form and concerns about the recent commercialization of hip-hop music. Perry points out that hip-hop has "both spewed American vices on the airwaves and aggressively introduced progressive politics, compelling artistic expression, emotion, and beauty into popular culture," but adds that "the commodification and commercialization of hip hop has forever altered the art form, at times challenging its integrity."[86]

In her book *When Chickenheads Come Home to Roost: A Hip-Hop Feminist Breaks It Down,* Joan Morgan also writes about the dissonance she feels toward hip-hop and its increasing objectification of women:

> Props given to rap music's artistic merits, its irrefutable impact on pop culture, its ability to be alternatively beautiful, poignant, powerful, strong, irreverent, visceral, and mesmerizing—homeboy's clearly got it like that. But in between the beats, booty shaking, and hedonistic abandon, I have to wonder if there isn't something inherently unfeminist in supporting a music that repeatedly reduces me to tits and ass and encourages pimping on the regular.[87]

---

82. Harris-Perry, *Sister Citizen.* Saartjie Baartman was a Khoi woman from Africa who was brought to Europe in the early 1800s. She was considered an oddity and was fetishized due to her body shape and proportions, particularly her buttocks, diverging from European cultural expectations. She was put on display during several "freak shows" during this period, where onlookers stared, and sometimes poked, at her body.

83. Collins, *Black Feminist Thought*; Harris-Perry, *Sister Citizen*; Rose, *The Hip Hop Wars.*

84. Rose, *Black Noise,* 1.

85. Ibid., 2.

86. Perry, *Prophets of the Hood,* 2–3.

87. Morgan, *When Chickenheads Come Home to Roost,* 66.

With the recent commodification of the male-dominated field of hip-hop, women have increasingly been portrayed as commodities themselves. When discussing the incorporation of women into the videos of male hip-hop artists, Imani Perry states, "They appear in the videos quite explicitly as property, not unlike the luxury cars, Rolex watches, and platinum and diamond medallions also featured."[88] In *Beyond the Lights,* by the time Noni has reached the peak of commercial success, she has been packaged and sold to the public. As a record executive tells Noni and her mother, they are "selling a fantasy." In the song for which she wins the Billboard Music Award, she is portrayed as Kid Culprit's plaything—his property. She may not literally be voiceless, like most women who are pictured in male hip-hop artists' videos, but her voice is overpowered by the in-your-face sexual explicitness of her image.

Noni's singing career did not begin within an "industry that wants to turn her into a slick, packaged, disposable commodity."[89] The film opens when Noni is a child with glasses and curly black hair on the verge of performing in her first talent contest. The night before the contest, her mother, Macy (Minnie Driver), walks the shy Noni into a hair salon that has closed for the night and desperately asks if the hairdresser can do something with Noni's hair. Macy, a White single mother with few resources, feels overwhelmed. She sees Noni's musical talent as a way out of their financial hardships, and uses Noni to advance their social status.[90]

Similar to *Love & Basketball,* Prince-Bythewood gives us a glimpse of the childhood of the lead character: we see Noni's talent and passion for singing at a very young age. The hairdresser who meets Noni the evening before the talent contest can also see Noni's passion for singing. Noni tells the hairdresser that she's going to perform the song "Blackbird" at the talent contest, and the hairdresser, impressed that she's performing Nina Simone's song, agrees to stay and help her. When Noni performs "Blackbird" at the talent contest and wins first runner-up, her face lights up. She is truly fulfilled. However, her smile turns to tears when she sees her mother's anger. As Macy pulls Noni off the stage and marches her out of the auditorium to the car, she furiously

---

88. Perry, *Prophets of the Hood,* 175.

89. Scott, "The Glamorous Life, With All Its Woes: 'Beyond the Lights,' a Diva's Romance."

90. Prince-Bythewood's inspiration for Macy's character came from the difficult experience of meeting the biological mother who put her up for adoption. The experience led her to consider how her life would have been different if she had been raised by someone who does not love her unconditionally: "When I was in my early 20s, I tracked down my birth mother, whom I had been trying to find for years . . . [W]hen I found my biological mother, it was pretty tough. She told me about the circumstances of my birth, which are a little too personal to talk about, but they were shocking and crushing. And to be in the presence of someone who gave birth to you, who loves and resents you at the same time." See Carter, "Reel Mama Drama."

says that the contest was "bullshit" and tells Noni to throw away her trophy. "You wanna be a runner-up or you wanna be a winner?" Macy asks. Noni looks disappointed and defeated. With this interaction, we see how Noni, like Shange's "lady in brown," has her girlhood stripped away. Noni does not want to give up the trophy or her happiness, but she throws down the trophy at her mother's insistence. Her love of singing slowly but surely transforms over the years as she becomes disconnected from her music and sense of self. "Noni, in the glare of her fame, feels invisible, as unloved and unrecognized as Nina Simone's blackbird."[91]

Noni's transformation into a commodity was spearheaded by her mother, who recognized that they would be rewarded with money and fame by participating in and conforming to the sexist system within the music industry. Noni's feeling of disconnection from herself and her art began early on and permeated her home and professional life. Her life became a juxtaposition of being highly visible, yet invisible. She was a modern version of the mythical "mammy." She may have become materially wealthy, unlike mammy, but she had no sense of personhood beyond what her mother or the record labels wanted her to be. She was working for everyone except herself. So, when Kaz (Nate Parker), the police officer who had been acting as security outside of Noni's room the night of the Billboard Music Awards show, runs over to Noni as she sits at the edge of the balcony, crying, she says to him, "You still can't see me" as she jumps—a metaphorical statement of feeling invisible in plain sight. Kaz grabs Noni's hand, in an attempt to stop her fall, and pleads with her to grab his other hand. But, it is not until he says, "I see you" that she grabs his hand and allows him to pull her up. After Noni makes the choice to live, she slowly begins to make other choices that resist her invisibility. She eventually reclaims her voice and career so that she can be true to herself.

Soon after Noni and Kaz meet, they begin to spend time together and develop a romantic relationship. Kaz is not caught in the trappings of fame that have constrained Noni, unlike her mother, who is the only family she has ever known. Because of this, when she is with Kaz, she feels more relaxed and lets go of her false public persona. She can just be Noni. As she sits in a car with Kaz, she tells him that she feels like her life is out of her hands. But, in the same conversation, she reveals that when she's singing, it's a high "greater than any drug." Kaz serves as a catalyst for Noni envisioning a life outside of the one her mother created for her; one in which she can be and express herself on her own terms. She shares with Kaz some of the song ideas that she has hidden in a box—because she has been conditioned to believe that no one else

---

91. Scott, "The Glamorous Life, With All Its Woes: 'Beyond the Lights,' a Diva's Romance."

will want to hear what she has to say. Through her interactions with Kaz, Noni reveals her desire for the self-definition that is essential to Black feminism.[92]

A significant turning point in Noni's effort toward self-definition comes when she performs at the BET Awards show. She is scheduled to perform with Kid Culprit, whom she had a relationship with that was initially "a label thing" (as she awkwardly explains to Kaz). But, she is becoming less willing to go along with other people controlling her career and life or to allow herself to be used as an object. Days before the show, Noni gently breaks things off with Culprit, telling him that she wants to go back to being friends. He acts unscathed at first, telling Noni that he will not "shed a tear." However, when the two are performing for the BET Awards, he attempts to reclaim power over her.

During the performance, Noni wears a trench coat that was originally choreographed to be pulled open by dancers to reveal Noni in her underwear. But Noni is no longer okay with this type of self-presentation, in which her body is put on display. When the dancers try to pull off the coat, Noni very subtly attempts to stop them from doing so. Culprit, clearly feeling that his power is being threatened by Noni's attempt to control her own body, attempts to pull off the coat himself and begins roughly pushing her around onstage. He then forces Noni down to her knees and pushes her head toward his groin to simulate oral sex during the performance. Noni's shocked reaction to his use of force and her attempt to pull herself away makes it clear that this was not part of the choreography. When the song ends, Kid Culprit loudly announces to the crowd that *he* was the one who ended things with Noni, apparently feeling his macho public persona was threatened by Noni's very public attempt at controlling her body, as well as her decision to break up with him to be with Kaz. He then aggressively rips Noni's coat off as Noni struggles to cover herself. As she stands exposed and vulnerable on the stage, Kaz comes on stage and punches Culprit. In response, Culprit yells, "You know that bitch is a freak."

Culprit's violent treatment of Noni, his attempt to sexualize her, and his reference to her as a "bitch" are all his ways of enacting socially constructed ideologies that equate masculinity with dominance, and reward men's use of violence and misogyny.[93] The use of violence against Black women has taken on a particular significance within recent commercial hip-hop. Tricia Rose explains that the portrayal of women as "bitches" and "hoes" is necessitated by the growth of the narrow form of masculinity that's promoted within con-

92. Collins, *Black Feminist Thought.*
93. Katz, *The Macho Paradox.*

temporary commercial hip-hop: "The gangsta rapper image *needs* 'bitches and hoes,' and so they continually invent them. If you can't have lots of women serving and servicing you, then how can you be a real player, a real pimp? So, the process of locating, labeling, partying with, and then discarding black women is part of the performance that enhances gangsta- and pimp-style rappers' status."[94] Noni's presentation as a sex object, a "freak," and Kid Culprit's use of force to overpower her are not only meant to degrade her—he needs Noni to be perceived as these things in order to increase and solidify his own status within the music industry.

Audre Lorde's often-cited declaration that "the master's tools will never dismantle the master's house" is useful to consider here.[95] How can Noni effectively dismantle the misogyny within hip-hop music when she is performing the very music that was designed to oppress her? She comes to the realization that she cannot truly change her situation as long as she is playing their game—or their music, to be exact. Instead of expressing concern about Noni's emotional well-being, Macy is worried that the BET Awards performance has ruined her record deal. She wants her daughter to go along with her own objectification in order to gain temporary monetary success. After all, "women are rewarded for participating in this system."[96]

It's at this point in the film that Noni disengages—at least, from the public eye, her mother, and the music industry. She covertly drives to Mexico with Kaz, where she has the privacy and space to go through a transformation that allows her to be herself without the pressure of conforming to the record label's or her mother's expectations. She is connecting to the person she was prior to her fame—when she was able to express herself through her singing—which gives her the strength to be "courageous" with her music and "in charge" (characteristics of a womanist) of her career. While in Mexico, after she and Kaz casually stroll the streets where no one recognizes her as Noni the pop star, she ends up onstage at a karaoke bar, singing "Blackbird" acapella. As she sings, she closes her eyes and begins to cry. She is once again *feeling* when she sings. The audience disappears from her conscious awareness. She is singing for herself. We see a brief flashback from her first talent contest performance of "Blackbird," before she began to feel like she was leading a life that was not her own.

Although Noni disengages from the hip-hop space in which she was embedded, several Black women have succeeded, using various approaches, in carving out a space for themselves within the hypermasculine world of

94. Rose, *The Hip Hop Wars*, 182.
95. Lorde, *Sister Outsider*, 112.
96. Rose, *The Hip Hop Wars*, 175.

hip-hop.[97] In *Black Noise,* Tricia Rose highlights that Black women have been "integral and resistant voices in rap music and in popular music in general who sustain an ongoing dialog with their audiences and with male rappers about sexual promiscuity, emotional commitment, infidelity, the drug trade, racial politics and black cultural history" since the 1980s.[98] Soon after hip-hop first gained mainstream success, there was a period in which several talented Black women rap artists emerged, like Salt-N-Pepa, Queen Latifah, and MC Lyte. These women artists gained mainstream success and contributed to hip-hop as a multifaceted form of Black cultural expression.[99] However, that period was short-lived.

Can Noni carve out a space for herself as a singer? Can she have a music career without conforming to the industry's expectations for Black women? Can she stay true to herself while pursuing her chosen vocation of singing? Imani Perry points out that the images of more contemporary commercially successful female hip-hop artists often play into dominant ideas about sexuality, rather than resisting dominant ideologies about sexuality and Black womanhood.[100] For example, beginning in the 1990s, commercially successful female rap artists, such as Lil' Kim, Foxy Brown, and more recently Nicki Minaj, blurred the line between sexual object and subject. Whether the highly sexualized images of these female artists indicate their sexual empowerment *or* their sexual objectification is an open question. However, within a society in which ideas about "sexiness" are largely based on "sexism," Perry suggests: "For women artists who have written and copyrighted their own lyrics, the lyrics might be one of their only areas of control."[101] The lyrics are the only area in which an artist's message and presentation of self can remain as she intended them to be.

Noni returns home with renewed energy and a new focus. She says to Kaz, "I can finally do it the right way. My way." She will present herself in a way that feels more authentic to who she is. Kaz tries to stop her from going back home, afraid that she'll lose her identity again. But Noni is determined to stay true to herself and reminds him that she has wanted to be a singer her whole life. Once she returns home, she has a meeting with record executives and insists on adding a song that she wrote to her album: Instead of saying what everybody else wants her to say, she declares, "*I* need to say something."

97. David, "More Than Baby Mamas: Black Mothers and Hip-Hop Feminism"; Perry, *Prophets of the Hood*; Rose, *Black Noise*.

98. Rose, *Black Noise*, 146.

99. Perry, *Prophets of the Hood*; Pough, *Check It While I Wreck It*; Rose, *Black Noise*.

100. Perry, *Prophets of the Hood*.

101. Ibid., 188.

By the end of the film, Noni has gotten rid of her record label, her mother/
manager, and the artifice that had become her physical appearance. She also
goes on television to publicly announce the reclamation of herself and her
career. When a reporter asks her if she is concerned about her image, she
replies, "I'm not concerned at all." Also, for the first time, she feels comfortable
honestly discussing her attempted suicide, which she had previously hidden
from the public: "I had to make the decision to stop being a victim. To stop
trying to be somebody I knew I wasn't . . . That fantasy girl on the posters,
she did go over the balcony. And the real Noni Jean got pulled back up," she
tells the reporter. As Audre Lorde states in her essay titled "The Transformation of Silence into Language and Action," the "visibility which makes us most
vulnerable is that which is also the source of our greatest strength."[102] Noni
expressing herself, rather than being concealed behind a manufactured image,
becomes a source of great strength.

The final scene of the film shows Noni performing one of *her* songs at a
concert—not one that the record label or her mother chose for her. She is no
longer using the tools from the "master's house" in order to design her career.
She is pursuing the life and career that she chose for herself. She has "become
like a swan: released in the grace of natural and spontaneous purpose."[103]

CENTRALIZING "BLACKBIRD" AND NINA SIMONE

Nina Simone's song "Blackbird" was such a perfect song for Noni's character
that when Prince-Bythewood heard it, she changed the script in order to centralize the song. When I spoke with Prince-Bythewood, she explained, "I just
went through all of my Nina Simone CDs and I came across 'Blackbird' and it
was like a lightning bolt. It just felt like it was written for the movie and for the
character." By including a Nina Simone song in her film, Prince-Bythewood
pays homage to one of the most talented and politically active Black women
musicians in recent history. Prince-Bythewood's films may not be openly political, but she does purposefully challenge the racial and gender status quo by
placing complex Black female characters at the center of her films. Her determination to centralize Black women's stories is an act that resists dominant ideologies and practices that marginalize women of color. This resistance is likely
why Prince-Bythewood feels a connection to the pianist, singer, songwriter,
and activist Nina Simone. "I create playlists for every script I write because I
write to music, and Nina Simone usually ends up on every playlist that I do

---

102. Lorde, *Sister Outsider,* 42.
103. Jordan, "The Creative Spirit."

. . . Nina was so authentic and so raw and so real, and spoke about real things," says Prince-Bythewood.[104] In the film, Noni also shares that she admires Nina Simone because Simone's voice evoked "so much pain and power."

Nina Simone was known for her hypnotic vocals and powerful lyrics. Her style was multifaceted, drawing from classical, jazz, soul, gospel, and folk music. Simone's music had a cultural impact on a global scale. But, her role as an activist has been largely overlooked.[105] Nina Simone expressed outrage at the racial discrimination and violence inflicted on Black people in her 1964 song "Mississippi Goddam," with lyrics such as "Yes, you lied to me all these years. You told me to wash and clean my ears, and talk real fine just like a lady, and you'd stop calling me Sister Sadie. Oh, but this whole country is full of lies." "Mississippi Goddam" was a "blend of the show tune, searing racial critique and apocalyptic warning," written in reaction to the assassination of civil rights activist Medgar Evers in Mississippi and the murder of four girls in a church bombing in Alabama; both murders were committed by White supremacists the year before Simone's song was released.[106] This was the first of many songs and activities in which Simone would engage, where "she dramatically commented on and participated in—and thereby helped to recast—black activism in the 1960s."[107]

The song "Blackbird" is less clearly a political song. But its message challenges the devaluation of Black womanhood, similar to Prince-Bythewood's films. "Blackbird" is a metaphor for the struggles faced by Black women. The song acts as a symbol throughout the film for Noni's struggle to find the courage and confidence to stand up for herself in a society that is constantly sending messages that devalue her:

No place big enough for holding
All the tears you're gonna cry
'Cause your mama's name was lonely
And your daddy's name was pain
And he called you little sorrow
'Cause you'll never love again
So why you wanna fly Blackbird

---

104. See appendix D.

105. Feldstein, "'I Don't Trust You Anymore': Nina Simone, Culture, and Black Activism in the 1960s"; Loudermilk, "Nina Simone & the Civil Rights Movement: Protest at Her Piano, Audience at Her Feet."

106. Tillet, "Nina Simone's Time Is Now, Again."

107. Feldstein, "'I Don't Trust You Anymore': Nina Simone, Culture, and Black Activism in the 1960s," 1350.

You ain't ever gonna fly . . .
You ain't got no one to hold you
You ain't got no one to care
If you'd only understand dear
Nobody wants you anywhere

Young Noni singing these lyrics at the talent contest foreshadows the emotional pain she will experience as she grows older. Noni expressing that she is not "seen," as she phrases it when Kaz pulls her up from the balcony, encompasses the feeling of not being recognized for who she really is and not being loved. When she tried to jump off the balcony and end her life, it was her desperate attempt to end her sorrow. Noni's public image was constructed based on the societal devaluation and objectification of Black womanhood—she had been forced to kneel down, bend over, and act as a sex object. She was told that she could not perform music that she wrote. She was forced to reveal her body, but hide her natural hair. The subtle message that she was given was "nobody wants you," like Simone's "Blackbird." It is that message that Noni confronts and fights in order to change her path. When Noni performs the song that she wrote at the end of the film, it is her first opportunity to "fly." Noni's original song is also titled "Blackbird" (on the film's soundtrack) and has the lyrics: "I'm free at last. Free from you. Free from the past. Freedom at last," and "Blackbird. Now I rise as the phoenix escapes from me." Drawing inspiration from Nina Simone, Prince-Bythewood illustrates how Noni is empowered by expressing herself, pain and all, through her chosen vocation as a singer *and* songwriter.

•

Both films analyzed in this chapter include a Black female lead who stands up for herself and her goals in the face of resistance. The films end with each lead character achieving the goal to which she aspired at the beginning of the film, connecting passion with purpose. In the final scene of *Love & Basketball*, Monica is playing for the WNBA, as Quincy and their daughter cheer for her on the sidelines. In the final scene of *Beyond the Lights*, Noni performs her original song, having pulled away the layers of artifice and misrepresentation that had previously made up her public persona, with Kaz backstage supporting her. These powerful images of Black women who "have it all" (to apply Prince-Bythewood's description) simultaneously acknowledge the socially constructed barriers that Black women face and resist dominant ideologies about Black womanhood. Prince-Bythewood's films and the characters Monica and Noni are direct challenges to the image of Black women as "mammies," who exist primarily to help *others* achieve their goals. Prince-Bythewood also challenges the perception that is the basis for the "black lady" stereotype, which is that Black women who are driven to succeed are cold, racially inauthentic, and problematic. Rather than portraying Black women as happy to work toward someone else's goals or as unfeeling when working toward their own goals, Prince-Bythewood creatively depicts Black women characters who experience empowerment, creativity, passion, and even the erotic through their work.

CHAPTER 3

Y'all Are My Children

Eve's Bayou and *Night Catches Us*

> We are African women and we know, in our blood's telling, the tender-
> ness with which our foremothers held each other. It is that connection
> which we are seeking. We have the stories of Black women who healed
> each other's wounds, raised each other's children, fought each other's
> battles, tilled each other's earth, and eased each other's passages into
> life and into death. We know the possibilities of support and connec-
> tion for which we all yearn, and about which we dream so often.
>
> —AUDRE LORDE[1]

THE MULTIDIMENSIONAL ROLE of motherhood has involved expressing ten-
derness and support, along with the potential to heal and the willingness to
fight for what matters. Black motherhood can also be an institution of self-
empowerment: "Motherhood can serve as a site where Black women express
and learn the power of self-definition, the importance of valuing and respecting ourselves, the necessity of self-reliance and independence, and a belief in
Black women's empowerment."[2] Additionally, in contrast to work performed
outside of the home, "historically, Black women have identified work in the
context of family as humanizing labor, work that affirms their identity as
women, as human beings showing love and care."[3]

Kasi Lemmons's *Eve's Bayou* (1997) and Tanya Hamilton's *Night Catches
Us* (2010) are rare films that, among other contributions, capture some of the
nuances involved in motherhood for Black women. In these two films, motherhood is portrayed in ways that demonstrate the devotion and agency of the
women who engage in this endeavor, along with the challenges that this role
involves. Each filmmaker also locates her characters within specific histori-

---

1. Lorde, *Sister Outsider,* 152.
2. Collins, *Black Feminist Thought.*
3. hooks, *Feminist Theory,* 133.

cal and cultural contexts that highlight Black motherhood as "dynamic and dialectical," and consisting of "a series of constantly renegotiated relationships that African American women experience with one another, with Black children, with the larger African American community, and with self."[4] Additionally, in *Eve's Bayou* and *Night Catches Us,* Lemmons and Hamilton draw from their childhood and family experiences for their creative cinematic depictions of motherhood and family.

Motherhood is one of the areas in which racial and gender cultural ideologies have had the most significant social impact on the lives of Black women. The fact that Michelle Obama, a Princeton and Harvard educated, married mother of two, was referred to as a "baby mama"[5] during her husband's presidential campaign demonstrates the power of ideologies of Black motherhood to distort the way Black women are viewed.[6] Stereotypes that misrepresent Black mothers as deficient, abusive, and destructive to Black families and communities have justified the withholding of much-needed resources.[7] In the following section, I provide a brief overview of the controlling images associated with Black motherhood, which Lemmons and Hamilton resist with the multidimensional Black women characters in their films.

CONTROLLING IMAGES OF BLACK MOTHERHOOD

Can you imagine a mother throwing a television set at her daughter, who is holding her infant grandson, out of anger that her welfare checks have been cut off? If you were among the many who saw the 2009 Academy Award–nominated film *Precious,* there is no need to imagine such a thing. "Mary" or "Mama" in the film *Precious,* a role for which actress/comedian Mo'Nique won an Academy Award, represents the mythology surrounding Black motherhood in dominant cultural discourse. Mo'Nique's Academy Award win for her role in the aforementioned film is a recent confirmation of the long-standing power of the controlling images of Black motherhood. Mo'Nique received considerable praise for her depiction of this verbally and physically abusive "mom from hell"[8] who manipulates the welfare system. Scholar Charlene Regester goes as

---

4. Collins, *Black Feminist Thought.*

5. "Baby mama" has a strong class and race connotation, and has been used, often derisively, to refer to a woman who has a child with a man to whom she is not married. The term is also suggestive of the myth of Black women as sexually promiscuous.

6. David, *Mama's Gun*; Harris-Perry, *Sister Citizen.*

7. Collins, *Black Feminist Thought*; Collins, *Black Sexual Politics*; Hancock, *The Politics of Disgust*; Roberts, *Shattered Bonds.*

8. Travers, "Precious."

far as reading *Precious* as a horror film and describes Mary as a "monstrous" mother: the images that the audience is confronted with are so "scandalous and disturbing that they invite reading the film as an extension of the horror genre."[9]

The filmic depiction of Black motherhood in *Precious* is especially noteworthy for its divergence from the literary text, *Push*, on which it was based. The novel *Push* is the creative work of a Black woman writer, Sapphire, and can be read as a feminist text that transgresses hegemonic ideology about Black women.[10] As scholar Kim Hester Williams argues, Sapphire's novel "forces a recognition of the ongoing violence of economic dispossession and the responsive 'oppositional knowledges' that Black women have formed in order to resist these oppressive paradigms of economic power."[11] However, unlike the novel, Lee Daniels's film adaptation "centers on the 'mental and emotional dysfunction' of Precious' abusive mother, Mama," and "produces a view that reinforces the pathology of the Black welfare mother, especially in the film's visual representation of Mama whose 'experience' is given no historical or institutional context."[12]

The fact that critics and the Academy embraced the film and Mo'Nique's depiction of Mary/Mama as having an aura of "realism"[13] reflects the cultural acceptance of this myth about Black women. Notwithstanding Mo'Nique's talent or ability to represent the character with which she was provided, her character in *Precious* is representative of the widespread stereotypes of Black mothers. The recent Oscar-winning film *Moonlight* (2016), which has been celebrated for its unconventional depiction of Black manhood, is another illustration of the villainization of Black motherhood in films that are celebrated by the Academy.[14] Interestingly, Naomie Harris, who was nominated in the Best Supporting Actress category for her role as a crack-addicted neglectful mother in *Moonlight,* explained that she was initially hesitant to portray such a "bad mother" in the film.[15] *Eve's Bayou* and *Night Catches Us* provide

---

9. Regester, "Monstrous Mother, Incestuous Father, and Terrorized Teen: Reading Precious as a Horror Film."

10. David, *Mama's Gun*; Hester Williams, "'Fix My Life': Oprah, Post-Racial Economic Dispossession, and the Precious Transfiguration of PUSH."

11. Hester Williams, "'Fix My Life': Oprah, Post-Racial Economic Dispossession, and the Precious Transfiguration of PUSH." 60.

12. Ibid., 63–64.

13. Mondello, "Movies: When Life Is This Hard, Stubbornness Is a Virtue."

14. *Moonlight* (2016), directed by Barry Jenkins, was nominated for several Academy Awards and won Best Picture.

15. Tapley, "Naomie Harris Had to Overcome Her Own Judgment to Play 'Moonlight' Role."

images that resist these hegemonic images of Black mothers as deficient, harmful, or abusive.

Whether they are working outside of the home or staying home to take care of their children, Black mothers have often been vilified as emasculating "matriarchs" or "welfare queens" for doing whatever they can to support and ensure the well-being of their families. "An emphasis on respectability, marriage, domesticity, self-reliance, normative gender roles, and heterosexuality permeates these controlling images both inter- and intra-racially, coding all black mothers as 'bad mothers' who are unfit child-bearers for the idealized white, heteropatriarchal nation."[16] Legal scholar Dorothy Roberts details how these socially constructed ideologies about Black motherhood have fueled government policies designed to maintain racial oppression by exercising control over Black women's fertility.[17] Patricia Hill Collins explains that in contrast to the subservient and obedient mammy mythical image that symbolizes the Black mother figure within White homes, who is depicted as selflessly taking care of White children, the negative matriarch and welfare mother images symbolize the mother figure in Black homes. Correspondingly, the mammy image represents the "good" Black mother figure and the matriarch and welfare mother are presented as "bad" mothers.[18]

The implied message behind the matriarch image is that she rejected the role of the submissive servant, and therefore she and Black communities are suffering. Rather than acknowledging the structural inequalities that have necessitated Black women to work outside of the home at higher rates than White women,[19] the matriarch depicts Black women as neglecting their families because they spend too much time away from home. Within the home, the matriarch is shown as having too much power, to the detriment of her family: she is a single mother or, if presented with a male partner, she overpowers and emasculates her male counterpart.

The depiction of Black women as unfeminine matriarchs did not emerge until the 1960s, even though there had been a higher percentage of Black families headed by single mothers than White families prior to that time.[20] It was during the peak period of Black activism and the feminist movement that the image of the unfeminine Black matriarch became part of the cultural

---

16. David, *Mama's Gun*, 5.
17. Roberts, *Killing the Black Body*.
18. Collins, *Black Feminist Thought*.
19. Collins, *Fighting Words*; Davis, *Women, Race, & Class*.
20. Collins, *Black Feminist Thought*.

mythology about Black women. The controversial 1965 Moynihan Report, which was officially titled "The Negro Family: The Case for National Action," written by Daniel Patrick Moynihan, an American sociologist serving as assistant secretary of labor, concluded that the high rate of families headed by single mothers was the root cause of the problems facing Black Americans in impoverished communities. "The Black matriarch thesis argued that African American women who failed to fulfill their 'womanly' duties at home contributed to social problems in Black civil society."[21] The matriarch stereotype blames Black women for issues that are caused by institutional factors, such as inferior housing, underfunded schools, the criminalization of young men, and employment discrimination.[22]

Bell hooks argues that sexist ideology was at the core of the Black matriarch myth:

> By labeling black women "matriarchs," Moynihan implied that those black women who worked and headed households were the enemies of black manhood . . . Implicit in the assertion that black women were matriarchs was the assumption that patriarchy should be maintained at all costs and that the subordination of the female was necessary for the healthy achievement of manhood. In effect, Moynihan suggested that the negative effects of racist oppression of Black people could be eliminated if black females were more passive, subservient and supportive of patriarchy.[23]

Because she is presented as unfeminine and emasculating, the "matriarch" justifies the lack of male partnership for Black women and perpetuates one of the "most popular sexist, racist myths about black womanhood—the myth that black women are inherently more assertive, independent, and domineering than white women."[24]

Instead of understanding Black mothers as women who are doing their best in tough circumstances, Melissa Harris-Perry explains that the Moynihan Report blamed them and labeled them "as unrelenting cheats who unfairly demanded assistance from the state."[25] This statement references the correlated, "welfare queen," stereotype of Black mothers. The welfare queen stereotype not only holds Black women responsible for the problems that essentially stem from institutional racism, it also presents Black women as opportunistic

21. Ibid., 75.
22. Davis, *Women, Race, & Class*.
23. hooks, *Ain't I a Woman: Black Women and Feminism*, 180.
24. Ibid., 181.
25. Harris-Perry, *Sister Citizen*, 93.

and immoral, taking advantage of undeserved benefits. This controlling image did not exist when poor Black women were denied welfare benefits.[26] The cultural ideology that Black women are welfare cheats was invented when Black women gained more political power and began demanding the same benefits White women had already been receiving.

The misperception that welfare recipients are primarily poor Black single mothers, who are undeserving of public assistance, has been central to the public discourse and policies that have ultimately called for the demise of welfare. Poverty has long been a harsh reality for a disproportionate number of Black families. However, prior to the 1960s, most Black people were excluded from government assistance.[27] As Black people were more visibly fighting for the same rights and access to resources enjoyed by Whites, there was a shift in the public perception of poverty: it was racialized as Black and the poor were stigmatized as "undeserving."[28] This shift in ideology laid the groundwork for the popularization of the myth of the welfare queen and was responsible for welfare reform that negatively impacted a significant portion of American families.[29] It was President Ronald Reagan who popularized the concept of the "welfare queen" in the 1970s as a campaign strategy (although he was not the first person to use this phrase). While campaigning in 1976, Reagan ran on an antiwelfare platform and provided the following anecdote about a woman who defrauded the government: "She used 80 names, 30 addresses, 15 telephone numbers to collect food stamps, Social Security, veterans' benefits for four nonexistent deceased veteran husbands, as well as welfare. Her tax-free cash income alone has been running $150,000 a year."[30]

Reagan's campaign story of this one woman shocked and angered crowds, which added fuel to the fire against welfare and the so-called welfare queen. Reagan did not mention race in his anecdote, because he did not need to. The guise of color-blindness[31] led to the practice of "dog-whistle" politics, in which racially coded language is effectively used in place of explicit references to race.[32] This image of welfare recipients as Black women had already begun to take root in the American psyche, so that it was unnecessary for Reagan to

---

26. Collins, *Black Feminist Thought*.

27. Black and Sprague, "The 'Welfare Queen' Is a Lie"; Katznelson, *When Affirmative Action Was White*; Quadagno, *The Color of Welfare*.

28. Quadagno, *The Color of Welfare*; Roberts, *Killing the Black Body*; Roberts, *Shattered Bonds*; Black and Sprague, "The 'Welfare Queen' Is a Lie."

29. Hancock, *The Politics of Disgust*.

30. Demby, "The Truth behind the Lies of the Original 'Welfare Queen'"; Levine, "The Welfare Queen."

31. Bonilla-Silva, *Racism without Racists*.

32. López, *Dog Whistle Politics*.

say "Black" in order to call upon the image of the Black welfare mother in his vilification of welfare recipients.

Stimulated by neoliberalism, this condemnation directed toward welfare recipients, who continued to be constructed as Black women, was amplified as we entered the Clinton era of the 1990s. Within the American neoliberal framework, there is an emphasis on economic independence and individualism, which means that social inequalities are perceived as resulting from individual deficiencies, and individuals who receive public assistance are easily deemed undeserving.[33] This emphasis on individualism combined with a call for "family values" vilified Black mothers in the minds of most Americans:

> Another powerful concept that has been vital to the project of racial neoliberalism is family values, a set of expectations that calls for patriarchal gender roles in nuclear family formations, with an emphasis on marriage, domesticity, and "good" mothering . . . Single mothers, mothers who work outside the home and same sex parents stand in stark contrast to the expectations of family values rhetoric, and the judgements against these kinds of families are moral in nature.[34]

This ultimately led to President Bill Clinton's campaign pledge to "end welfare as we know it" and the passage of the Personal Responsibility and Work Opportunity Reconciliation Act of 1996, which left poor families even more vulnerable.[35] These changes were "not simply an attempt to reform welfare . . . [T]he welfare program was to be eliminated in its entirety."[36] As a recent article highlights, "Put simply: in the aftermath of welfare reform, people most in need—disproportionately families of color—fall through the shredded public safety net, making it increasingly difficult to escape poverty."[37]

When rapper 2pac speaks the words, "A poor single mother on welfare, tell me how ya' did it. There's no way I can pay you back. But the plan is to show you that I understand. You are appreciated" in the now classic tribute to his

---

33. Goldberg, *The Threat of Race.*

34. David, *Mama's Gun,* 17.

35. Hancock, *The Politics of Disgust*; Semuels, "The End of Welfare as We Know It"; Ehrenfreund, "The Major Flaw in President Clinton's Welfare Reform That Almost No One Noticed."

36. Hester Williams, "'Fix My Life': Oprah, Post-Racial Economic Dispossession, and the Precious Transfiguration of PUSH."

37. Marchevsky and Theoharis, "Why It Matters That Hillary Clinton Championed Welfare Reform."

mother in the song "Dear Mama," he demonstrates that Black motherhood has been viewed differently through the lenses of Black men.[38]

A controlling image that is correlated with, and partly a reaction to, the previously mentioned images of Black motherhood is that of the "superstrong black mother."[39] This image was, in part, an attempt within Black communities to valorize Black mothers' intensive attempts to raise their children in a society within which racism is entrenched. This ideology expects Black mothers to regularly place the needs of others above their own, have an almost superhuman ability to protect their children from the harsh surrounding environment, and overcome the dangers of living with institutionalized racism, all while facing deteriorating economic and social support. Within Black communities, this image of motherhood is predominant. This is illustrated through hip-hop's discourse surrounding motherhood, in which Black mothers are either "honored or pitied" for the sacrifices they make and the struggles they endure for their children.[40] Like the mammy image, the superstrong Black mother image recognizes Black women as significant only to the extent to which they sacrifice themselves for others. Like the matriarch and welfare queen myth, the "superstrong black mother" stereotype blames Black women for issues with which Black communities have been burdened, by mythologizing Black women as having extraordinary powers to change that which was created by structural factors. Additionally, the myth of the "superstrong black mother" justifies the withholding of resources and minimizes the "extent to which black women are likely to be victimized in this society."[41]

Lemmons and Hamilton directly challenge the ideologies behind the "matriarch," "welfare queen," and "superstrong black mother" images in the counter-hegemonic characterizations of Black motherhood in their films. Central to the narrative of *Eve's Bayou* (1997) is the experience of an affluent stay-at-home mother of three. Lemmons's depiction of this wealthy stay-at home mother, who is portrayed as providing care and discipline for her children as she faces the emotional challenges of being a wife and mother, calls into question the dominant ideology of Black mothers as absent, negligent, or abusive. *Night Catches Us* (2010) features a lead character who is a member of the Black Panther Party, an attorney, and a widowed mother of one daughter. Although

---

38. "2Pac's 'Dear Mama' Selected for Inclusion in Library of Congress' National Recording Registry."

39. Collins, *Black Feminist Thought*; Elliott and Reid, "The Superstrong Black Mother."

40. David, "More Than Baby Mamas: Black Mothers and Hip-Hop Feminism."

41. hooks, *Feminist Theory*, 15.

struggling with the loss of her husband, due to his involvement with the Black Panthers, she does the best that she can to ensure her daughter's well-being. Over the course of each of these films, the audience sees both of these women deal with family and personal challenges and comes away from both films having seen much more nuanced images of Black motherhood than most films provide.

Whereas the controlling images of Black motherhood seek to justify the exploitation of Black women, Lemmons and Hamilton depict Black women exercising agency as mothers by applying adaptive strategies in response to their specific social contexts. Specifically, *Eve's Bayou* and *Night Catches Us* highlight motherhood as a collective effort, in which the role of biological mothers as well as other female members of the extended family and fictive kin play an important role in raising children. These approaches to motherhood are a reflection of the agency exercised by Black women and act as "culturally specific, resilient lifelines that can be continually refashioned in response to changing contexts."[42] These films portray Black motherhood in ways that highlight what Audre Lorde so powerfully articulates: "the possibilities of support and connection for which we all yearn, and about which we dream so often."

EVE'S BAYOU

"Certainly, *Eve's Bayou* is a place where I felt that very close to 100 percent of what I wanted got on the screen . . . and, that was, kind of, a magical experience," says Kasi Lemmons about her first feature film.[43] That magic jumped off the screen and was experienced by viewers and critics, as well. Famed film critic Roger Ebert referred to *Eve's Bayou* (1997) as one of the best films of the year[44] and Lemmons as one of "today's most gifted young American writer-directors."[45] *Eve's Bayou* won the Independent Spirit Award for Best First Feature and received seven NAACP Image Award Nominations, including Best Picture. Lemmons also won the National Board of Review Award for Outstanding Directorial Debut. Additionally, *Eve's Bayou* became one of the highest-grossing independent films of 1997, earning over $14 million at the box office domestically.[46]

42. Collins, *Black Feminist Thought,* 177.
43. See appendix C.
44. Ebert, "Eve's Bayou Movie Review & Film Summary (1997)."
45. Ebert, "'Eve's Bayou' a Remarkable Directing Debut."
46. Nocenti, "Writing and Directing Eve's Bayou: A Talk with Kasi Lemmons."

Although the film was a success with critics and audiences,[47] it was a "tough sell—a rural period piece centered around a group of independent-minded black women."[48] *Eve's Bayou* is set in 1962 in a Creole community in Louisiana and focuses on a well-to-do Black family. As film scholar Mia Mask points out, "Lemmons' portrait of a rural, affluent, French-speaking black family does threaten essentialist notions of black experience as definitely urban, ghetto-centered, and youth-culture dominated."[49] Lemmons stated, in an interview with journalist George Alexander, that her focus on a wealthy African American family during this time period was perceived as radical: "Most White people in the industry gravitated towards an aesthetic of Black filmmaking that was gritty and in your face and, I mean, it's *Boyz 'N The Hood* and, wow, the Black experience . . . So this was a whole different Black experience and nobody in the film mentioned White people, which was radical."[50] To market a film that had an African American cast and did not focus on racism or violence, like the Academy Award nominated *Boyz 'N the Hood* (1991), challenged film executives' tendencies to homogenize Blackness and discount the specific and varied standpoints of Black women.

Several Black women characters are at the center of *Eve's Bayou* and, significantly, Lemmons refers to the women who star in her film as "fabulous."[51] The women (and girls) in the film, to which Lemmons is referring, are ten-year-old Eve (Jurnee Smollett); Eve's older sister, Cisely (Meagan Good); Eve's mother, Roz (Lynn Whitfield); and Eve's aunt (Debbi Morgan). The story is told from the perspective of the youngest daughter of the Batiste family, Eve, which is also radical. Veteran actor Diahann Carroll is also in the film, as Elzora, a practitioner of voodoo, who is not onscreen for much of the film, but whose role is central to Eve's perspective of the events that occur over the course of the film. "The fact that I had two children under fifteen as the stars and all the women, let's say, were over thirty was radical. There were no hot twenty-five-year-olds in the movie," says Lemmons.[52] Although Lemmons's story and casting of the film may have been considered "radical," her reference to the women as "fabulous" expands dominant cultural ideologies about what

47. Mask, "Eve's Bayou: Too Good to Be a 'Black' Film?"; Young and Kim, "'Eve's' Plum."
48. Nocenti, "Writing and Directing Eve's Bayou: A Talk with Kasi Lemmons."
49. Mask, "Eve's Bayou: Too Good to Be a 'Black' Film?"
50. Alexander, *Why We Make Movies.*
51. Ibid.
52. Ibid.

a fabulous woman is. Her statement emphasizes that "fabulous" is inclusive of Black women as well as women who are not "hot twenty-five year-olds."[53]

CREOLE CULTURE AND MOTHERING IN *EVE'S BAYOU*

Eve's Bayou (1997) is a film that transcends social expectations, yet fully embraces its cultural roots. Kasi Lemmons has artfully captured the historical, cultural, and aesthetic environment of the Creole community in the bayous of Louisiana in which the film takes place. Lemmons describes herself as having come from a Southern family,[54] which connects her to the region and inspired her to place her characters within that context. But her decision to use the South as the setting was in part a creative one: "It is the rhythms, and the poetry, and a certain way of speaking . . . even though it's not true, the South seemed heightened, more dramatic, more emotional."[55] Additionally, she completed research about the region and Creole culture, including reading about the history and working with an expert in the Louisiana Creole language.[56] The result is a film that merges the realities of history and culture with the personal experiences and creative imagination of Kasi Lemmons. This combination reflects the womanist artistic standpoint by centering (1) Blackness, specifically Creole identity, and (2) Lemmons's particular perspective, or artistic standpoint.

The region's connection to the institution of slavery and the development of a Creole community from which it emerged is weaved into the film's opening sequence. When the film begins, the audience is presented with black and white imagery, symbolizing the past, as a voiceover of Eve narrates the film. She begins by telling the story of her ancestor, an enslaved woman named Eve, after whom she and the region were named: "The town we lived in was named after a slave. It's said that when general Jean Paul Batiste was stricken with cholera, his life was saved by the powerful medicine of an African slave woman called Eve. In return for his life, he freed her. And gave her this piece of land by the bayou. Perhaps in gratitude she bore him sixteen children. We are the descendants of Eve and Jean Paul Batiste. I was named for her." As Eve narrates this history, an image of a woman, who is presumably Eve's ancestor, appears in the midst of a field. The imagery then shifts to the bayou. As the

---

53. See chapter 5 for more details about how Black women filmmakers challenge hegemonic standards of beauty.

54. Nocenti, "Writing and Directing Eve's Bayou: A Talk with Kasi Lemmons."

55. Ibid, 128.

56. Alexander, *Why We Make Movies*; Katz, *Conversations with Screenwriters*.

camera moves forward through the bayou, the picture changes from black and white to color. The story shifts from past to the present as the camera arrives at the Batiste residence in 1962 and the tale of what happened to Eve and her family during one fateful summer begins to unfold. Lemmons visually depicts the relationship between history and the present, connecting Eve and her family to their ancestor. In the spirit of the womanist artistic standpoint's emphasis on incorporating nuanced images and narratives that draw from Black women's histories, Lemmons acknowledges Black womanhood as a significant part of the history of the region.

The story of Eve's ancestor introduces the institution of slavery that was a central part of the region's economic and cultural context. Though brief and contained within the opening sequence, this history provides the backdrop for the film and a sense of the family's connection to the bayou. Lemmons explains: "Without going into the specific history of slavery, I wanted that sense of oppressiveness, and a rich past."[57] The region's history of interracial relationships between Black women and White men that resulted in the multiracial community of Creoles, and the centrality of Black motherhood within these families, are also central to this historical context. It is important to note that "the open and usually uncoerced social and sexual relationships" that are referred to in the opening sequence of Lemmons's film were distinct from the more typical forced "sexual encounters involving violence and rape in the case of African enslaved women."[58] Specifically, "in the case of the Creole-Indian/ free women of color, because of their open and quasi-legal social and sexual relationships with French men, they were able to acquire large amounts of property and wealth. In contrast, enslaved African and Indian women were the literal producers of capital as they reproduced offspring that were destined to become slaves."[59] The descendants of these interracial relationships formed communities of relatively prominent American-born people of African, Indian, and French descent, who lived independently among other Creole people. Distinct cultural practices that combined the French, African, Indian, and American ancestry of the group, such as the Louisiana Creole language, emerged within these communities.[60]

The specific story of Eve's ancestor, an enslaved woman who was freed, given land, and bore the children of a French man, is atypical, and Lemmons explains that it was a product of her imagination.[61] However, it does mir-

---

57. Nocenti, "Writing and Directing Eve's Bayou: A Talk with Kasi Lemmons," 198.

58. Jolivette, *Louisiana Creoles*.

59. Ibid, 12.

60. Kein, *Creole*.

61. Katz, *Conversations with Screenwriters*.

ror the story of a woman named Marie Thereze, an enslaved woman of African and Indian ancestry who became a legend in Creole society. Thereze was born into slavery, but saved the life of her ailing mistress. In return, she was freed and given support for a land grant. She later had several children with a French man named Claude Metoyer, and was able to pass on her wealth to her children.[62] The similarities in these stories further illustrate the relationship between artistic vision and social context for Black women filmmakers.

Lemmons situates her characters within this high-status Louisiana Creole context from the moment the Batiste family first graces the screen. The Batistes are throwing an extravagant and lively party at their grand and picturesque house, as music, dancing, and champagne fill every corner. The level of material wealth displayed at the party, along with the fact that we hear a partygoer refer to Louis Batiste, the family's patriarch, as "the best colored doctor in all Louisiana," signify the high level of status that the family enjoys. Although the dialogue is primarily in English, we also hear the Creole language spoken throughout the first scene. This opening scene demonstrates the sociohistorical context in which the characters exist, including the cultural and economic status enjoyed by members of these communities.

All members of the Batiste family are in attendance at the party, including the children; however, it is Roz Batiste, Eve's mother, who most strikingly personifies the glamour and sophistication exuded by the family. She wears a dress that is tailored to flatter her figure, including tasteful (and expensive-looking) jewelry to accent her ensemble, has her hair expertly coiffed in an updo, and displays the most charming and welcoming smile. Roz Batiste simultaneously exhibits confidence, warmth, and beauty. Through these initial images of Roz, we see that she is a far cry from the dominant cultural ideologies that exist related to Black women's roles in the family. She is no mythical angry "matriarch" or conniving "welfare queen." She initially appears to be the antithesis of *Precious*'s "Mama" in every possible way: wealthy, sophisticated, glamorous, and gracious.

These images of Roz and the Batiste household represent Lemmons's memory of her childhood. She was recreating the glamour that she saw in her parents when she was a child, but that she never saw portrayed in film.[63] "It was more the reality of my memory of the time. My memory as a child of my family . . . They were glamorous and beautiful and all their friends were glamorous and beautiful, that's true . . . That's what I wanted. I wanted deep

---

62. Jolivette, *Louisiana Creoles*.

63. Alexander, *Why We Make Movies*; Nocenti, "Writing and Directing Eve's Bayou: A Talk with Kasi Lemmons."

southern glamour because I just hadn't seen that in a movie."[64] These images not only represent the memories that Lemmons has of her family, they also represent Lemmon's desire to present a counter-hegemonic image of Black femaleness—one that signifies beauty and status.

The initial picture-perfect images that we see of Roz and the Batiste family at the party mask a more complex family dynamic. Roz is a loving mother and wife who adores her husband and children. But she is married to a man who is "supposed to be a healer," and instead "destroys the things he loves."[65] Roz has devoted her life to her family, and when she finds out that her husband can't seem to control his sexual desires for other women, she does her best to keep her family together without compromising her family's status or image. Lemmons explains, "Her position as a doctor's wife, and as woman of the household is very important to her. She is a Jackie Kennedy. She is a Princess Di. Women like this exist in high places. All the time. She bought into a comfort zone, and not just materially."[66]

Because the story takes place from the perspective of Eve, the audience sees her mother, as well as the situation in which Roz finds herself, through Eve's eyes. Roz *is* glamorous, but Eve begins to get a glimpse of the complexities involved with being a wife and mother within this family when she unexpectedly and astonishingly sees her father in a compromising position with one of his mistresses in the carriage house the night of the party. Louis tries to comfort Eve, who is shocked and distraught after seeing her father with another woman. He then attempts to save face by acting as though he was doing something innocent with the other woman. But Eve, now unsure of the relationship between her parents, asks her father if he loves her mother. Louis says he does love his wife and replies that she is "the most beautiful perfect woman" he has ever met. "Your mama's a lady," he adds. Louis may be unfaithful and attempting to cover his tracks, but his comments about his wife ring true to Eve. Roz *is* beautiful. She *is* someone whom her family and community should look upon with the utmost respect. Later that night, Eve also confides in her older sister, Cisely, about seeing her father with another woman. Cisely denies that their father could ever be with anyone other than their mother, and says to Eve, "Mama's the most beautiful woman in the whole world."

Referring to Roz as a "lady" and as "beautiful" signifies a type of femininity that is rarely applied to Black women. The status of being viewed as a "lady" or as "beautiful" has historically been reserved for White women,[67]

---

64. Alexander, *Why We Make Movies*.

65. Nocenti, "Writing and Directing Eve's Bayou: A Talk with Kasi Lemmons," 193.

66. Ibid.

67. Craig, *Ain't I a Beauty Queen?*

usually to justify the idea that they are in need of protection from men. There are, of course, negative implications of this for White women. However, Black women have been viewed through the lens of other, racially specific, controlling images—none of which characterize Black women as worthy of status or respect. Hearing Louis and Cisely apply these characteristics to Roz challenges dominant ideologies about Black women. Because Roz is the wife of a respected doctor, who is not expected to work outside of the home, and is portrayed as a "lady" and as "beautiful," she challenges stereotypes of Black motherhood. However, we learn that Roz is *more* than a "beautiful lady."

As the film progresses, Roz's character allows the audience to see behind the façade of the mythic "superstrong black mother" who can miraculously overcome any and all wrongs inflicted upon her. Lemmons developed the character of Roz to be multidimensional, and though she embodies confidence and refinement at the party and in other social situations, we also see her express a range of emotions related to the vulnerability and stress of her role as a doctor's wife and mother. When one day, Eve and her Aunt Mozelle come home to find Roz sitting on a bench in her foyer, crying with her hands over her face, Eve gets a glimpse of the emotional impact of her father's infidelity on Roz. Roz and Mozelle (her sister-in-law) move into another room and close the door for privacy, but Eve eavesdrops outside the room. Eve only hears pieces of the conversation, but it is clear that Roz is upset about Louis and his mistress when Eve hears Roz angrily declare, "How dare that woman call my house!" Another night, Roz waits up for her husband, who has been out late. The children are in bed, but Eve is woken up by the sound of her parents yelling. Eve does not understand much of what is being said, but it is implied that Roz is not willing accept her husband's unfaithfulness when we hear her yell, "You get your shit straight or you're out of here!" In front of her children and in public, Roz maintains her composure, but Lemmons strategically reveals a more complex character that is more than what she initially seems to be.

Roz's anger toward her husband is presented in a way that is justifiable and as an understandable reaction to her situation. One display of the complex reaction to her situation occurs during a conversation with Mozelle. Roz thoughtfully and calmly considers out loud why she was drawn to Louis when she met him: "I said to myself, here's a man who can fix things. He's a healer. He'll take care of me. So, I leave my family and I move to the swamp. And I find out he's just a man." She left her home and moved to the bayou for Louis. She gave him three children. She trusted him. Yet, he has repeatedly deceived her. Her anger is not irrational or exaggerated. On the contrary, despite the friction between Roz and Louis, caused by his infidelity, the film shows that the two are still able to discuss the welfare of their children when necessary. In the midst of the tension that infuses the household, Roz and Louis are shown peacefully sitting together, discussing their oldest daughter, Cisely. Although just days before this conversation, Roz and Louis had a loud argument about his betrayal and Roz had threatened to kick him out of the house, Roz is willing to temporarily push her anger to the side in order to try to do what is best for her daughter. The two of them then talk to Cisely together, presenting a united front. Roz is angry with her husband, yet Lemmons represents Roz as displaying a capacity for a variety of concerns and emotions, unlike the one-dimensional ideology of Black women as emasculating matriarchs.

OTHERMOTHERING IN *EVE'S BAYOU*

Roz is the primary, though not sole, mother figure in the Batiste household, reflecting a communal, multigenerational, and woman-centered approach to parenting. When Roz moved away from her family of origin to marry Louis, the women of the Batiste family became an important source of support for her and her children. Patricia Hill Collins explains that "othermothers," women who assist biological mothers by sharing mothering responsibilities and supporting each other, have been central to the institution of Black motherhood. "The centrality of women in African-American extended families reflects both a continuation of African derived sensibilities and functional adaptations to intersecting oppressions of race, gender, class and nations."[68] Sisters, aunts, grandmothers, or cousins often help care for children and support biological mothers. Roz's sister-in-law, Mozelle, and her mother-in-law, Gran Mere, are often shown taking part in family activities within the Batiste household, such as preparing meals and disciplining the children. Additionally, when Roz is upset about Louis's infidelity, she turns to Mozelle and Gran Mere for emotional support.

Eve is close to her parents and siblings; however, she visits her Aunt Mozelle's house so much that it seems like Eve's second home. Eve's aunt becomes her emotional anchor when her parents' marriage appears to be on shaky ground. The dynamic between Eve and her Aunt Mozelle is based on Lemmons's own childhood relationship with her aunt. "Eve and Mozelle are myself and my Aunt Muriel . . . absolutely,"[69] Lemmons exclaims. On numerous occasions, Mozelle provides guidance to Eve after she finds out about her father's infidelity. During one of the many visits between Eve and Mozelle,

---

68. Collins, *Black Feminist Thought*, 178.
69. Alexander, *Why We Make Movies*.

Mozelle explains to Eve that she is not physically able to bear children. "Y'all are my children," she tells Eve, emphasizing her feeling of being a mother figure, or "othermother," to the Batiste children.

During my interview with Kasi Lemmons, she explained how perceptions of her own family, and the way that love was always at the core of it, inspired the interactions between Roz and her children: "I wanted to explore a way of speaking that felt very southern, and felt like my family. And, even the way of talking to children that had a poetry to it, that could be harsh—but it also had a love behind it." There is one particular situation that highlights this combination of harshness and love. One day, Cisely blatantly disobeys her mother's direct order to stay in the house. After Roz cannot find her, she becomes hysterical and calls the police for fear that her daughter might be hurt. When Cisely finally walks in to the house, she gloats that she went to the beauty parlor and to visit her father. As an emotional reaction to this blatant disobedience, which was perhaps intensified by the tension between herself and her husband, Roz slaps Cisely across the face. Roz immediately appears to be shaken by her reaction to her daughter's behavior. Later that evening, Roz, who has calmed down since the afternoon's chaos, has a talk with Cisely. In an attempt to reconcile with her daughter, yet still maintain her position of authority, Roz tells Cisely: "I love you. And it's my job to protect you as best I can. If you disobey my orders and leave this house again, I swear I'll lock you in your room." Although Roz threatens to lock Cisely in her room, she is never depicted as a "bad" mother. She may be riding the emotional roller coaster of managing the relationships with her husband and children, but there is never a doubt that Roz loves her children.

SPEAKING THE "SAME LANGUAGE" AS JULIE DASH

"*Daughters of the Dust* was one of those films where I said, oh, we speak the same language," said Lemmons in an interview.[70] The connections between *Eve's Bayou* and *Daughters of the Dust* have been explored in the work of a handful of film scholars—a few that discuss both films' incorporation of West African cultural practices.[71] In Sandra Grayson's book *Symbolizing the Past*, these two films are explained as providing symbolic representations of the continuity of West African and African American cultures. Grayson focuses on Dash's incorporation of the Nigerian Yoruba deities into her film and

---

70. Nocenti, "Writing and Directing Eve's Bayou: A Talk with Kasi Lemmons," 197.

71. Biccum, "Third Cinema in the 'First' World: 'Eve's Bayou' and 'Daughters of the Dust'"; Grayson, *Symbolizing the Past*; Missouri, *Black Magic Woman and Narrative Film*.

Lemmons's incorporation of the traditional West African cultural belief that supernatural power is inherited from women.[72] The two films have also been compared for the ways they "remember the history of slavery, employ cinematic space, constitute objectivity, subjectivity, and desire."[73] In addition, Lisa B. Thompson, who focuses on displays of middle-class sexuality in her book *Beyond the Black Lady,* compares the two films for their depiction of Black women who reclaim sexual agency in the context of the Southern United States.[74]

I discuss Dash's film here in order to emphasize one of the ways that Black women filmmakers provide validation of other Black women's contributions. Although Lemmons's *Eve's Bayou* is the result of her own personal experience and creative vision, she has openly drawn comparisons between her work and that of Dash's, which I argue is a way of honoring Dash's significance within the film industry and culture, in general.

The combination of research and a visionary approach to filmmaking make Dash's *Daughters of the Dust* (1991) truly groundbreaking. The film takes place at the turn of the twentieth century and tells the story of three generations of Gullah women living on an island off South Carolina. Dash, incredibly, completed ten years of research on the Gullah people for her film. However, *Daughters of the Dust* moves beyond reality or accuracy into a realm of imagination.[75] An unborn child and ancestors who have passed on become part of the present story. The voiceover at the beginning of the movie acknowledges: "I am the first and the last. I am the honored one and the scorned one . . . I am the barren one and many are my daughters." These statements recognize the connection between the past, present, and future. They also reinterpret reality in a way that allows the simultaneous existence of seemingly contradictory ideas. Dash's goal was to take fact and infuse it with an imaginative construction.[76] In her analysis of *Daughters of the Dust,* Gloria Gibson explains that "memory emerges as a powerful cinematic device to frame historical content. Further, as memory functions within the filmmaker's creative process and also as a filmic device, it remains intimately connected to cultural history and identity formation."[77]

---

72. Eve and Mozelle inherited their power to see the future from their ancestor Eve.

73. Biccum, "Third Cinema in the 'First' World: 'Eve's Bayou' and 'Daughters of the Dust,'" 60.

74. Thompson, *Beyond the Black Lady.*

75. Dash, *Daughters of the Dust.*

76. Ibid.

77. Gibson, "The Ties That Bind."

The significance of history, the fusion of imagination and reality, and the role of memory in recalling one's history play a central role in Lemmons's *Eve's Bayou,* as they do in *Daughters of the Dust.* The recognition and respect given to one's ancestors, particularly women, is essential to the story of both films. The opening sequence of *Eve's Bayou* (described earlier in this chapter), in which it is revealed that a woman named Eve was given the land around the bayou and bore sixteen children, highlights the significance of honoring one's ancestors, acknowledges the history of slavery, and pays tribute to the women from whom the current generations were descended.

Lemmons's decision to tell the story from young Eve's perspective high-lights the inherently personal nature of memory: "I was interested in how two different people can look at their past and see two different things," explains Lemmons.[78] The audience is immediately drawn in to the film and learns that the interpretation of memory is central to *Eve's Bayou* with Eve's opening line: "Memory is a selection of images. Some lucid. Others printed indelibly on the brain. The summer I killed my father, I was ten years old." The idea that Eve killed her father is an imaginative reconstruction based on Eve's memory of the summer. Eve witnesses a few key events throughout the course of the film that she perceives as possibly relating to the death of her father, but the only thing that is clear is that the events are open to more than one interpretation.

An example of the interpretive nature of memory is illustrated when Eve tries to make sense of seeing her father with one of his mistresses in the carriage house the night of the party, as described earlier in this chapter. She is in shock and begins to hyperventilate because of what she has seen. When her father sees her, he comforts her and acts as though he was doing nothing wrong. When Eve goes to her room that night and tells her sister Cisely that she saw their father with another woman, Cisely tells her that she was mistaken about what she saw and gives Eve an alternate explanation for what she witnessed between her father and the other woman. Eve now seems a little less sure about what she saw her father doing in the carriage house. Her memory of the events is slightly altered with each new encounter.

Eve's memory of her father's death is also open to interpretation. After Cisely discloses a traumatic interaction between herself and their father, Eve is angered to the point of telling Cisely, "I'll kill him for hurting you," asks her Aunt Mozelle if it's possible to kill someone with voodoo, and visits Elzora (the voodoo practioner). Not long after, Louis is killed by the husband of one of his mistresses, but Eve wonders if she is responsible. This concern affects her recollection of the events during the days prior to his death. Had her actions caused

78. Alexander, *Why We Make Movies.*

her father's death? "The questions in Eve's Bayou are more interesting to me than the answers," says Lemmons.[79]

Perhaps memory is, as explained by Toni Morrison, "not an effort to find out the way it really was . . . The point is to dwell on the way that it appeared and why it appeared in that particular way."[80] Eve's memory of these events consists of several, sometimes conflicting, ideas that are simultaneously part of her history. After Louis's death, Eve finds a letter from her father that explains the traumatic interaction between Cisely and Louis from *his* point of view. Eve then confronts Cisely and accuses her of lying. Both of the sisters are tearful and Cisely emotionally confesses, "I don't know what happened." By the end of the film, we see that Eve and Cisely are aware of the interpretive nature of memory. The two sisters and the audience are left to wonder whose interpretation of the events should be believed.

Like Dash's *Daughters of the Dust*, *Eve's Bayou* reveals how reality can be interpreted in ways that allow the simultaneous existence of seemingly contradictory ideas, yet connect us to our history. In the closing of *Eve's Bayou*, we hear the voiceover of adult Eve acknowledge the interpretive nature of memory and its connection to one's past: "The truth changes color, depending on the light. And tomorrow can be clearer than yesterday. Memory is a selection of images . . . Each image is like a thread. Each thread woven together to make a tapestry of intricate texture. And the tapestry tells a story. And the story is our past."

Lemmons's refusal to give the audience one definite version of the truth in *Eve's Bayou* reflects the embrace of multiple standpoints that Patricia Hill Collins calls for in *Black Feminist Thought*. A necessary tenet of Black feminism is the realization that "individual African-American women have long displayed varying types of consciousness regarding our shared angle of vision. When these individual expressions of consciousness are articulated, argued through, contested, and aggregated in ways that reflect the heterogeneity of Black womanhood, a collective group consciousness dedicated to resisting oppression becomes possible."[81] Lemmons's acknowledgement of the existence of multiple perspectives reflects the womanist artistic standpoint. By problematizing the perception that there exists a single perspective, she resists the homogenization and marginalization of Black womanhood.

79. Nocenti, "Writing and Directing Eve's Bayou: A Talk with Kasi Lemmons," 193.
80. As cited in Gibson, "The Ties That Bind."
81. Collins, *Black Feminist Thought*, 36.

NIGHT CATCHES US

Night Catches Us (2010) focuses on a part of American history that is as complicated as it has been overlooked: the period immediately following the Black Panther Party movement and the impact of the movement on its members. But Tanya Hamilton does not give audiences the familiar and simplistic images of radical and militant Black Panthers that one might expect. Instead of playing it safe, she takes an intimate look at the interpersonal relationships of the people who had devoted so much of themselves to the movement. She "chooses the riskier path of examining its emotional and political fallout" for its members.[82] The film takes place in 1976, a time when the memory of the movement is still fresh, but there is a sense of "loss, sadness and regret, and the feeling that history has moved on."[83]

The film centers on the relationships between people whose lives have been intimately and forever impacted by their connection to the Black Panthers. Patricia/Patty (Kerry Washington) was married to a member of the Black Panther Party who was killed by law enforcement officers because of his involvement with the group (evoking the memory of the 1969 assassination of Black Panther Fred Hampton). Patricia remains in their home, raising their daughter, Iris, and continues to fight for former members of the Black Panthers through her career as an attorney. Marcus (Anthony Mackie) is a former member of the Black Panthers, who left the area after he was labeled a "snitch" and blamed for causing the murder of Patricia's husband. The film begins when Marcus returns to his old Philadelphia neighborhood in 1976 for his father's funeral, following a four-year absence. His return leads Patricia, Marcus, and Iris to come to terms with their connections to the movement and each other.

When Tanya Hamilton's *Night Catches Us* premiered at the Sundance Film Festival in 2010, she was the only Black female director to screen a film.[84] Because of her original narrative and skillful ability to write relatable characters, the film has received multiple awards and nominations. It was awarded the "FIPRESCI Award" at the 2010 Seattle International Film Festival for Best American film for its "profound exploration of a chapter of American history that is woefully underexplored."[85] It was named Best Screenplay by the African-American Film Critics Association. Additionally, the film received a

---

82. Anderson, "Night Catches Us Takes a Brutally Honest Look at Black Power."
83. Ebert, "Night Catches Us Movie Review (2010)."
84. Sharkey, "Tanya Hamilton's 'Night Catches Us' Captures a Point in Time."
85. Brown, "Movie Director Tanya Hamilton Talks about Debut Film 'Night Catches Us'"; "Seattle International Film Festival Winners Announced."

nomination for the Sundance Film Festival Grand Jury Prize and a nomination for an Independent Spirit Award in the Best First Feature category, and it was a finalist for the 2010 Humanitas Prize. It was nominated for several NAACP Image Awards, including Outstanding Independent Motion Picture and Outstanding Directing in a Motion Picture. Hamilton was also nominated for Breakthrough Director at the 2010 Gotham Awards.

ACTIVIST MOTHERING IN *NIGHT CATCHES US*

How does a mother explain her connection to a group labeled by the government as "terrorists" and the greatest "threat"[86] to the nation? How does a mother explain to her child that her father was murdered by agents of the government in his own home? *Night Catches Us* illustrates the ways that motherhood takes on a complicated meaning within the context of the Black Panther movement and its aftermath.

Black women have been integral to struggles against injustice. In 1970, Toni Cade Bambara wrote about the centrality of social activism to Black womanhood: "Now the young look to emulate Nina Simone, Abbey Lincoln, Kathleen Cleaver, not because they're gorgeous in that old way, but beautiful in a new Black way. We measure their womanhood in terms of their connection to the struggle."[87] It would follow that being a good mother and being a social activist were viewed as overlapping goals for Black women: "Their very definitions of good mothering went beyond a simple measure of caring for their own biological children. Instead, they saw good mothering as comprising all actions, including social activism, that addressed the needs of their children and community."[88]

In *Night Catches Us,* the emphasis on self-determination and self-defense advocated by the Black Panthers merges with an ideology of family and kinship that extends to those outside of the nuclear family to create a complex web of meaning and responsibilities associated with motherhood. Patricia not only takes care of her daughter, Iris; she also acts as a protector, advocate, and mother figure for many others in her Philadelphia neighborhood.

Tanya Hamilton sets the historical, cultural, and political context for her artistic vision of activist mothering by skillfully weaving images of the Black Panthers throughout the film. The first images that the audience sees include

---

86. Davis, *Freedom Is a Constant Struggle*; Workneh and Finley, "27 Important Facts Everyone Should Know about the Black Panthers."

87. Bambara, *The Black Woman*, 106.

88. Collins, *Black Feminist Thought*, 191.

black and white archival video footage of the Black Panthers, standing together in their uniform of black berets and leather jackets. As the opening credits are displayed on the screen, so are black and white images that highlight symbols of the movement, such as the clenched fist and messages in support of Black businesses. There is also an image of a child carrying a bag of groceries, indicating the Black Panthers' free food program for children, and an image of a gun juxtaposed with images of the Ku Klux Klan, referencing their emphasis on self-defense. As the opening credits end, the words "Philadelphia, 1976" flash across the screen as the camera cuts to an image of kids playing outside in a residential neighborhood. With the merging of these images—the footage of the Black Panthers followed by the children playing outside—the relationship between Black motherhood and social activism is foregrounded.

Patricia's family is forever affected by their connection to the movement and the government's violent reaction to it. Patricia lives in limbo with her daughter, not willing to move on or move out of the house where her husband was killed. Iris, Patricia's daughter, is unfailingly curious about her father, whom she never had the opportunity to know. Patricia's younger cousin Jimmy, who feels alienated and disempowered, idolizes the Black Panthers and makes failed and misguided attempts to emulate their militant approach in his interactions with law enforcement.

Much of *Night Catches Us* takes place through the eyes of Iris, similar to Lemmons's use of a child as a narrator in *Eve's Bayou*. Additionally, Hamilton draws from her own childhood memories to cinematically frame the historical content of her film, comparable to Lemmons incorporating her childhood memories and centralizing the relationship between memory and history in *Eve's Bayou*. In *Night Catches Us*, Iris is constantly seeking answers to questions about her family's past from her mother. Her thirst for knowledge about her family is similar to the curiosity that Tanya Hamilton experienced as a child. In my interview with Hamilton, she discussed her childhood fascination with the political involvement of a family friend, whom she referred to as her "aunt." "She was my second mother and everything about her history fascinated me . . . I loved what she did. I loved how she did it. All of it, I thought was so interesting. So, she's the Pat character. I've just stolen huge swathes of her life, because I loved it and I wanted to become it," explained Hamilton. Also, when Iris first meets Marcus, he offers her some of his old Black Panther comic books, which she happily accepts and eagerly begins reading. Iris's enthusiastic reaction to receiving the comic books is inspired by Hamilton's memory of her own childhood fascination with the memorabilia that her aunt had collected: "I would go into the basement all the time and she had all these civil rights books. And I got a bunch of them after she passed away, and they were awesome. Some were civil rights and some were straight up Black militant books, which I loved. They were fascinating. I have a bunch of them. They're basically newsletters. They were done by local organizations and stuff from the NAACP. And I was like, 'This is beautiful.'"

Patricia's connection to the Black Panthers and the violent way in which her husband was killed necessitates that she engage in a challenging balancing act as a mother. Although Patricia exemplifies an activist spirit in many ways, she also struggles with exactly how much information about the violence that has resulted from this involvement to share with her daughter. Iris, inquisitive and interested in learning about her father, regularly pushes for answers. However, when Iris asks her mother questions about her father, Patricia often does her best to distract her and change the subject. For instance, early on in the film, we see Iris looking through some old heirlooms when she finds a photograph of Patricia sitting with two men, one being her father. The collection of mementos around the house, such as the photographs of her husband, suggests that Patricia has discussed at least some of the details related to her husband's involvement with the Black Panthers, but when Iris asks why they "never" talk about her father, Patricia abruptly brings the conversation to an end by telling Iris to go brush her teeth. Patricia's reluctance to disclose more information about her husband is her attempt to protect Iris from something that may be difficult for her to hear, which reflects the unique situation in which Patricia finds herself as a Black activist mother during this time period.

Patricia is doing her best, in a difficult situation, to protect herself and her daughter, while struggling with the emotional aftermath of her involvement with the Black Panthers and her husband's death. At one point, Iris reveals to Marcus that the FBI follows them and taps their phone. She also shares that she knows that her father died in their living room, although her mother thinks she doesn't know this piece of information, but she does not know *how* he died. When Patricia and Marcus are alone one night, after Iris has gone to sleep, Patricia cautions Marcus, "We don't talk about the past. It's too painful." Marcus asks, "For her or for you?" Patricia says it's for both of them, demonstrating that she is struggling to protect her daughter from something that is equally difficult for her to face.

The pain that Patricia has been living with, and trying to protect Iris from, is eventually revealed. One day, Iris stares at the worn wallpaper in their living room. She senses that there is something significant hiding behind the wallpaper and begins tearing it down. As the wallpaper comes down, blood stains underneath are exposed—symbolically exposing the circumstances that led to her father's death. This scene is interspersed with black and white images of police with guns and riot gear, and a funeral procession that is attended by Black Panthers.

The bloodstained walls that Iris discovers offer physical evidence of the history of oppression within Black communities. That Patricia and Iris live among these bloodstains just under the surface demonstrates the impact of this history of oppression on Black women—a recognition of this shared history of oppression is a central element of Black feminist thought, according to Patricia Hill Collins, and an important part of the womanist artistic standpoint.[89] Wallpapering over the bloodstains and continuing to raise her daughter in the house that she shared with her husband was Patricia's reaction to the challenges that she faced as a widow, mother, and former Black Panther. The bloodstains that remained on the wall years after the murder of her husband connected her to the past, while wallpapering over them allowed Patricia to exercise some agency in the way that she reacted to this history.

Continuing to live in her Philadelphia neighborhood after the murder of her husband was important to Patricia in part because she felt connected to that community in a way that, I argue, was similar to that of an extended family, or what is referred to as "fictive kinship." The concept of fictive kin, which is used to refer to social bonds shared by individuals who are not related by marriage or blood, has often been applied to the social networks within African American communities.[90] A shared history of violence perpetuated by the state, and other forms of social and economic oppression, connects members of communities such as the one depicted in the film. The Black Panthers' emphasis on self-determination further advanced this kinship. As a result, in addition to protecting her daughter, Patricia is also concerned for the well-being of others in her community. For instance, when Marcus first comes to her house, Iris is sitting outside and tells him that her mother is in the kitchen "feeding the whole neighborhood" with the tone of a slightly annoyed child, implying that this is a regular occurrence. When Marcus walks inside, he sees kids sitting around her dining room table while Patricia makes sure they eat their fruit and vegetables. We also see a bag full of groceries with the words "Free Food Program" written in bold letters, in recognition of the Black Panthers' community outreach activities. Another occasion that indicates Patricia's interest in taking care of others in a way that goes beyond mainstream societal expectations is when she holds a potluck in her backyard to raise funds for one of her clients who can't afford bail. Some of the Black Panthers

---

89. Ibid.

90. Stack, *All Our Kin*; Collins, *Black Feminist Thought*.

come to this potluck and bring food, showing their support for Patricia and her cause. Thus, Patricia's house seems to feel like a home and source of support for many people in her neighborhood.

One person in particular that Patricia regularly supports is her younger cousin, Jimmy, who lives with Patricia and Iris. He idolizes the Black Panthers but was never involved with the group and has a flawed idea of what the Panthers did when they were more active in the neighborhood. Faced with the realities of living in an under-resourced community that has a pervasive police presence, he reacts based on a misinterpretation of the Black Panthers' goal of self-defense. One evening, after Iris watches Jimmy get arrested for starting an argument with the police, Patricia sits at the table with her boyfriend, who is also an attorney. Patricia tells him that she wants to get her cousin out of jail that night. He replies that he can't do it *this time,* implying that Jimmy has been to jail before and that Patricia has in the past leveraged her position as an attorney to help her cousin. The next day, Patricia picks Jimmy up from the police station, but on the way home she takes on the motherly role of scolding him for constantly engaging in behavior that puts him in danger.

Although Patricia's desire to take care of her family and community could be presented as a version of the "superstrong black mother" trope, filmmaker Tanya Hamilton also fashioned Patricia's character as vulnerable, which humanizes her beyond the controlling image. For example, one day Marcus and Iris witness Jimmy attempting to provoke the police by yelling at them and calling them "pigs." Marcus, concerned for Iris and Patricia, tells Jimmy to stay away from Iris and the house. Patricia becomes upset with Marcus for threatening her cousin, to which Marcus responds that she should stop acting like "Mother Teresa," emphasizing and reproaching her for the mothering role that Patricia plays for others in her community. Marcus is worried that Patricia's desire to take care of others is putting herself and Iris in a vulnerable position, which calls out the problematic potential for Black women to place others' needs above their own.

The history and threat of violence that lurk under the surface of the lives of Patricia and Iris, as symbolized by the bloodstains on the walls, is illustrated when the police are searching for Jimmy toward the end of the film. As sirens blare outside of their house, Patricia frantically says to Iris, "What did mama tell you to do?" And Iris recites the following: "When face to face with a policeman I should keep my mouth shut. Say nothing unless asked. Answer questions with 'Yes, sir. No, sir.' Unless they violate my civil rights. Then put my hands on my head where they can clearly see them and ask for a lawyer. Never make sudden moves and never get angry." It is obvious that Patricia has anticipated herself and Iris being placed in a potentially dangerous situation with law enforcement. She recognizes that Iris's life may depend on Patricia's ability to prepare her on how to survive. It is the ever-present threat of this kind of confrontation with law enforcement that necessitates the merging of Black motherhood and social activism, which Patricia exhibits throughout the film.

Patricia's character also challenges the dominant cultural ideology of Black mothers as neglectful or abusive. Her primary interest throughout the course of the film is protecting her daughter—from the pain that the past may cause to the continuing threats that her family faces—and she struggles with the decisions that she has made for the sake of her family. Her character is more multidimensional than the emasculating "matriarch," manipulative "welfare queen," and "superstrong black mother" images. She regularly puts on a tough face for her daughter, although her vulnerability is portrayed through her conversations with Marcus, with whom she feels a sense of comfort because of their history. There are also many times that we see Patricia and Iris talking one-on-one while sitting close to each other, signaling a comfort and affection between the two of them. As one film critic puts it, "Hamilton depicts a world of familiar domesticity. The occasional gunshot and crime may violate the setting, but the will to preserve family and community is still strong."[91] Patricia also aims to paint a positive picture of her husband for Iris, so as to not damage Iris's image of the father she never had a chance to know. She is portrayed as a thoughtful and concerned parent who is actively involved in the daily life of her child and community.

RECOGNIZING THE WOMEN OF THE MOVEMENTS

Through Patricia's character, *Night Catches Us* honors the women of the movements that led to significant cultural and political changes, and without whom the movements and the more visible male leadership would not have been nearly as effective. Few women have been recognized for their activism and leadership during the civil rights and Black Power movements, from the iconic Rosa Parks to women like Kathleen Cleaver, Angela Davis, Ella Baker, and Fannie Lou Hamer, whose names have been left out of far too many history books. Countless other women influenced the direction and success of these social movements and groups such as the Black Panther Party, Student Nonviolent Coordinating Committee, and Southern Christian Leadership Conference.

---

91. Ventura, "Night Catches Us: A Criminally Overlooked Film about the Legacy of the Black Power Movement."

Although recent scholarship highlights the centrality of Black women to the social movements of the 1960s and 1970s, Black women have not been granted the recognition enjoyed by men.[92] The autobiographies of Assata Shakur and Angela Davis provide rare firsthand narratives of the experiences of Black women who were active in social movements during this time period.[93] Additionally, Angela Davis, who is herself "one of the few great long-distance intellectual freedom fighters in the world,"[94] addresses the way that the nation's collective historical memory has identified men as the central figures in these social movements. "Even though numbers of books, both scholarly and popular, have been written on the role of women in the 1955 [Montgomery bus] boycott, Dr. King who was actually invited to be a spokesperson for a movement when he was entirely unknown—the movement had already formed—Dr. King remains the dominant figure."[95] She explains that she never tires of "urging people to remember that it wasn't a single individual or two who created [the civil rights] movement, that, as a matter of fact, it was largely women within collective contexts, Black women, poor Black women who were maids, washerwomen and cooks. These were the people who collectively refused to ride the bus."[96]

The film and Patricia's character, specifically, were inspired by a close friend of Hamilton's family (mentioned earlier in this chapter), Carol Lawson-Green, whom Hamilton refers to as her aunt and with whom Hamilton was fascinated as a child. Lawson-Green was a civil rights activist who was arrested with a group of six students for taking part in a sit-down protest in the White House four days after protesters were attacked in Selma, Alabama, in 1965.[97] "All got at least a six-month jail sentence. Normally they would get a $50 fine. But they threw the book at them," says Hamilton about Green's arrest. "I was fascinated . . . I love the idea that these people did a thing that may not be the final moment in their life, but shaped the rest of their lives."[98] Hamilton adds that by the time Green became friends with her family, she focused her

92. Davis, *Women, Race, & Class*; Davis, *Freedom Is a Constant Struggle*; Farmer, *Remaking Black Power*; Ransby, *Ella Baker and the Black Freedom Movement*; Robnett, *How Long?*; Spencer, *The Revolution Has Come.*

93. Davis, *Angela Davis*; Shakur, *Assata.*

94. West, Forward to *Freedom is a Constant Struggle*, vii.

95. Davis, *Freedom Is a Constant Struggle*, 66.

96. Ibid., 118.

97. Adams, "Simmering in the City"; Brown, "Movie Director Tanya Hamilton Talks about Debut Film 'Night Catches Us.'"

98. Brown, "Movie Director Tanya Hamilton Talks about Debut Film 'Night Catches Us.'"

energy on social activism within her community instead,[99] as does Patricia in *Night Catches Us.*

Patricia's involvement and interactions with the Black Panthers signify the role of Black women as the backbone of the movement, while highlighting the tendency for the actions of women to be less conspicuous than those of the men. Patricia is a leader in her community in many ways. In particular, as an attorney she makes concerted efforts to defend people within her neighborhood, who are under an intense amount of scrutiny from the sometimes corrupt and often unjust criminal justice system. Because of this, along with her status as a widow of one of the leaders of the Black Panthers, she is treated with a modest amount of deference within the group.

Although Patricia does not officially take on a leadership role within the Black Panthers and she is never shown publicly overpowering the male leadership, she is nonetheless influential. Patricia attempts to use her influence to defend Marcus's presence in the community, after he had been threatened several times by the group. When Marcus attends a potluck fund-raiser at Patricia's house, he urgently feels the need to leave as soon as he sees members of the Black Panthers arriving. She offers to talk to them and emphasizes, "They listen to me."

Patricia's influence within the group is further illustrated when she visits the head of the Panthers, DoRight, after he and Marcus were in a fist fight. She cautions DoRight to "stay away" from Marcus. When he asks her why she is standing up for Marcus, she replies, "'Cause that's what I do. For *all* of you," emphasizing her centrality to the group. He warns her that Marcus should not be trusted, and reminds her that Marcus sold out Patricia's husband to the authorities—they "own him," DoRight says. But she insists that it was not Marcus who told the authorities about her husband. He finally concedes to her request and tells her that no one will "lay a hand on" Marcus. To reassert his authority, DoRight adds that she should not ask for any more favors. However, Patricia laughs at this comment, knowing that she has done them more favors than he is willing to admit. Her point is made when another man immediately walks into the room and eagerly asks if she has any news about *his* legal case. This conversation that takes place between the public leader of the Panthers and Patricia is indicative of the covert power of Black women within the movement. Patricia's actions exemplify the value and beauty of Black women, as measured by their "connection to the struggle."[100] This is creatively illus-

---

99. Adams, "Simmering in the City."
100. Bambara, *The Black Woman,* 106.

trated in the way that Tanya Hamilton highlights the relationship between Black motherhood and social activism in *Night Catches Us*.

•

Kasi Lemmons's and Tanya Hamilton's characters are modern representations of the words written by Audre Lorde: "Black women who healed each other's wounds, raised each other's children, fought each other's battles." Lemmons's and Hamilton's cinematic depictions of motherhood also highlight the ways that Black women have redefined motherhood in ways that assist in their navigation of social challenges, while embracing the networks within their communities. These characters resist negative cultural ideologies of Black motherhood: Roz and Patricia are respected within their communities and families. In Lemmons's *Eve's Bayou*, Roz is married to a doctor who comes from a family that has enjoyed a high status in their community for generations. Her husband and children refer to her as "beautiful" and "perfect." In Hamilton's *Night Catches Us*, Patricia is an attorney who goes above and beyond to take care of her daughter and community. As a member of the Black Panther Party whose husband was killed because of their cause, and who continues to fight for the group while raising her daughter alone, she challenges hegemonic images about single mothers.

The ending of each film transgresses dominant ideologies about families and motherhood. Kasi Lemmons and Tanya Hamilton refuse to accept the narrow idea of "good" mothering being tied to a woman's embrace of the patriarchal nuclear family. Roz has everything that the dominant culture idealizes for women: wealth, a husband, and children. But, her marriage is far from ideal for her. When she visits a fortune teller, she is told: "You are in pain . . . [T]here is an end to your problem. Though not one you imagined." She is then told that she will be happy again in three years. The death of her husband by the end of the film suggests that her happiness is facilitated by the fact that her husband is no longer part of her life. She can be happy raising her children without Louis, and perhaps with the continuing involvement of her sister and mother-in-law. Patricia is a widow, but by the end of the film, Marcus has asked that she and Iris come live with him. Although Patricia has feelings for Marcus, she chooses to stay in her home and community rather than go with him. When during my interview I asked Hamilton why Patricia did not choose to leave with Marcus, her response reflected the complexity of Patricia's situation: "I don't know that I understand fully her choice of not going . . . And, you know, I guess it depends on your experience. On some days, I feel like it's heroic . . . On my more real days I feel like she's afraid. You know, of upending all that she knows." At the end of each film, a nuclear family is not portrayed as the only or ideal option for the women. The combination of qualities exhibited by Roz and Patricia, in addition to the contextualization of their experiences, provide a much more complicated and humanizing picture of motherhood than the one-dimensional stereotypes of Black mothers that overwhelm most media.

CHAPTER 4

Rebellious Love

Middle of Nowhere and *Pariah*

> I am a feminist, and what that means to me is much the same as the
> meaning of the fact that I am Black: it means that I must undertake
> to love myself and to respect myself as though my very life depends
> upon self-love and self-respect.
>
> —JUNE JORDAN[1]

"*LOVE? AH, ASK* the troubadors [*sic*] who come from those who have loved
when all reason pointed to the uselessness and foolhardiness of love. Perhaps we
shall be the teachers when it is done. Out of the depths of pain we have thought
to be our sole heritage in the world—O, we know about love!"[2] Love of and
between Black people is rebellious. Loving Blackness is to resist dominant cultural ideologies that tell us otherwise.[3] Yet, as Lorraine Hansberry states, Black
people have chosen love, beyond all reason. Choosing love is a form of liberation. Patricia Hill Collins describes love relationships between Black people
as something that can challenge systematic oppression—love of and between
Black people calls into question the system that seeks to devalue Blackness.[4]

It is no wonder, then, that Black women filmmakers, whose work and very
presence in the film industry challenge the status quo, would choose to create stories about Black women and love. Ava DuVernay's *Middle of Nowhere*
(2012) and Dee Rees's *Pariah* (2011) each compassionately explores the love
life of Black women. Whereas DuVernay explores the emotional journey

---

1. Jordan, *Some of Us Did Not Die*, 270. (From *Some of Us Did Not Die: New and Selected Essays* by June Jordan, copyright © 2003. Reprinted by permission of Civitas Books, an imprint of Hachette Book Group, Inc.)
2. Hansberry, *To Be Young, Gifted and Black: Lorraine Hansberry in Her Own Words*, 256.
3. Collins, *Black Sexual Politics*.
4. Collins, *Black Feminist Thought*, 170.

and depth of a woman whose marriage is suddenly disrupted when her husband is arrested and imprisoned, Rees provides a coming-of-age story about a teenager who is learning about love in a space where she struggles to fit in and within a family where this love is perceived as problematic. Each of these directors affirms the value of love for Black women by providing a story about love relationships and their complexities that are rarely afforded Black women characters in film. DuVernay and Rees also link the desire for love to social contexts specific to Black women: mass incarceration and perspectives of homosexuality within working-class Black communities.

There are countless ways to define love. Novelist Zora Neale Hurston[5] says the following of love: "When I fall *in,* I can feel the bump. That is a fact and I would not try to fool you. Love may be a sleepy, creeping thing with some others, but it is a mighty wakening thing with me. I feel the jar, and I know it from my head down."[6] Hurston describes love as something one *falls in* to—love is something, a feeling, that happens to you. On the other hand, in *All about Love,* bell hooks describes love as a verb, a choice one makes that requires a mix of various ingredients—care, affection, recognition, respect, commitment, trust, and open and honest communication.[7] Audre Lorde uses the term "erotic" to describe the deep powerful feeling that can be expressed, but is too often suppressed, by women: "The erotic is a resource within each of us that lies in a deeply female and spiritual plane, firmly rooted in the power of our unexpressed or unrecognized feeling."[8]

Something Hurston, hooks, and Lorde share with many Black women writers is an emphasis on the exploration of self-love,[9] which is a key element of a womanist perspective. As Alice Walker states, a womanist "Loves herself. *Regardless.*"[10] According to June Jordan, choosing self-love is so important for Black women that it must be undertaken as though one's "very life depends upon self-love and self-respect."[11] In their films, Ava DuVernay and Dee Rees explore these various dimensions of love: deep feeling, caring, affection, recognition, respect, commitment, trust, and communication. Also, like many

5. Hurston is best known for her novel *Their Eyes Were Watching God,* in which she created one of the most complex stories about love, from a Black woman's perspective, in literary history.

6. Hurston, *I Love Myself When I Am Laughing and Then Again When I Am Looking Mean and Impressive,* 67.

7. hooks, *All About Love,* 5.

8. Lorde, *Sister Outsider,* 53.

9. hooks, *Salvation*; Hurston, *I Love Myself When I Am Laughing and Then Again When I Am Looking Mean and Impressive*; Lorde, *Sister Outsider.*

10. Walker, *In Search of Our Mothers' Gardens,* xii.

11. Jordan, *Some of Us Did Not Die,* 269.

other Black women writers, DuVernay's and Rees's films illustrate that self-love is valuable in and of itself, and as a basis for all loving relationships.

THE ABSENCE OF LOVE IN
CONTROLLING IMAGES OF BLACK WOMEN

In 2002, Halle Berry became the first Black woman to win an Academy Award for Best Actress in a Leading Role (*Monster's Ball,* 2001).[12] In her Academy Award–winning role, Berry plays Leticia Musgrove, a struggling waitress and single mother living in the deep South, whose husband is on death row, and who is verbally and physically abusive to her son. There is no relationship or feelings—no love—between Leticia and her husband. She takes her son to visit his father hours before his execution, and it is clear that she is doing this strictly for her son, not because she has any interest in seeing her husband; "visiting the State Penitentiary has become another burden, one indistinguishable from her financial and provisional needs," writes film scholar Mia Mask.[13] During the course of the film, Leticia loses her husband and her son—they are both killed at different times and in different ways, but both violently so. In the midst of a life that seems to be defined by the absence or loss of love, she enters into a relationship with Hank, a bigoted White prison guard, whose life is equally devoid of love. Hank participated in the execution of Leticia's husband, although he keeps this from her, at first. He was raised by a father who also has no love in his life, who regularly spews overtly hateful racist insults (of which Leticia becomes a target).

Monster's Ball is known not just for Halle Berry's Oscar win, but for the fact that in the film, Berry participated in an explicit sex scene—a sex scene that Berry herself describes as "animalistic."[14] Instead of exploring the complicated history or circumstances of the relationship between Leticia and her husband or the role of the prison industrial complex in the lives of poor Black men and women, their marriage is glossed over. The relationship between Leticia and her husband is minimized and quickly eliminated in order to set the stage for Leticia seeking comfort in a sexual relationship with Hank—one where she desperately pleads for Hank to make her "feel good" during their first sexual encounter. Collins poses a question that was on the minds of many

12. Halle Berry has discussed her multiracial heritage (a White mother and Black father), but she self-identifies as Black and is often cast in roles in which she plays a character who is racialized as Black.

13. Mask, "Monster's Ball," 49.

14. Brooks, "'Now I'm Really at the Party.'"

after Berry's win: "Halle Berry's career had included many fine films, yet she won best actress for *Monster's Ball*, a film in which Berry engages in a torrid interracial sex scene . . . Of all of the actresses and films that might have been selected, why *Monster's Ball* with its depiction of Black female sexuality?"[15]

Mia Mask describes the portrayal of Leticia as a Black woman living in the South with no extended family or other social networks as "implausible."[16] It is this contrived setup that places Leticia in a position in which she is only able to find comfort, after tragedy, in a sexual relationship with a bigoted White man. By the end of the film, Leticia has moved in with Hank, after being evicted from her home. Hank tells Leticia that he wants to take care of her, which is an offer that she readily accepts because, as she tells Hank, she really needs to be taken care of. The film is centered on Hank's redemption, not Leticia's liberation, emotional or sexual, according to Mask—Hank "takes care" of Leticia and is rewarded with a restored sense of masculinity, and with sex.[17] Ultimately, the Black female body is used to atone for Southern White racism through Hank's sexual and paternalistic relationship with Leticia.

The explicit sexuality of Halle Berry's role in *Monster's Ball* and the fact that it stands as the sole Academy Award win for a Black actress in a leading role has caused strong reactions.[18] Although many praised Berry for her performance, many were also critical that she was recognized for a role in which an "animalistic" sexual relationship is central. Additionally, Berry's character is shown having dysfunctional relationships with her son and husband—she is portrayed as an abusive "bad mother" who "has no affection at all" for her ex-husband.[19] These characteristics draw from two of the most damaging controlling images of Black womanhood—"Jezebel" and "Sapphire"—both of which characterize Black women as unloving and undesirable romantic partners.

Critiques of *Monster's Ball* are driven by the paucity of Black women film characters who are in loving relationships or deemed as capable of being in one. Often Black women are portrayed without a romantic partner, but if Black women are shown in any type of romantic or sexual interaction, they are frequently portrayed as cold, emasculating, angry, verbally abusive, and/or in ways that are associated with sexual deviance or excess. Similar to the matriarch image (discussed in chapter 3), which portrays Black women as emasculating "bad" mothers, the controlling image of "Sapphire" (also referred to as an "angry black woman") characterizes Black women as argumentative,

15. Collins, *Black Sexual Politics*, 181.
16. Mask, "Monster's Ball," 51.
17. Ibid., 54.
18. Braxton and Valdespino, "Dust-Up Over an Oscar Role."
19. Ebert, "Monster's Ball Movie Review & Film Summary."

unfeminine, and irrationally angry "bad" partners. Collins argues that the image of the angry Black woman affects Black men's desire for Black women as partners: "Many Black men reject Black women as marital partners, claiming that Black women are less desirable than white ones because we are too assertive."[20]

Like the matriarch and welfare queen images discussed in the previous chapter, the angry Black woman stereotype is also meant to justify the lack of public support for Black women. This stereotype masks the true social and institutional problems faced by Black women, and instead, places the blame on Black women themselves. "This stereotype does not acknowledge black women's anger as a legitimate reaction to unequal circumstances; it is seen as a pathological, irrational desire to control black men, families, and communities. It can be deployed against African American women who dare to question their circumstances, point out inequities, or ask for help."[21]

The media image of Black women as irrationally angry "Sapphires" can be traced back to the *Amos 'n' Andy* radio and television show (1928–1960), in which a Black female character named Sapphire Stevens was often portrayed nagging and belittling her husband.[22] Bell hooks identifies Sapphire from *Amos 'n' Andy* as the first media image of Black womanhood she encountered as a child. She recalls, "*She was not us.* We laughed with the black men, with the white people . . . We did not want our construction to be this hated black female thing—foil, backdrop. Her black female image was not the body of desire."[23] Since *Amos 'n' Andy*, there have been numerous Black female television characters that follow the archetype of Sapphire. These characters are harsh and never, or rarely, show vulnerability, suggesting that Black women's anger should not be taken seriously and they can take whatever insults and injustices are thrown their direction. A recent iteration of the Sapphire stereotype can be seen on the overwhelming number of "reality" television shows, such as *The Real Housewives of Atlanta* and *Flavor of Love,* that continuously portray Black women as loud and angry.[24] Black women film and television characters that exhibit intense, unreasonable anger are so commonplace that this is rarely questioned or challenged. Melissa Harris-Perry notes that it is a comparatively understudied stereotype of Black womanhood because this myth is accepted by many as truth.[25]

20. Collins, *Black Feminist Thought,* 77.
21. Harris-Perry, *Sister Citizen,* 95.
22. Harris-Perry, *Sister Citizen*; hooks, *Reel to Real.*
23. hooks, *Reel to Real,* 260.
24. Ward, *Real Sister.*
25. Harris-Perry, *Sister Citizen,* 89.

In sharp contrast to the asexual image of the mammy, who was stereotyped through dominant cultural ideology as the only moral Black woman, images of Black women as sexual beings label them as immoral, sexually aggressive, promiscuous "Jezebels." In *Black Sexual Politics,* Patricia Hill Collins argues that images of Black sexuality have long been used to oppress Black women and men, and persist in order to facilitate a new racism that is integral to the myth of a post-racial society.[26]

The cultural myth of Black women as hypersexual has origins in the enslavement of Black women and was created as a way to justify the forced commoditization and widespread sexual assault of enslaved Black women.[27] The sexual exploitation of Black enslaved women was the result of several motives. One motive was economic—slave owners had economic motivation to force their female slaves to produce more slaves and used their bodies for breeding. "If Black slave women could be portrayed as having excessive sexual appetites, then increased fertility should be the expected outcome."[28] Another motive was power or intimidation—by degrading and abusing Black women, White slave owners were able to effectively exercise control over them.[29] Hooks refers to the rape of Black female slaves as "an institutionalized method of terrorism which had as its goal the demoralization and dehumanization of Black women."[30] In addition to sexual assault, enslaved Black women were subjected to public nudity during slave auctions and beatings. The labeling of Black women as animalistic sexual beings allowed White Southerners to reconcile their dehumanizing treatment of Black women within a context that claimed to value modesty and chastity in women. "The idea that black women were hypersexual beings created space for white moral superiority by justifying the brutality of Southern white men."[31]

The controlling image of Black women as animalistic "Jezebels" persists, as do sexual assaults on Black women's bodies.[32] The lack of relative economic and political resources compared to White women places them in a more vulnerable position: "Even though the current statistics indicate that Black women are more likely to be victimized than White women, Black women are

26. Collins, *Black Sexual Politics.*

27. Collins, *Black Feminist Thought*; Collins, *Black Sexual Politics*; Harris-Perry, *Sister Citizen*; hooks, *Ain't I a Woman: Black Women and Feminism*; Jewell, *From Mammy to Miss America and Beyond*; Roberts, *Killing the Black Body.*

28. Collins, *Black Feminist Thought,* 81.

29. Frankenberg, *White Women, Race Matters*; Harris-Perry, *Sister Citizen*; hooks, *Ain't I a Woman: Black Women and Feminism.*

30. hooks, *Ain't I a Woman: Black Women and Feminism,* 27.

31. Harris-Perry, *Sister Citizen,* 55.

32. Richie, *Arrested Justice.*

less likely to report their rapes, less likely to have their cases come to trial, less likely to have their trial result in convictions, and, most disturbing, less likely to seek counseling and other support services."[33]

The myth of the hypersexuality of Black women has become a common theme in contemporary popular culture in general, but no other medium has received more attention and public scrutiny than the hypersexualization and objectification of Black women's bodies in the male-dominated arena of hip-hop.[34] As hip-hop grew into a multi-billion-dollar industry, "hip hop made black women into silent, scantily clad figures who writhe willingly behind male artists."[35] Women are dehumanized as sexual objects that exist for the sole purpose of satisfying the physical needs of (hypersexualized) men. The persistence of this myth creates barriers to the development of love relationships between Black people. It aims to deny them the power of the erotic: the "power which comes from sharing deeply any pursuit with another person."[36] "How can seemingly 'wild' women and men learn to love one another?"[37] asks Collins.

Ava DuVernay and Dee Rees portray Black women as worthy of love, in addition to being loving, caring, and thoughtful, and as trying to figure out this often-elusive thing called love. Their films challenge the dominant ideologies of Black women as hard and unfeeling, or as purely sexual beings or objects. In *Middle of Nowhere* (2012) and *Pariah* (2011), the human desire for personal connection—for love—is central to the narrative. The characters fall in love, experience pain, and make decisions about how much of themselves to devote to a relationship. They deliberate issues such as commitment, trust, communication, and expressing physical affection in relationships.

Collins emphasizes that there is a need to recognize the dissonance between popular ideologies of love relationships and the realities of such relationships within various contexts for Black women and men.[38] DuVernay and Rees disrupt mainstream expectations and narratives about love and relationships in their films. In *Middle of Nowhere*, DuVernay asks the audience to consider the meaning of love and commitment for Black women when the

33. Collins, *Black Feminist Thought*, 148.
34. Black women's hypersexualization in hip-hop is also discussed briefly in the analysis of *Beyond the Lights* (see chapter 2).
35. Harris-Perry, *Sister Citizen*, 65.
36. Lorde, *Sister Outsider*, 56.
37. Collins, *Black Sexual Politics*, 258.
38. Ibid.

prison industrial complex has so many poor and working-class young Black men under its control. In *Pariah*, Dee Rees provides a window into the life of a young Black woman who is exploring how to express her love within the context of a gay Black community and within a family that does not embrace her homosexuality. In challenging circumstances, these characters choose love. Ultimately, in each film, the lead character learns the importance of self-love—that the most important relationship is the one with herself.

MIDDLE OF NOWHERE

Is sacrifice an essential part of love? And if so, how much should one give up for someone else in the name of love? If marriage means committing one's life to another, are there limits to how much of one's life to commit? *Middle of Nowhere* (2012) tells the story of Ruby, a young working-class Black woman who is, in many ways, putting her life on hold while her husband is incarcerated. The film's title acts as a metaphor for their situation: her husband is *physically* in the middle of nowhere serving an eight-year prison term, while she is *mentally and emotionally* in the middle of nowhere, with her life on hold during his imprisonment. Unlike the aforementioned film *Monster's Ball, Middle of Nowhere* compassionately explores the impact of incarceration on relationships between Black men and women.

Middle of Nowhere is the second narrative feature film released by DuVernay, for which she became the first African American woman to win Sundance's award for Best Directing of a Feature Film. Although this was the first narrative film that she wrote, the film's production was delayed because of difficulty finding financial support. DuVernay made the decision to release her film through her new distribution company AFFRM, and amazingly, she shot the film in only nineteen days.[39] But DuVernay took her time doing research for the script. In preparation for the film, she interviewed several women whose partners were incarcerated.[40] After a successful showing at the Sundance Film Festival, the film was released in a limited number of theaters in 2012. It was released on DVD in 2015, after the increased attention DuVernay received for directing the 2014 Oscar-nominated film *Selma*.

Ruby (Emayatzy Corinealdi) is at the center of the story in *Middle of Nowhere*. She is a young, married medical student who drops out of medical school to work as a nurse when her husband is imprisoned. Her life revolves

---

39. Rickey, "She's a Graduate of an Unusual Film School: Ava DuVernay and 'Middle of Nowhere.'"

40. "Ava DuVernay: A New Director, After Changing Course."

around *waiting* and *anticipation*—she waits by the phone for her husband's daily phone calls and she anticipates seeing her husband as she takes the long bus trip to visit him every weekend. Amidst this waiting and anticipation, she numbly walks through her days, clinging to the happy memories she has of married life prior to her husband's imprisonment. She is living for the promise of her husband's early release. Much of the story and progression of the film is based on the internal emotional journey of Ruby. Although film scholar Michael Gillespie describes Ruby as "an affective vessel of temporalities" and states that she "abides black love as grief and absolution,"[41] Ruby's perspective toward love and her marriage evolve over the course of her husband's incarceration, as she begins to revise her vision for love and sense of self. Below, I detail the social context in which Ava DuVernay has situated Ruby, which causes Ruby to grapple with making sense of marriage and love in an era of mass incarceration.

LOVE, MARRIAGE, AND MASS INCARCERATION

The film opens with Ruby engaging in an activity that the audience soon learns is a now routine, although time- and energy-consuming, part of her life as a woman married to a man serving a prison sentence. She is sitting on the bus as she journeys back home after visiting her husband, Derek, in prison. She appears calm. But Ruby's calm exterior masks the thoughts that are racing through her mind as she sits motionless. The images on the screen alternate between Ruby sitting on the bus and flashbacks of her recent conversation with Derek. The long journey that she takes to visit her husband and the conversation she has with him immediately reveal the level of commitment and sacrifice that she is making for her marriage. While sitting across from Derek in prison, she tells him that she is dropping out of medical school. She needs to do this so that she can take the four-hour bus trip to visit him on the weekends and be available to answer his phone calls during the weekdays: "I can't get down here on weekends around labs. I'll miss every call you make during the day," she tells her husband. He tells her that he doesn't want this life for her. She was on her way to something—something better than the life that he is living, is implied. But Ruby insists. "*We* were on our way," she says. "I'm your wife. I'd fully expect you to be here if the tables were turned." Derek resists: "I can't do this. I can't take care of you. I can't even hold your hand." Derek tells her to keep going on with her life: "Don't stop for me," but Ruby

---

41. Gillespie, *Film Blackness*, 160.

replies, "You are me." When Derek pleads with Ruby to move on with her life, she tells him *he* needs to make things right, like he promised, and he'll be out in five years. Ruby desperately asks him to repeat the words "Five years with good time" to show that he'll do his part, and he does. Derek was pleading with Ruby to move on with her life because, while he's in prison, he is not able to express love and care for her in the way that he thinks he should—they can't hold hands and he can't contribute financially. Whereas Derek stresses his desire to express love through physical affection and financial security, Ruby emphasizes love as commitment and sacrifice. She is willing to sacrifice her plans for medical school—to take on his punishment as her own—because of the commitment that she made to her husband. In return, she asks that her husband commit to doing everything he needs to do to be out, and back with her, in five years.

The situation of Ruby and Derek is not unusual. In fact, it is becoming increasingly common in Black poor and working-class communities. Mass incarceration. Prison industrial complex. Prison nation. New Jim Crow. All of these phrases reflect the substantial and highly disproportionate number of Black people, men and women, who are under the control of the criminal justice system.[42] In *The New Jim Crow*, Michelle Alexander describes the recent growth of the prison population as a legalized form of racial discrimination in a country that claims colorblindness: "It is no longer socially permissible to use race, explicitly, as a justification for discrimination, exclusion, or social contempt. So we don't. Rather than rely on race, we use the criminal justice system to label people of color 'criminals' and then engage in the practices we supposedly left behind."[43] Because "crime" is a social construct, what is considered criminal behavior, as well as how this criminal behavior is punished, has evolved over time, depending on the goals of those with the power to make these decisions. Alexander discusses the targeting of African American communities during the "war on drugs" as being the catalyst for the substantial increase in incarceration rates of Black people: "When the war on drugs gained full steam in the mid-1980s, prison admissions for African Americans skyrocketed, nearly quadrupling in three years, and then increasing steadily until it reached in 2000 a level *more than twenty six times* the level in 1983."[44] Although the majority of illegal drug users and dealers nationwide are White, three-fourths of all people imprisoned for drug offenses have been

42. Alexander, *The New Jim Crow*; Davis, *Are Prisons Obsolete?*; Richie, *Arrested Justice*.
43. Alexander, *The New Jim Crow*, 2.
44. Ibid., 98.

Black or Latino. As Ava DuVernay highlights in her 2016 documentary *13th*, while White men have a one in seventeen chance of ending up behind bars, for Black men this chance is one in three.[45]

In California, where *Middle of Nowhere* takes place, African Americans and Latinos comprise two thirds of the state's prison population.[46] Geography scholar and activist Ruth Wilson Gilmore details the growth of California's prison system, which she refers to as "the biggest prison-building project in the world."[47] She provides the startling statistic that the California state prison population grew nearly 500 percent between 1982 and 2000. This prison expansion, Gilmore explains, is a partial solution to political economic crises, organized by the state—"resolutions of surplus land, capital, labor, and state capacity congealed in to prisons."[48]

It is within this context of unprecedented prison growth in which Ava DuVernay sets *Middle of Nowhere*. Mass incarceration is a topic that DuVernay also explores in depth in her Oscar-nominated documentary *13th* (2016). DuVernay's riveting documentary, which convincingly traces the relationship between the history of enslavement in the United States and the criminalization of Black people, demonstrates her recognition of the continuing need to bring attention to the problem of mass incarceration and its impact on Black communities. In *Middle of Nowhere*, DuVernay does not provide statistics or a history lesson about the California prison boom. What she does is provide a narrative about how the everyday lives of people within poor and working-class Black communities are directly impacted by this growth. Through the character Ruby, DuVernay highlights the ways that families and marriages are affected by the loss of their loved ones. "The film is not only a meditation on losing a loved one to the criminal justice system; it also manages to humanize those in the system's grasp."[49]

In *Arrested Justice: Black Women, Violence, and America's Prison Nation*, Beth Richie refers to the "ideological and public policy shifts that have led to the increased criminalization of disenfranchised communities of color, more aggressive law enforcement strategies for norm-violating behavior, and an undermining of civil and human rights of marginalized groups" as a "prison

---

45. It is also noteworthy that in 2014 the imprisonment rate for African American women (109 per 100,000) was more than twice the rate of imprisonment for White women (53 per 100,000). See http://www.sentencingproject.org/wp-content/uploads/2016/02/Incarcerated-Women-and-Girls.pdf and https://www.bjs.gov/content/pub/pdf/p15.pdf.

46. Gilmore, *Golden Gulag*, 7.

47. Ibid., 26.

48. Ibid., 28.

49. Beverly, "No Medicine for Melancholy: Cinema of Loss and Mourning in the Era of #BlackLivesMatter," 95.

nation."[50] This prison nation has left Black women in poor communities especially vulnerable to marginalization—and violence—within their communities, at the same time that it has placed more and more people of color behind bars. The disturbingly large portion of African American men who are incarcerated is often overlooked in public discussions about Black women and families in poor and working-class Black communities.[51]

By focusing on the character Ruby, DuVernay is centralizing the stories of the women who are affected by this "prison nation." Collins points out that the high rate of incarceration is a class- and gender-specific site of racial oppression that disproportionately affects poor and working-class African Americans.[52] In all of DuVernay's films, she prioritizes the contributions and experiences of Black women—women she knew personally or women she admires for their contributions to our society.[53] DuVernay made *I Will Follow* (2010), a story about a woman coming to terms with the loss of her beloved aunt, in remembrance of her own aunt.[54] When DuVernay directed *Selma* (2014), she expanded and added several women historical figures, such as Coretta Scott King and Diane Nash, in honor of their contributions to the civil rights movement. And, when she wrote and directed *Middle of Nowhere,* she honored the *women* whose lives are affected by the loss of loved ones to the criminal justice system—women who live in the Los Angeles area in which DuVernay grew up.

DuVernay spoke to several women who have been affected by the incarceration of a loved one. In an interview with NPR, she describes the "ordeal" that the women experienced in order to visit someone in prison:

> Many of them will travel in the wee hours before dark, before visiting hours begin so they can be in line. And then the series of screenings . . . Bags are being checked. Children are involved. And then there may be issues with your incarcerated loved one even coming out . . . certainly in California, they're out in the high desert areas, so that's quite a drive. And if you don't have a car, then it's quite a bus ride. So it's an ordeal . . . And then you get in that chair, and you're facing someone who you have to become reacquainted with. And you have to share what's going on with you—it might be financial

50. Richie, *Arrested Justice.*

51. Alexander, *The New Jim Crow.*

52. Collins, *Black Sexual Politics,* 253.

53. Kovan, "Interview with Ava DuVernay on 'Selma' and Telling the Stories of Black Women."

54. King, "For Ava DuVernay, Making 'I Will Follow' Is Personal."

issues he can't help with. And then also trying to balance that with what's going on with him back there—it's a very, very complicated experience.[55]

DuVernay's goal was to make these women's stories visible and call into question many of the assumptions that many people have about the poor and working-class women of color in this situation. The assumption is often: "This couldn't be a bright, smart, articulate woman. You know, this couldn't be someone who'd had goals for herself for more than waiting for a man behind bars. And all of that's just not true. There are women—and there are millions and millions and millions of them—women in waiting, women in this kind of middle place, and they're disregarded, they're invisible to us," says DuVernay.[56] Her discussions with the women whose loved ones are behind bars shed light on their struggles, but also their humanity. DuVernay brings this sense of humanity to the screen through "Ruby."

After Ruby's first trip to visit Derek in prison, the film jumps ahead four years. Four years of Ruby putting medical school on hold while working as a nurse. Four years of long bus rides to visit Derek in prison. Four years of waiting for phone calls from her husband. Four years of working tirelessly with his attorney to ensure that he can be released early. As we see Ruby going through her day, it is clear that although her husband is behind bars hours away from her, he is her life. While she is at work, we see her write and send a card to Derek. When she comes home, she has an expression of pure joy when she sees flowers from Derek on her doorstep. As she lays in bed, she thinks about kissing her husband and imagines him lying next to her, holding her. One night, after having dinner with her sister and nephew, she comes home to a letter, stating that Derek is eligible for early release. She enthusiastically runs out and hugs her sister. This is what she has been *waiting* for.

The film paints a picture of Ruby as a loving, loyal, and intelligent woman. She is strong, but not like the stereotypical aggressive "Sapphire." Although it takes strength to make the sacrifices that she has for her marriage, this strength is not an impenetrable wall that dehumanizes her. On the contrary, DuVernay created Ruby as a character that the audience can relate to. As Audre Lorde explains, "The need for sharing deep feeling is a human need."[57] Whether or not one has been in Ruby's specific situation, it is difficult not to be empathetic toward Ruby and the feeling of longing she has for her husband.

---

55. "Ava DuVernay: A New Director, After Changing Course."
56. "Indie Appeal and Black Experience Meet In 'Middle.'"
57. Lorde, *Sister Outsider*, 58.

Ruby loves her husband, but as the film progresses, the question of whether she is sacrificing too much of herself in the name of love becomes more pressing. If, as bell hooks describes it, love is a choice, is she making the right choices? Furthermore, are the other "ingredients" that hooks lists as necessary for love (trust, open and honest communication) present?

The most audacious critique of the sacrifices that Ruby has made for her husband comes in the form of Ruth, Ruby's mother. Ruth openly disagrees with the choice that Ruby made to stop attending medical school and devote her life to her incarcerated husband. The very first time we see Ruby with Ruth, she references Ruby's need to "get on" with things. At a tense dinner with her daughters, Ruth's frustration with Ruby's situation comes to a head. She turns to Ruby and tries to make her daughter see the problem: she says that things are "always about soon—the job, the car. But soon never comes." Ruth is disappointed, even angry, that Ruby no longer mentions medical school because she spends her "entire days sitting in a dark apartment waiting by the phone" for her husband to call from prison. When Ruby says that she is trying her best, Ruth replies "This is *not* your best." As Ruby sits silently at the table, not responding, Ruth yells "Speak up for yourself, Goddammit!" Although there is anger in Ruth's voice, there is also a sense that this intensity comes from the feeling of wanting something better for her daughter. She is trying to elicit an emotional response from Ruby to end her numbness. Ruby's insistence that she is trying her best means that she is trying her best to make her commitment to (and love for) her husband work. But, Ruth's passionate plea stems from her concern that Ruby is not loving or respecting *herself* by sacrificing so much for her husband.

The more time we spend with Ruby, the more we understand her mother's pleas. The "complicated, contradictory, and flawed motivations and loyalties"[58] in Ruby's marriage become more apparent. We begin to see the extent to which several of the "ingredients" that are needed to create a loving relationship are missing from Ruby's marriage—aspects of her relationship that her unwavering commitment, exacerbated by the physical separation from her husband, did not allow her to see. For example, when Ruby runs into one of Derek's ex-girlfriends, with whom he has a daughter, Ruby suggests that she visit Derek with her daughter. Derek's ex-girlfriend replies, "You're not as smart as people say you are . . . If I were you, I wouldn't want me coming around too much," calling into question Derek's trustworthiness and commitment to Ruby. Ruby also learns that Derek has been charged with assault and instigating a melee in

---

58. Rastegar, "Evolving Narrative Structures Forge New Cine-Love at the 2012 Sundance Film Festival."

prison, for which he denies responsibility. Neither of these pieces of information cause Ruby to question her love and commitment to her husband. At the parole hearing, though, Ruby learns something that shifts her perspective. The board brings up a "disciplinary action" involving consensual "sexual contact" with a female officer two years ago. In response, Derek looks down, ashamed, and Ruby, for the first time, looks hurt by Derek's actions. During her ride home, we see Ruby cry for the first time in the film. Respect. Trust. Commitment. Communication. Ruby realizes that Derek has offered her none of these in return for her love, commitment, and sacrifice.

"The intersecting oppressions that produce systems of domination such as slavery aim to thwart the power [of feeling] as energy available to subordinate groups," writes Collins.[59] Derek regularly expresses his desire to "take care" of Ruby, which reflects his interest in conforming to the dominant gendered expectations for men. But Derek's desire to take care of Ruby and Ruby's expectations of a loving relationship were unrealized. Being married to a partner who is behind bars is not conducive to the expectations of sharing a powerful feeling, not to mention communication, respect, or trust.

In Joan Morgan's *When Chickenheads Come Home to Roost,* she writes: "In the interest of our emotional health and overall sanity, black women have got to learn to love brothers realistically, and that means differentiating between who they are and who we'd like them to be. Black men are engaged in a war where the real enemies—racism and the white power structure—are masters of camouflage."[60] Morgan is referencing the necessity of understanding the power of institutional racism when navigating love relationships with Black men, and that expectations based on dominant cultural gender roles may lead to unfulfilling relationships.

Ruby's emotional release following the parole hearing was the first time she allowed herself to *feel deeply* since her husband's incarceration. This opens her up to a deeper loving relationship with herself—and a relationship with another man, Brian (David Oyelowo). The first time Ruby and Brian meet for a date is soon after Ruby's alarming discovery at the parole hearing—they dance, kiss, and spend the night together, allowing Ruby to experience an intimacy that had been missing from her life for the previous five years. As the two of them embrace, Ruby's expression suggests that she is not only receiving physical comfort but emotional release, as well. Unlike the hypersexual "Jezebel" controlling image, Ruby is portrayed as experiencing a physical *and* emotional connection. Brian demonstrates care and respect toward Ruby—he

---

59. Collins, *Black Feminist Thought,* 151.
60. Morgan, *When Chickenheads Come Home to Roost,* 75.

even goes as far as stepping outside of his comfort zone to watch a movie with *subtitles,* after Ruby tells him that she only likes seeing independent, sometimes foreign, films ("The ones a brother's gotta read?" he asks. "Alright. I can swing with subtitles"). The two of them hold hands as they leave the movie theater. They communicate openly and honestly with each other. With Brian, Ruby appears to have an opportunity for a loving relationship in which she can fully express and receive love.

Ruby's relationship with Brian may lead one to conclude that it is "no story book romance" (which is how Patricia Hill Collins refers to love relationships within Black communities).[61] After all, Ruby is married to another man—she tells Brian that her husband has been in prison for five years and she doesn't know what's happening next. Additionally, Brian is divorced and has a daughter—but, he tells Ruby *he's* going to try to be "what's happening next" for her. Despite the divergence from the typical "story book romance," DuVernay depicts the potential for Ruby to experience a deep connection and commitment—to experience the various elements of love. One morning, after Brian asks Ruby if she plans to wait for her husband, he expresses his hope for a committed relationship with Ruby: "We could have a life," he says. "I still love my wife, but it's not happening. It's not gonna happen. But you and me . . ." he says to Ruby, expectantly.

As Collins explains, the chances for mutual recognition and understanding become greater in love relationships within working-class Black communities when both partners recognize how the impact of racism affects their ability to fit into the dominant gender role expectations. Restricted employment opportunities, single parenthood, and mass incarceration, for example, often mean that people within poor and working-class Black communities will not fit into dominant gendered expectations within heterosexual love relationships.[62] Redefining loving relationships in this context is of central importance. Ruby's relationship with Brian may not fit the description of a "story book romance" by dominant cultural standards, but by providing Ruby with romantic love in *Middle of Nowhere,* DuVernay has rewritten the narrative of love within a Black working-class context.

Derek also loves Ruby. He is remorseful for all that he has put Ruby through—he calls her and leaves several messages after the parole hearing and is very apologetic when she finally visits him in prison. But, the apologies are not enough. The apologies do not absolve him of the choices that he

---

61. Collins, *Black Sexual Politics,* 247.
62. Collins, *Black Feminist Thought*; Collins, *Black Sexual Politics.*

had made that undervalued the love they had for each other. Perhaps Ntozake Shange[63] says it best in her choreopoem:

> One thing I don't need / is any more apologies / I got sorry greetin' me at my front door / you can keep yours. I don't know what to do wit 'em / they don't open doors / or bring the sun back. / They don't make me happy

When Ruby visits Derek in prison for the first time since his parole hearing, she tells him that they are not supposed to live like *this*. "I'm not gonna do another four years with you," she says, making the decision that love will no longer mean sacrificing herself. DuVernay does not minimize the role of the institution of prison on the lives of poor and working-class Black men and women. Ruby's statement reflects the recognition of prisons as systems of domination that aim to thwart love and the power that comes with it.[64] In a letter to Derek, which we hear as the film ends, Ruby states that there are no clear answers and she is not sure what the future holds. She recognizes that her relationships will not fit neatly into the dominant cultural narratives of love. As she goes to work in the light of day, happily greeting those around her, no longer sitting at home waiting for her husband to call, we see that although Ruby is open to love, she has chosen "a new start outside of the context of her relationship with either man."[65] Ruby chooses to love herself—as though her very life depends upon self-love and self-respect.[66]

PARIAH

Whereas DuVernay's *Middle of Nowhere* centers on an adult woman's choices related to her marriage, Dee Rees's *Pariah* (2011) focuses on a teenager who experiences the "mighty wakening"[67] feeling of *falling* in love for the first time. Alike, or "Lee" (Adepero Oduye), is a teenager living in a socially conservative household in New York. Her parents know, but do not want to accept, that their daughter is gay. Alike knows and accepts that she loves women, but struggles with *how* to find love. The cinematic depiction of love between Black women is rare, for sure. "As a general rule, Black gay and lesbian characters are

63. Shange, *for colored girls who have considered suicide / when the rainbow is enuf.*
64. Collins, *Black Feminist Thought.*
65. Martin, "Conversations with Ava DuVernay—'A Call to Action': Organizing Principles of an Activist Cinematic Practice."
66. Jordan, *Some of Us Did Not Die.*
67. Hurston, *I Love Myself When I Am Laughing and Then Again When I Am Looking Mean and Impressive.*

denied both love relationships and sexual expression in film."[68] One exception is Cheryl Dunye's 1996 film *The Watermelon Woman,* which was the first theatrically released narrative feature film written and directed by an openly gay Black woman filmmaker.[69] Yvonne Welbon also explores love between Black women in her short film *Sister in the Life: First Love* (1993). Film scholar Kara Keeling writes, "Black lesbian and gay film" emerged as a way of "resisting the marginalization and the exclusion of black homosexuality and of black lesbians and black gay men within existing (white) U.S. lesbian and gay culture and politics."[70] However, depictions of love between Black women remain rare—there were nearly fifteen years between the release of Dunye's film and *Pariah.* One writer declares, "The fact that this film's protagonist (in *Pariah*) is a black lesbian teenager is nothing short of a cinematic landmark."[71]

Black women loving each other poses a threat to systems of power—"How dare these women love one another in a context that deems Black women as a collectivity so unlovable?"[72] If love between Black people is a rebellious act, "'out' LGBTQ African Americans are inherently rebellious, regardless of their choice of love interest, the sexual practices they prefer, and/or whether they are sexually active at all," writes Collins.[73] Black feminist scholar and activist Cheryle Clarke writes, "For a woman to be a lesbian . . . is an act of resistance"[74] in her seminal essay, fittingly titled "Lesbianism: An Act of Resistance." Although it may challenge dominant ideologies, Black women loving other Black women is anything but unheard of. Audre Lorde, E. Patrick Johnson, and bell hooks, to name a few, have written about the long history of the existence and awareness of love between women (and between men) within Black communities.[75] However, dominant cultural and cinematic narratives about love have largely ignored or disparaged love between Black women. As an "out" Black filmmaker, then, Dee Rees is rebelling against social expectations. Her first narrative feature film, *Pariah* (2011), challenges systems of power with its semiautobiographical portrayal of a young Black woman's search for love.

Kara Keeling argues that "black lesbian film" challenges the marginalization of love between Black women by making visible that which has gener-

68. Collins, *Black Sexual Politics,* 271.

69. Anderson, "25 Years Later, Writer-Director Julie Dash Looks Back on the Seminal 'Daughters of the Dust.'"

70. Keeling, "'Joining the Lesbians': Cinematic Regimes of Black Lesbian Visibility," 216.

71. Landis, "GBF Looking for Love."

72. Collins, *Black Feminist Thought,* 167.

73. Collins, *Black Sexual Politics,* 270.

74. Clarke, "Lesbianism: An Act of Resistance."

75. hooks, *Salvation;* Johnson, *Sweet Tea;* Lorde, *Sister Outsider.*

ally been invisible. However, she also cautions that what "black lesbian film" often *leaves out* of the image it designates as "black lesbian" includes "precisely that which might challenge the logical connections that currently rationalize existing social relations, including some of those that support homophobia, classism, heterosexism, sexism, and racism."[76] I propose that Rees's film challenges existing social relations through Alike, who explores, embraces, and complicates various elements of her identity (race, sexuality, gender, and class). Rees, having been influenced by Audre Lorde, incorporates elements of Lorde's critical work related to the multidimensionality of identity in her representation of various aspects of Alike's sense of self.

FINDING FIRST LOVE . . . FINDING ONESELF

"You're a grown ass woman, bruh." With this line, Dee Rees captures the nuances of navigating social and romantic interactions for Alike. Laura (Pernell Walker), Alike's best friend, is confident in how she expresses herself within her community of gay working-class Black women. When Laura says to Alike, "You're a grown ass woman, bruh," she's encouraging Alike to be confident in who she is, in addition to invoking the comparatively flexible gendered presentations within Black gay communities. Alike is confident that she wants to find love—that she loves Black women—but the film centers on her progression toward becoming confident in herself, as she makes decisions about how to fit in to the world as a gay Black woman, and the meaning of love within this context.

In *Invisible Families: Gay Identities, Relationships, and Motherhood among Black Women,* sociologist Mignon Moore provides a rare empirical study that examines how openly gay Black women shape their identities, form relationships, and structure their lives in predominantly Black social spaces.[77] Moore found that gendered presentations of self play an important role in shaping identities and relationships:

> Whereas one influential legacy of 1970s lesbian-feminism has been White middle-class lesbians' rejection of the use of gendered physical presentation, and particularly lesbian butch/femme presentation, as a way of organizing relationships and lesbian community life, I find that many Black gay women are not influenced by this legacy. Instead, they have modified the

76. Keeling, "'Joining the Lesbians': Cinematic Regimes of Black Lesbian Visibility."
77. Moore, *Invisible Families.*

older butch and femme identities into three fairly distinct categories of gender presentation.[78]

Moore refers to the gendered presentations that Black gay women may adopt as "transgressive," "femme," and "gender blender."[79] The recognition and acceptance of various gender displays allow for a sense of empowerment to move away from the dominant social constructions of gender for women. This sense of empowerment that comes from the ability to choose a gender presentation, rather than conform to dominant gender norms, reflects a key aspect of Black feminism. Collins explains that self-definitions are essential: "The struggle lies in rejecting externally defined ideas and practices, and claiming the erotic as a mechanism for empowerment."[80]

Alike's attire is regularly depicted as a symbol of her gendered expression, which she alters depending on her social environment. Her attire is central to her identity and her attempts to find a romantic partner. When we are introduced to Alike, she is at a dance club in which the majority of the clientele are Black women. She's wearing a baseball cap and a baggy shirt and pants—a style that is read as "masculine." When she rides the bus home after the club, she sheds her masculine attire, taking off her cap and baggy shirt, and replaces it with a more "feminine" look—earrings and a more form-fitting shirt. This wardrobe change is a common practice for Alike. Alike's mother (Kim Wayans) is aware that Alike's attire may be an expression of her sexual identity, and insists that she wears clothes that are perceived as feminine. For instance, when Alike gets dressed for church one morning, her mother demands that she put on a pink, fitted, ruffled sweater that she purchased for Alike. Alike reluctantly wears the sweater, but laments, "It isn't me." As a result of her mother's constant scrutiny, Alike regularly changes out of and into her comfortable, baggy clothing on her way to and from her house.

Alike's self-presentation is what Moore refers to as "transgressive."[81] Women who adopt a transgressive gender display usually wear attire that is read as masculine (men's pants, shirts, hats, etc.). Moore explains that "transgressive women described themselves as dressing in a way that makes them feel 'comfortable,'" which is associated with "feeling good or having a sense

---

78. Ibid., 67.

79. "Transgressive" women usually wear men's shirts, pants, and shoes, which may be coordinated with other masculine-looking accessories. "Femme" involves wearing clothing such as dresses, skirts, and form-fitting or low-cut tops. "Gender-blenders" combine specific aspects of both to create a unique look (Moore, *Invisible Families*).

80. Collins, *Black Feminist Thought*, 131.

81. Moore, *Invisible Families*.

of authenticity in their self-expression that is conveyed through their clothing and overall comportment."[82] Moore also finds that transgressive/nonfeminine gender displays were more common among working-class (as opposed to middle-class) Black women, as an act of resistance to social norms: "Asserting a transgressive gender presentation is one way they express feelings of difference from larger society based on the multiple marginalized statuses they occupy."[83] In this sense, Alike's self-presentation can be read as a chosen gender display that is an act of resistance, and influenced by her sexuality, race, and class position.

The gender displays are not only a form of self-expression and act of resistance, they also play an important role in romantic relationships, according to Moore—attracting a person with a certain gendered style often means displaying a complementary gender presentation. "The eroticism engendered by complementary gender display makes visible the expression of women's sexuality."[84] Alike awkwardly attempts to add an accessory to her gender presentation when she is interested in a woman with a "feminine" look. She overhears her love interest having a conversation in which Alike is referred to as "in the middle" and "not hard enough," meaning that they do not perceive her self-presentation as adequately diverging from a feminine display. In an effort to attract her love interest, and display a more "transgressive" self-presentation, Alike asks her friend Laura to buy her a "strap on" to wear to a dance club, where she hopes to see her love interest. However, while at the club, Alike feels so uncomfortable wearing the strap-on that she won't stand up and dance when given the opportunity, so her love interest moves on to someone else.

The strap-on mishap that Alike experienced is just one example of her efforts to form a relationship and situate herself within the community of young gay Black women in her neighborhood. With her friend Laura, Alike spends time in the social spaces that are frequented by other Black gay women in her community, such as a local dance club and "the piers." Alike *is* a young, Black, gay woman, but there are other facets of herself that she does not feel she can express at the club or piers. Alike is also a poet, for example, and at one point, she suggests to Laura that the two of them go to an open mic night because she's not sure if "the piers" is her thing anymore.

Alike's desire to express her full self is echoed in the following statement made by Audre Lorde: "As a black lesbian feminist comfortable with many different ingredients of my identity, and a woman committed to racial and

82. Ibid., 75.
83. Ibid., 69.
84. Ibid., 90.

sexual freedom from oppression, I find I am constantly being encouraged to pluck out some one aspect of myself and present this as the meaningful whole, eclipsing or denying the other parts of self. But this is a destructive and fragmented way to live."[85] Alike begins to spend more time with a female classmate, named Bina, with whom she bonds over their shared interest in writing and music. When Alike is with Bina, listening to music and talking about her poetry, she can express a side of herself that she cannot when she is at the clubs or piers. This friendship leads to the development of romantic feelings and an intimate night together—Alike's first. She immediately feels the power that comes from "sharing deeply any pursuit with another person."[86] For the first time, Alike *falls* and she feels an emotional, physical, and psychic connection—"the passions of love."[87]

The passion that Alike experiences turns to pain very quickly. When Alike wakes up the next morning, she is elated and tells Bina that last night was "amazing." Bina coldly replies, "Last night was just playing around." She tells Alike that she's not "*gay* gay," and as Alike rushes out of Bina's room, her heart broken, Bina asks her not to tell anybody what happened between them. Although Bina recognizes and embraces the poet in Alike and expresses physical affection toward her, this is ultimately negated by her lacking other important ingredients of love: honesty and openness about her own feelings and willingness to commit herself to Alike.

Bina's immediate disavowal of being gay, despite having just been intimate with Alike, stems from the homophobia within the larger U.S. culture. Black feminist lesbian writers, such as Audre Lorde, Cheryle Clarke, and Barbara Smith, have passionately written about the need to challenge homophobia in Black communities and the United States in general. At the same time, bell hooks, E. Patrick Johnson, Mignon Moore, and Audre Lorde point out that, contrary to a common misperception, homophobia is no worse in Black communities than in White communities. Black gay women and men have long made spaces for themselves within predominantly Black social contexts.[88] Lorde writes, "women identified women . . . have been around in all of our communities for a long time . . . the unmarried aunt, childless or otherwise . . . was a familiar figure in many of our childhoods."[89] Bell hooks emphasizes, "without idealizing the past, it is important for black people to remember that love was the foundation of the acceptance many gay individu-

---

85. Lorde, *Sister Outsider*, 120.

86. Ibid., 56.

87. Ibid.

88. hooks, *Salvation*; Johnson, *Sweet Tea*; Moore, *Invisible Families*.

89. Lorde, *Sister Outsider*, 49.

als felt in the segregated communities they were raised in. While not everyone loved them or even accepted their lifestyle, there was enough affirmation to sustain them."[90] However, the acknowledgement and love of gay people by a portion of society within a larger homophobic culture is nonetheless problematic.

Dee Rees captures this contradiction of experiencing and expressing love within a homophobic culture through Alike's relationships. Alike's mother, Audrey, is the person who expresses the most forceful rejection of Alike's identity as gay. Audrey regularly polices her daughter's clothing, friends, and activities in an attempt to police her sexuality. She often tells Alike that she does not like her (gay) friend Laura and expresses contempt toward her. Alike's father, Arthur, regularly tells Audrey to go easy on Alike, but he insists that Alike is *not* gay. While Audrey is openly homophobic, Arthur claims ignorance and tries to distance himself from any discussion of Alike's sexuality (though he occasionally makes subtle remarks to Alike that reflect his heterosexism).

"That there is homophobia among black people in America is largely reflective of the homophobic culture in which we live,"[91] begins Cheryl Clarke in the essay in which she critiques Black activists and intellectuals for their homophobia. Audrey's contempt, Arthur's denial, and Bina's rejection are all a reflection of the larger homophobic context in which they live. Toward the end of the film, and after Bina's rejection, Alike intervenes in a heated argument between Audrey and Arthur. Audrey yells at Arthur: "Your daughter's turning into a damn man right in front of your eyes!" When Arthur says to Alike, "Tell your mother that's not true," Alike openly tells them, for the first time, that she *is* gay. Audrey begins angrily hitting Alike.

Alike's revelation is necessary for her sense of self: as Audre Lorde states, "the transformation of silence into language and action is an act of self-revelation, and that always seems fraught with danger."[92] Dee Rees drew from her own experience with her family in her depiction of Alike's self-revelation. Although Rees did not experience violence from her parents when she told them that she was gay, Audrey's violent reaction to Alike represents the rejection that Rees felt when she came out: "My mother, father and grandmother flew to New York and tried to have an intervention with me. Then they sent me a lot of Bible verses, and I had to tell them not to write to me."[93]

---

90. hooks, *Salvation*, 192.
91. Clarke, "The Failure to Transform: Homophobia in the Black Community," 190.
92. Lorde, *Sister Outsider*, 42.
93. Zack, "'Pariah' Director Dee Rees Confronts Disapproval."

In Moore's research on Black gay women living in New York, she explains that the women who participated in her study "make their homosexuality a salient component of the selves they project to others in predominantly Black social spaces,"[94] which highlights the fact that there are Black spaces that embrace homosexuality. For Alike, love comes from her sister, who lies in bed with Alike one night, as they listen to their parents arguing, and says to Alike, "I hope you know it doesn't matter to me." Although her sexuality is not stated overtly in this conversation, it is understood that her sister is letting her know that she loves her—unconditionally. Alike's best friend Laura often tries to protect her from getting hurt, acutely aware of the homophobia that exists within the culture. When Alike first falls for Bina, she cautiously tells Alike that she's glad Bina makes her happy and adds, "'Cause I love you." Alike feels cared for and recognized/seen with Laura. In fact, after Alike is rejected by Bina and her parents, she stays with Laura, who welcomes her with open arms.

For Alike, whose desire to find love is central to the film's narrative, it is loving herself that allows her to embrace the deep feeling that Audrey Lorde refers to as "erotic." The relationship that Alike had with Bina, although it was not fully realized because of Bina's rejection, allowed a temporary awareness of a previously "unexpressed or unrecognized feeling"[95] within Alike. After this encounter, followed by coming out to her parents, Alike is able to go deeper with her poetry. In the final scenes, Alike tells her father that she has been accepted early to a college program at Berkeley, and she's not going back home: "I'm not running, I'm choosing," she tells her father. As Alike heads toward the bus with her father, sister, and Laura, we hear a voiceover of her reading a poem to her English teacher: "Heartbreak opens onto the sunrise. For even breaking is opening. And I am broken. I am open . . . See the love shine in through my cracks . . . My spirit takes journey. My spirit takes flight . . . I am not running. I am choosing." Tears form in Alike's eyes as she reads the poem to her teacher, who smiles and says, "Yeah," approvingly. Alike's openness to deep feeling led her to choose self-love. The final image shows Alike sitting on the bus, smiling: "For having experienced the fullness of this depth of feeling and recognizing its power, in honor and self-respect we can require no less of ourselves."[96]

94. Moore, *Invisible Families*, 3.
95. Lorde, *Sister Outsider*, 53.
96. Ibid., 54.

THE POETRY OF AUDRE LORDE AND ALIKE

Dee Rees's admiration for the work of Audre Lorde is made clear as soon as the film begins.[97] *Pariah* opens with a quote from Lorde displayed on the screen: "Wherever the bird with no feet flew, she found trees with no limbs." This quote represents Alike's search for a place where she feels like she can be her true self, but it also represents the influence of Audre Lorde on Rees's film. Alike's struggles to find spaces in which she can fully embrace her various identities, and her desire to express herself through her poetry, reflect the ideas expressed in the work of Audre Lorde.

When Alike's teacher reads one of her poems toward the beginning on the film, her teacher tells her that they're "lovely"—but she is not moved. "Is it your best? No," she says to Alike and adds, "I think you can go deeper." By the end of the film, after Alike expresses deep love and feels deep pain, and is honest with her parents about her sexuality, she is able to go deeper in her poetry. Alike and her teacher can both feel the pain, joy, and liberation that comes through her poetry. When Alike reads the last line of the poem, "I am not broken. I am free," it reflects the sentiment of Audre Lorde's essay *The Transformation of Silence into Language and Action*: "I have come to believe over and over again that what is most important to me must be spoken, made verbal and shared, even at the risk of having it bruised or misunderstood. That the speaking profits me, beyond any other effect."[98] By expressing herself to her parents and Bina, Alike makes herself vulnerable, and that is how she finally feels free. It is this freedom that opens herself up to the love within herself.

•

"Who speaks about LOVE OF BLACKNESS with a swagger that feels wonderfully dangerous. A swagger that feels militantly proud. This is something that has fallen out of favor among those truly in the spotlight. To be loud and proud about one's Blackness. To be bold and brash with it. Is that so wrong?" asks Ava DuVernay in a 2011 article that she penned.[99] Ava DuVernay and Dee Rees are bold in their cinematic depictions of Black love. They rebel against dominant narratives about love with their creative visions of Black women's love relationships, which reflect the womanist artistic standpoint. Ruby and Alike are not portrayed as emasculating, hypersexual, or incapable of love. They seek and receive relationships that are based on physical and emotional

---

97. Swadhin, "GLAAD Interviews 'Pariah' Director Dee Rees."
98. Lorde, *Sister Outsider*, 40.
99. DuVernay, "Watch the Throne."

connections. In the face of institutional racism and homophobia, Ruby and Alike experience love. DuVernay and Rees also embrace a womanist perspective by highlighting the necessity of *self-love*. They move from a position of unrecognized or unexpressed feelings[100] to the empowerment that comes with embracing love. "Out of the depths of pain,"[101] they choose love. And, choosing love is as liberating as it is rebellious. As bell hooks writes, "To give ourselves to love, to love blackness, is to restore the true meaning of freedom, hope and possibility in all our lives."[102]

---

100. Lorde, *Sister Outsider*.

101. Hansberry, *To Be Young, Gifted and Black: Lorraine Hansberry in Her Own Words*.

102. hooks, *Salvation*, xxiv.

CHAPTER 5

Transformative Beauty

> As I dance, whirling and joyous, happier than I've ever been in
> my life, another bright-faced dancer joins me. We dance and
> kiss each other and hold each other through the night. The
> other dancer has obviously come through all right, as I have
> done. She is beautiful, whole and free. And she is also me.
>
> —ALICE WALKER[1]

> Learning to love ourselves as Black women goes beyond a
> simplistic insistence that "Black is beautiful." It goes beyond
> and deeper than a surface appreciation of Black beauty,
> although that is certainly a good beginning.
>
> —AUDRE LORDE[2]

I WILL END this book with a topic that, according to Audre Lorde, is a good way to *begin* transforming ideologies about Black womanhood: appreciating the *beauty* of Blackness. In the epigraphs above, Alice Walker and Audre Lorde both embrace beauty as something that can open us up to an appreciation of Blackness. Whereas Walker experiences the recognition of herself as beautiful as a *freeing* sensation, Lorde urges us to *deepen* our understanding of beauty and Blackness.

As Patricia Hill Collins points out in *Black Feminist Thought,* prevailing ideologies of beauty have negated the physical features associated with Black womanhood.[3] Because of this, expanding ideologies of beauty to include Black women is an important part of cultural transformation. Black women filmmakers challenge prevailing standards of beauty by creating films that identify Black women as, among other attributes, beautiful.

Representations of Black women's bodies have often been central in efforts to challenge racism. In *Ain't I a Beauty Queen: Black Women, Beauty, and*

1. Walker, *In Search of Our Mothers' Gardens,* 393.
2. Lorde, *Sister Outsider,* 174.
3. Collins, *Black Feminist Thought,* 169.

the Politics of Race, scholar Maxine Craig details the ways that Black women's physical appearance has intersected with race, gender, and politics in the process of racial rearticulation:[4] "Though both black men and women live in 'marked' bodies, many African American efforts to reclaim the honor due to the race have particularly focused on celebrating and defending the beauty and dignity of black women."[5] Scholars acknowledge that race and gender are socially constructed categories, similarly emphasizing the extent to which these identities are performed.[6] However, discussions of race in popular discourse generally focus on Blackness and femaleness as a state of "being," suggesting that dominant conceptions of Blackness and womanhood exist in the physical body. Additionally, whereas men are evaluated based on their accomplishments, women are generally evaluated based on the degree to which their physical features compare to dominant standards of physical beauty. In order to disparage and devalue Black womanhood, Black women's bodies have been socially constructed as "unfeminine," based on a perceived capacity for labor or excessive sexuality, rather than as beautiful.[7] Therefore, Black women filmmakers' representations of Black women as beautiful, as opposed to laborious or hypersexual, challenge dominant narratives of Black womanhood.

Patricia Hill Collins points out that it is the construction of Black womanhood as the opposite of White womanhood that has created and sustained the limiting, dominant standards of beauty: "Within the binary thinking that underpins intersecting oppressions, blue-eyed, blond, thin White women could not be considered beautiful without the Other—Black women with African features of dark skin, broad noses, full lips and kinky hair."[8] Dark skin and "kinky" (or tightly coiled) hair, which are constructed in opposition to the skin tone and hair of White women, are the primary characteristics for which Black women's bodies and beauty are devalued within dominant culture.

The social and personal significance of hair texture and skin tone for Black women has been explored by several Black women filmmakers in documentary and short films, such as Celeste Crenshaw's and Paula Caffey's *Black Women On: The Light, Dark Thang* (1999), Nadine Valcin's *Black, Bold and Beautiful: Black Women's Hair* (1999), Ngozi Onwurah's *Coffee Colored Children* (1988), Maureen Blackwood's *Perfect Image?* (1988), Ayoka Chenzira's

---

4. Racial rearticulation is the process by which racial social identities are redefined. See Omi and Winant, *Racial Formation in the United States.*

5. Craig, *Ain't I a Beauty Queen?,* 14.

6. Butler, *Gender Trouble*; Omi and Winant, *Racial Formation in the United States*; Johnson, *Appropriating Blackness.*

7. Collins, *Black Feminist Thought*; Collins, *Black Sexual Politics*; Craig, *Ain't I a Beauty Queen?*

8. Collins, *Black Feminist Thought,* 89.

Hair Piece: A Film for Nappy-Headed People (1985), and Alile Sharon Larkin's *The Kitchen* (1975) and *A Different Image* (1982). A 2012 documentary titled *In Our Heads About Our Hair* also explores the relationship between hair and personal identity for Black women (directed by Hemamset Angaza, a Black man, and produced by several women: Anu Prestonia, Maitefa Angaza, and Paulette Maat Kesa Tabb).[9] Although filmmaker Spike Lee famously addresses the problem of colorism in his feature film *School Daze* (1988), scholar Michele Wallace questions the film's absence of a transformative critique of the social ideologies associated with color and hair. In response to Lee's depiction of two opposing images of Black womanhood (centering on physical appearance) in *School Daze,* Wallace asks viewers, "Which would you rather be? For black women, either/or is really neither/nor."[10]

Contemporary Black women filmmakers incorporate images of Black women that disrupt binary thinking about Blackness, femaleness, and beauty. They recognize that resisting ideologies of beauty must do more than reverse the current binary—that definitions of beauty must allow for more freedom of expression and recognition of beauty in various features and forms. "Redefining beauty requires learning to see African American women who have Black African features as being capable of beauty . . . creating an alternative Black feminist aesthetic involves . . . rejecting binary thinking altogether."[11] Because of the centrality of hair and skin tone to the binary construction of race, gender, and beauty, I focus below on how Black women filmmakers challenge and expand ideologies of beauty through their representations of Black women of various skin tones and hair textures.

BEAUTY AS A FLOWER GARDEN

"Mama, why are we brown, pink, and yellow, and our cousins are white, beige, and black? . . . Well, you know the colored race is just like a flower garden, with every color flower represented."[12] With this dialogue between a mother and child, Alice Walker presents a metaphor for broadening ideas of beauty to include the diversity of the physical features of Blackness as part of her

9. Chris Rock's popular documentary *Good Hair* (2009) focuses on Black women and hair, as well. However, the film has been critiqued for lack of contextualization related to the role of White supremacy and the politics of hair. It was also critiqued for reinforcing the stereotypes of Black women as financially irresponsible and as "gold-diggers" due to hairstyling expenses. See Byrd and Tharps, *Hair Story.*

10. Wallace, "Spike Lee and Black Women."

11. Collins, *Black Feminist Thought,* 169.

12. Walker, *In Search of Our Mothers' Gardens,* xi.

definition of "womanism." In Walker's description of the flower garden (symbolizing the beauty of Blackness) as having every color flower represented, she is embracing the diversity of skin tones, as well as challenging colorism within Black communities. Colorism is an experience that is not unique to Black women.[13] However, Patricia Hill Collins posits that Black women have been "most uniformly harmed by the colorism that is a by-product of U.S. racism."[14] Depicting Black women of various skin tones as beautiful has the potential to transform ideologies about beauty and the narratives about Black womanhood.

Alice Walker is often credited with coining the term "colorism."[15] In her collection of essays, *In Search of Our Mothers' Gardens,* first published in 1983, she writes, "Unless the question of Colorism—in my definition, prejudicial or preferential treatment of same-race people based solely on their color—is addressed in our communities and definitely in our black 'sisterhoods' we cannot, as a people, progress. For colorism, like colonialism, sexism, and racism, impedes us."[16] Colorism has had and continues to have a particularly strong impact on Black women, which results in differential outcomes that advantage Black women with lighter skin in marriage, schooling, income, employment, and even prison sentencing—this social hierarchy based on skin tone has been referred to as a "pigmentocracy."[17] Valuing lighter skin within Black communities is based on a larger system of racism that devalues Blackness: "Colorism in the U.S. context operates the way that it does because it is deeply embedded in a distinctly American form of racism grounded in Black/White oppositional differences."[18]

Along with Alice Walker, many Black women artists have challenged colorism through their written and visual work. For example, in the book *Troubling Vision: Performance, Visuality, and Blackness,* scholar Nicole Fleetwood theorizes that two plays by Black women playwrights, Dael Orlandersmith's *Yellowman* (2002) and Zora Neale Hurston's *Color Struck* (1926), "trouble vision" by depicting characters whose visions fail them due to their invest-

---

13. Herring, Keith, and Horton, *Skin Deep*; Hunter, *Race, Gender, and the Politics of Skin Tone*; Rondilla and Spickard, *Is Lighter Better?*

14. Collins, *Black Feminist Thought,* 90.

15. Norwood, "'If You Is White, You's Alright . . .' Stories about Colorism in America"; Tharps, "The Difference Between Racism and Colorism."

16. Walker, *In Search of Our Mothers' Gardens,* 290.

17. Glenn, *Shades of Difference*; Hannon, DeFina, and Bruch, "The Relationship between Skin Tone and School Suspension for African Americans"; Herring, Keith, and Horton, *Skin Deep*; Hunter, *Race, Gender, and the Politics of Skin Tone*; Norwood, *Color Matters*; Viglione, Hannon, and DeFina, "The Impact of Light Skin on Prison Time for Black Female Offenders."

18. Collins, *Black Feminist Thought,* 90.

ments in colorist ideology.[19] Also, in addition to the Black women filmmakers mentioned previously in this chapter, who address the significance of skin tone for Black women, Julie Dash's seminal feature film *Daughters of the Dust* (1991) broke new ground in its cinematic portrayal of darker-skinned Black women as beautiful.[20]

The Black women filmmakers who are the focus of this book challenge the ideologies that equate beauty with light skin color. The lead characters in their films are portrayed with a range of skin tones—and significantly, these skin tones are not differentially constructed as more or less beautiful or feminine. It is especially important in the transformation of ideologies of beauty that the two films that highlight self-love and romantic love for Black women, *Middle of Nowhere* (2012) and *Pariah* (2011), feature women with deep brown skin tones. In Ava DuVernay's *Middle of Nowhere,* Ruby is the object of affection of two men who identify her as desirable. Her beauty is inclusive of her brown skin. In Dee Rees's *Pariah,* Alike is also a dark-brown-skinned woman who is presented as beautiful and desirable on many levels. That DuVernay and Rees depict brown-skinned women as self-respecting, loveable, and desirable expands dominant meanings of beauty.

In the two films in which the lead characters have the lightest skin tones, the filmmakers contextualize this through the characters' multiracial heritage. Kasi Lemmons's *Eve's Bayou* takes place in a Louisiana Creole community, which consists of a group of people with a combination of African, French, and American Indian ancestry. Lemmons makes this multiracial history clear from the film's opening sequence, in which Eve narrates the family's history of being descendants of a woman of African ancestry and a man of French ancestry. The women of the Batiste family in *Eve's Bayou* have skin tones that range from light (such as Eve) to deep brown (Gran Mere). In Gina Prince-Bythewood's *Beyond the Lights* (2014), Noni has a White mother and Black father. Although Noni is racialized as Black (her mother refers to her as "Black," and as distinct from her own racial identity as "White"), her light skin tone is explained by her parents' interracial relationship. Together, all six of the films discussed in this book include leading Black women characters with a broad range of skin tones—all presented as beautiful.

---

19. Fleetwood, *Troubling Vision,* 73.

20. Dash, *Daughters of the Dust*; Donalson, *Black Directors in Hollywood.*

THE BEAUTY OF BLACK HAIR

Noni stands alone in the bathroom in front of a mirror. Looking at her reflection, it seems that she is really seeing herself for the first time. What does she do in this moment of revelation? She does not wash off her makeup or discard uncomfortable clothes. Instead, she begins to slowly take out the pieces of long, straight (purple) hair extensions that had been hiding her natural hair. This hair represents the false persona she had been forced to project to the public for her singing career. As she walks out of the bathroom with her natural black, curly, and shorter hair, she feels vulnerable and exposed. But we soon see a genuine smile form on Noni's face. Embracing her hair is symbolic of embracing herself—curly, short hair and all—as beautiful.

The scene described above, from *Beyond the Lights* (2014), uses hair as a symbol of personal identity and transformation. Noni altering her self-presentation to reveal her curly hair indicates that she has gone through a transformation that embraces a more authentic self—she is embracing her "Blackness." For Black women, hair is a part of their self-presentation that has taken on gendered and racialized, cultural and political, symbolic and personal meanings.[21] Unlike skin tone, hair is largely malleable (in texture, length, and color). Therefore, although both aspects of physical appearance are important in challenging dominant beauty ideals, the personal, cultural, and political meaning of hair has provided a sense of empowerment and self-love, in addition to being an aesthetic feature, for Black women.

"Black is beautiful," is a phrase that became popular in the 1960s and 1970s in response to the widespread devaluation of Black skin and tightly curled hair. In *Ain't I a Beauty Queen?* Maxine Craig points out that during this period of time, "a new standard of beauty that celebrated dark skin, naturally kinky hair, and full lips offered redress to those women who had been devalued by earlier beauty standards."[22] The previously common practice of Black women straightening their hair was abandoned by many women of this generation, in place of the hairstyles known as the "afro" or "natural," which emphasized the texture of tightly coiled Black hair. Craig notes the political and cultural significance that these hairstyles began to represent: "Hair in its kinky, untamed state, whose coils had not been pressed into straight submission and whose texture was distinctively African, was readily transformed into a symbol of both pride and defiance."[23]

---

21. Banks, *Hair Matters*; Byrd and Tharps, *Hair Story*; Craig, *Ain't I a Beauty Queen?*; Gill, *Beauty Shop Politics*; Rooks, *Hair Raising*.

22. Craig, *Ain't I a Beauty Queen?*, 23.

23. Ibid., 80.

It is within this political and cultural context, in which naturally "kinky" hair is embraced as a symbol of racial pride and beauty, that we see Patricia in Tanya Hamilton's *Night Catches Us* (2010). The film takes place in the late 1970s, and focuses on Patricia's connection to the Black Panther Party: she's the widow of a leader of the party and continues to be involved with the Black Panthers after her husband's death. Whether she is dressed in a suit for work or dressed more casually in her home and neighborhood, her hair is styled in an afro, embracing a style and texture of hair that is perceived as symbolic of Black pride. Although the Black men in this film are shown with naturally textured hair, like Patricia's, their hair is cut shorter than hers and is often covered with a hat. Because gender shapes the relationship between racial identity and hair,[24] it is Patricia's hair that represents racial pride, as well as femininity and beauty, in this context.

The meaning of hair for Black women has been more complex than embracing naturally tightly coiled hair as beautiful during the 1960s and 1970s, although this was a seminal time in the process of racial rearticulation. Contrary to the belief system embraced during the "Black is beautiful" movement, many Black women also have positive associations with straightened Black hair. A common assumption that reduces straightened hair to self-hatred misses the various meanings that hair alteration has had for Black women.[25] Maxine Craig traces the different meanings that have been attached to straightened and naturally curly hair for Black women over the twentieth century. During the early part of the twentieth century, hair straightening was a common practice that was popularized by entrepreneur Madame C. J. Walker. Walker emphasized hair straightening as a process that should allow Black women the luxurious feeling of being "pampered" so that they felt "beautiful inside and out." To be beautiful, Walker stressed, "does not refer alone to arrangement of the hair . . . To be beautiful, one must combine these qualities with a beautiful mind and soul."[26] During this time period, straightened hair was perceived as "good grooming and was a symbol of personal and racial pride" by Black women and men.[27] By the 1960s, when "Black is beautiful" was associated with naturally tightly coiled hair, straightened hair within Black communities had been "transformed into a symbol of racial shame."[28] However, by 1980 the afro and natural had evolved into a stylistic choice, rather than a political statement, for many women. Once again,

---

24. Banks, *Hair Matters*; Craig, *Ain't I a Beauty Queen?*
25. Banks, *Hair Matters*; Byrd and Tharps, *Hair Story*; Craig, *Ain't I a Beauty Queen?*
26. Byrd and Tharps, *Hair Story*, 35.
27. Craig, *Ain't I a Beauty Queen?*, 15.
28. Ibid., 16.

straightened hair was considered socially acceptable for Black women—"in the 1980s most Black women, regardless of their political orientations, wore straightened hair."[29]

Straightened hair was not only a style; the process of straightening hair became part of a ritual that allowed Black women to bond with each other at home and in the beauty salon. In her essay "Straightening Our Hair," bell hooks fondly discusses the weekly Saturday morning ritual of having her hair straightened by her mother, along with her sisters. Hooks acknowledges that straightening hair probably emerged from the ideological framework that privileges Whiteness, but she emphasizes that it was expanded to become a "ritual of black women's culture of intimacy."[30]

In Gina Prince-Bythewood's *Love & Basketball* (2000), Monica has these moments of bonding and pampering with the women in her family when her older sister, Lena, styles her hair in what appears to be an intimate ritual for the two of them. For instance, eleven-year-old Monica sits on the floor of her bedroom as Lena braids her hair before she walks to school with Quincy. During the process, Monica and Lena talk and she asks Lena to make her hair "look pretty" (for Quincy, is the implication). Monica and Lena are in a similar position when she is in high school and Lena helps Monica prepare for the school dance. When Camille, their mother, walks in the room to see Monica's hair styled for the dance, she lovingly tells her daughter to "enjoy being beautiful." In a moment of closeness between the two of them, Monica smiles at her mother and says, "Do you really think I'm beautiful?" In these two cases, the ritual of styling and straightening Monica's hair became an activity that brought the women in the family closer together.

As a child, Noni (*Beyond the Lights*) is brought to the hair salon by her mother, in preparation for her first talent show performance. It is implied that Noni and the hairdresser (a Black woman) who agrees to style Noni's hair bond during the process when we see the hairdresser in the audience during Noni's subsequent performance. It is also apparent that the two of them form an *enduring* bond through the process of hairstyling when we see the hairdresser again at the very end of the movie, backstage as Noni prepares to perform the song that she wrote. Monica and Noni are both portrayed forming intimate connections with other Black women through the ritual of having their hair styled or straightened.

Noni revealing and embracing her naturally curly hair as she stands in front of the mirror, as described at the beginning of this section, is indicative

---

29. Ibid.
30. hooks, "Straightening Our Hair."

that the ideology that naturally curly (unstraightened) hair is beautiful has not disappeared. In fact, in the last decade, the portion of Black women who embrace the beauty of naturally textured, loosely curled, and tightly coiled hair has slowly increased.[31] At the same time, a large portion of Black women straighten their hair as part of their self-presentation. Black women's reasons for choosing a particular hairstyle are varied and complex, ranging from racial ideology, to personal aesthetics, to convenience.[32] Choosing a hairstyle can be one of the ways in which Black women reject externally defined ideas and practices and claim self-definition and empowerment, as discussed by Collins in *Black Feminist Thought*.[33] By presenting various hairstyles and textures in their films as beautiful—from Patricia's afro to Noni's curly hair and Monica's straightened hair—Black women filmmakers are engaging in acts of resistance that challenge dominant ideologies of beauty.

•

At the beginning of this book, I argued that the womanist artistic standpoint framework recognizes the multiplicity of representations in the work of Black women filmmakers—Black women filmmakers create nuanced cinematic images and narratives that draw from their histories, experiences, and perspectives. In this final chapter, I discussed their embrace of multiple skin tones and various styles and textures of Black hair as indicative of this approach. By presenting Black women with a range of skin tones and with tightly coiled, loosely curled, straightened, long and short hair as part of the beauty of Black women, they are expanding the limited cultural ideologies of beauty and Black womanhood.

Ava DuVernay, Tanya Hamilton, Kasi Lemmons, Gina Prince-Bythewood, and Dee Rees move beyond a surface appreciation of the beauty of Blackness in their films. *Part* of the appreciation of the beauty of Black womanhood is a recognition and love of the various skin tones and hair textures of Black women—these filmmakers expand the narrative about what constitutes physical beauty to include Black women and the physical features that are associated with Blackness. But social resistance and transformation involve changing the stories that are told—the narratives about Black women—in addition to the visual imagery of beauty. By *resisting* dominant narratives of Black womanhood, *creating* new narratives about Black women's lives, and

31. Byrd and Tharps, *Hair Story*; Edwards, "Relaxer Hair Sales Continue Decline as Black Hair Industry Aimed to Be Worth Over $774 Million."

32. Banks, *Hair Matters*.

33. Collins, *Black Feminist Thought*, 131.

sharing their narratives with film audiences, contemporary Black women filmmakers are engaging in a process of social transformation. These transformative narratives embrace an appreciation of Black *motherhood*. They recognize and value the *work* of Black women. And at their core, the narrative films of contemporary Black women filmmakers are based on the ultimate act of resistance—*love* of Black womanhood.

APPENDIX A

Narrative Feature Films by Black Women

*Note: Only films with an original (not adapted) screenplay and a single Black woman writer/director are included in this table.

FIGURE 1. Tanya Hamilton. Used with permission from Tanya Hamilton.

APPENDIX B

Tanya Hamilton Interview

CB: Do you think of yourself as an artist?

TH: I think it's in my genes. I was a painter for a long time. It's how I learned to express myself early on and I don't think I could ever be disentangled from that. I look at my kid who's ten and she's a wonderful artist. And I didn't put her in art class. It's in her makeup. And so, yeah, it's just how I see the world. And mind you, there are times when I wish I didn't see the world that way. When I could be more practical. Less lofty. But, that's just who I am. And I want to make movies that are respectful of the notion of art as a way to communicate. And art as a way to educate and to uplift and to make us self-reflective. And I think what's nice for me is that as a visual artist this has never been disentangled from who I am. I can never make it go away, even if I wanted to. It really aids in a way to my filmmaking. Everything that I think about is visual. And that has been a really great gift to me, I think.

CB: What caused you to make the transition from being a painter to making films?

TH: I just think that stuff happens. I never one day said, "I'm going to now do this." I went to an arts high school where I'd go to art classes at noon through the rest of the day. You know, academics first half, arts second half. And then I went to art school and I loved it. I loved every inch of it. But I think that if I look back on my early paintings, they were always telling stories. There's a constant storytelling piece to all of this and I think that I only recognized it as I look back later, and I was like, "Oh yeah, my stuff was abstract." But there were always these giant narratives and figures, but abstracted. There was always a story. And I think that it was just inevitable. I think that it sort of happened. When I was in art school, even while I was still painting very heavily, I would go to the film division and take little film classes. I made a bunch of shorts and I just love it. It's just another way of doing what my brain is already set up for. Which is just to tell stories. I think that it's always in an effort to tell a story.

CB: *Night Catches Us* tells a pretty amazing story. Did you have an audience in mind when you wrote *Night Catches Us?*

TH: I didn't at all. And in many ways, I'm not a good marketing person. I can't think that way. It's purely selfish and narcissistic, frankly. And just so much about an experience and a time that I admired. And that I wanted to be close to. And that I've known people who were a part of in various ways, and I admired their stories—my aunt, who was not my biological aunt, who was my mom's best friend from the time that my mom came to this country in her twenties. And I loved her story. I always say that I learned to be a Black American from her because she grew up with me. She was my second mother and everything about her history fascinated me. She was a tough cookie. You couldn't please her very well, but I loved everything that she had to say. I loved what she did. I loved how she did it. All of it, I thought was so interesting. So, she's the Pat character. I've just stolen huge swathes of her life, because I loved it and I wanted to become it.

CB: Would you say that you made the story for her?

TH: I think I made it because of her. I don't know if that makes any sense. Although she was hard to please and a lot of my life was spent trying to please her with very little success. Actually, she died just before I finished the film. But, I think I made it because of her. I made it for my own very selfish reasons. It was something I needed to purge. I remember when I was about sixteen, she lived around the corner from us. I'd go into her basement and their house was chaotic. I came here when I was almost nine and they were always in my life and my brother's life and my mom's life. They were a second family. I would go into the basement all the time and she had all these civil rights books. And I got a bunch of them after she passed away, and they were awesome. Some were civil rights and some were straight up Black militant books, which I loved. They were fascinating. I have a bunch of them. They're basically newsletters. They were done by local organizations and stuff from the NAACP. And I was like, "This is beautiful." It's my love song, in a way, to all of that.

CB: Do you see yourself in the character Iris?

TH: I do. It's me. It's my brother. My cousin. It's all of us. I love *To Kill a Mockingbird*. In a lot of ways the script began there . . . about the perspective of these kids. And then I think what happened, in a way, is that the early drafts were all about the kid and her friends. And it took so long to get the money, frankly, that it changed so much. And my perspective changed. And I think as a writer I grew up a lot. I just became, hopefully, a better writer in my ability to understand other people's perspective. I think it became easier and suddenly the other characters took over. So it was a very organic experience, in a way.

CB: I thought it was really interesting that it was told, in part, through the eyes of Iris. Especially in the way the audience learns the history of her family through her eyes. Were you inspired by any other filmmakers or films as far as how you told the story?

TH: I think that there were many. I love Nicolas Roeg. He's a really amazing filmmaker. I love his film *Walkabout*. I think in a lot of ways *Walkabout* inspired me. The film is about the journey of these two kids that get left in the outback by their father, who tries to kill them, and then they have to go on this journey. They meet this Aboriginal boy, and the politics are messed up, okay. But the essence of the characters and the journey is very simple. Just the walk and the landscape, I always loved. So that was a really big one. I love Raoul Peck. I thought a lot about simple stuff like *Lumumba*, which is this extraordinary, way underrated, film. In some ways those are two good ones for me. I love *Hope and Glory*, which is a film about the experience of a kid set against the backdrop of something larger, World War II. So those are some examples of films I just loved at the time and just spent a lot of time thinking about them.

CB: Do you feel that there was some resistance to making your film because of its focus on the aftermath of the Black Panther Party? Was it difficult to find support for the story?

TH: That's interesting. I think that's a two-part answer. I think that we had lots of support. Tons. We went to the Sundance writing and directing labs. They were with us and me from the very beginning and always there for every resource that I needed. If I needed to find a cinematographer or if I needed to find a producer. I could always call, especially Michelle Satter who runs Sundance, and say "please help me" and they were always there. So we had a lot of support. But I think in a lot of ways the film was sort of . . . looking back now, because it came out in 2010, it's now seven years . . . big arc of time. And when I think, just looking at where we are now to where we were then, I think it was in a way just before its time. In a way I think it would be so much more relevant being made now. Reflective, in a way, of what's happening around us. But I think back then people were sort of like, "Why do you want to make this story? And who really cares?" And by that, I mean, not the people that were our supporters, who are very ardent, but the people who we were looking for money from. It took us a really long time to get financing, and I think in part because socially it made no sense to them. It was throwback in a way that wasn't relevant.

CB: Are you referring to recent social movements, such as Black Lives Matter?

TH: Yeah. Black Lives Matter. The fact that in our film the whole centerpiece, in a way, of the film is about a disaffected youth who acts out against the police because of what's going on in his community and how he feels that he's being treated and you see so much of that around us at the moment. It's risen up in the last several years. But I think back then it wasn't to the surface. It's always been there, but it hadn't bubbled to the mainstream media. So, there was not a large countrywide conversation. And there still isn't, about that emotional piece of it. But just in terms of events. So, I think it was that people didn't know why it was relevant, and therefore, I think as far as "I can help you make this movie, for real. I can help you go find money. I can give you money," we couldn't find anybody. And that was hard for a long time.

CB: How long were you working on the film before you got the financial support?

TH: It took us nine years to get the financing. From the very beginning of the project and, probably in all fairness, I don't think the script was really ready until maybe a couple years after I started writing, so maybe I can pare it down to seven years. But it took us a long time.

CB: Do you think that was a longer process than a lot of other filmmakers face?

TH: I don't know. I don't think so. I think a lot of people spend a long time trying to find a way to make a movie and I think a lot of people don't succeed. So certainly, it's important to know how grateful I am that we were able to do it. It was a mountain to climb and we got over it. So we were able to do it but I think it takes a long time. It's a hill for many people.

CB: Were there things that you saw, watching films, that you really wanted to try to change or improve with your film? As far as the kinds of films that are out there and the characters? Black characters, specifically?

TH: I don't know if I would draw a direct correlation. What I think is that I feel the responsibility to make the best film that I can. And to illustrate the Black experience, and not only the Black experience, just anything that I do . . . I don't have to work in the Black sphere and that's it . . . but I do I feel like it's important for me to do my best to illustrate the Black experience in the most complicated and layered way possible. I do not believe that that is something the Black experience is often afforded. And it's certainly not afforded to other groups of people, like people who are Asian or Latino, for sure. But if I speak about this corner of the Black experience that I understand really well . . . I feel like it's not a space that rises up to the mainstream in ways that I want. So, to me, I wanted to make a movie about people. I didn't want to make a movie about a move-ment, because that's not why I loved that basement as a teenager. I didn't love it because I thought civil rights as a mechanism was so extraordi-nary. It is, of course. But everybody thinks that. I love the people. And I thought, it in a way, that's not often afforded in the Black experience.

And there are places that love this . . . the depraved Black person. And, you can be depraved because you're an addict. You can be depraved because you're fighting the man. So, I just wanted people. I just wanted the thing that unites all of us and the thing that we are often not allowed. Both, we don't allow it of ourselves and it's not allowed in terms of the mainstream. And I think that's why I set it in the aftermath. Because I think, to me, the movement is another character, but it's not the world. The world is these people doing what we all do, which is trying to survive. Trying to take care of our kids and trying to love. And I think that to me is what I endeavor to do all the time in everything I do. But, what I don't love is the Black experience as one thing: we are struggling in one way or another. Well, how about struggling just as ordinary people? How about struggling because you love somebody and they don't love you back? Or you've got to raise your kid and your kid's a problem and you don't know how to deal with it? So I think I didn't want any more struggling porn. I don't want that in my life, particularly. I'll take this much of it, but I feel like the Black experience extends so far beyond that.

I do not believe that the Black experience, that includes the people as well as the events, is given a broad enough and empathetic enough sketching. I don't think that that's what exists. Again, we can be struggling for civil rights or trying to get our dues and that's fine. Except when it's *this*. But, if it's this, okay, I'm cool. And then everything else around it is what everybody else gets, which are normal things: crappy person, awesome person; interesting story, story about the struggle. You know, shake it up. And so, that's my goal. Just that balance. To participate and contribute to a balanced perspective about what the experience is.

CB: The ending of the movie was unexpected and it was sort of left open. We don't really know what's going to happen with the characters. We don't have this happy ending, so to speak, that you might see in a lot of formulaic films, where you would expect Patty and Marcus to walk off into the sunset together. It's kind of messy and complicated, like life is.

TH: Yeah. A lot of people don't love that ending, but I do.

CB: And that would be, perhaps, what other movies would do. But that's not necessarily the way that things work. Patty seems to have this family life or kinship with former members of the Black Panther Party, and so she has this connection to the neighborhood. Although Marcus feels like he can't stay there, she feels like she has to stay there.

TH: And, I think that the Marcus character is someone who has never been able to commit. Not really. And he's got a fundamental problem, too, which is that he's not willing to put it all on the line. And in a lot of ways she is.

CB: Patty had this family-like relationship, not just with her daughter, and not just the members of the Black Panther party, but really the entire neighborhood. It seemed like they were all family. In one scene, she's feeding *all* the kids in the neighborhood. Did your experiences with your family inform how you portrayed that sense of community?

TH: In a way. I think that the house I grew up in was half and half. My mother, as the immigrant from Jamaica, she would never do that. It's all about your family and your yard and that's the world. And Jamaicans, the Jamaicans in my family, are tight-knit and nationalistic. The butcher the baker the candlestick maker are all going to be Jamaican. But, Carol, my aunt, was very much like that. Her door was always open. When your door is wide open, anyone can come in and it doesn't mean that you're all that safe and all that happy and always feeling like you're at the top of the food chain. Sometimes you get put at the bottom.

So, I think I saw both. I saw what it means to always have an open heart and to say, "Sure, come in." And for not necessarily these perfect reasons—the need to save people. The need to take in every stray animal. I think that complexity is something I was really interested in in the film. And in some ways I imagined that's why Marcus couldn't stay. 'Cause sometimes you don't want to be at the bottom of the food chain. Sometimes you want to be right there at the top with the person you love. And if they don't have room for you today because ten people need to come in . . . And so that was what my aunt was like. I don't know how my uncle did it. It was kind of like the third floor was always occupied by somebody: So and so, who'd come back from Liberia, and so and so, who was running from this. And so I thought that was something I really wanted. And yet, Marcus in some ways represents the other half of what I knew or what my mom was like. "No. My door is not open like that. And I can't hang with that. So you guys work that out and I'll be over here." And so that push and pull was always in my life when I was a kid. I thought it was interesting.

CB: What would you say Patty prioritizes in her life? Her career? She seems to do a lot of informal social activism to help out people in the community. She has the connections to the Panthers. To her daughter. Her husband. Marcus.

TH: I think she wants it all. I think that that's the thing. That, I think, is the complicated part, though. Because you can't have it. For her as a character, and the way that I envisioned her, and I think this is separate from the way anyone else might see her and experience her, she was always somebody who wanted everything. She wanted him. She wanted him to be there right at her side. Doing whatever he needed to do, but to be there. And she wanted the kid to participate. To understand that she couldn't be at the top of the food chain, but she was there. And she wanted to be the martyr in helping everybody that she could because she was driven by all sorts of personal means. And then she wanted the façade of being somebody that was climbing the ladder. And I don't know that anything took precedence. It depended on the day and the hour and what was going on. But, I think in the end it's why she, for me at least, ends up not with the man she loves. As much as for him, he's not able to give himself over to anybody: in that he gets a wife, he gets a child, he gets a family, and he gives it all up. Because he doesn't know how to connect. And how to just be.

CB: I found myself wondering if her choosing not to go with him was choosing herself. Or, was it choosing the other people in the neighborhood? I wasn't completely sure.

TH: I don't know that I am either. I don't know why. I feel like she's bound. I don't know that I understand fully her choice of not going. But, I do feel like she's tethered. And, you know, I guess it depends on your experience. On some days I feel like it's heroic. You know. She's gonna stay with the community. And she's gonna be what her husband was. And honor his memory. On my more real days I feel like she's afraid. You know, of upending all that she knows. And trusting him.

CB: And she is never really honest with the community. So I kind of wonder, is she being honest with herself about what she's doing there?

TH: Yeah.

CB: So, you talked about this a little when you discussed your aunt and her activism with . . . was it the Black Panthers specifically or the civil rights movement?

TH: It was all of it. To me, I think they were much more realistic in terms of normal people at that time. Like how many members of Black Lives Matter do you know? And if you do, is it just some girl who has a very specific view on the world and who goes to some protests? But who also has to go walk her dog. And, that's something I kinda loved about them. That she and her sister—they used to date Black Panthers. And they just had very specific ways of thinking about the world. But, it was in their world. My aunt was the first person to protest inside the White House in '65, right after Selma. I found this file of old letters because they went to jail after they did it and there were all these letters because the mothers went on this letter-writing campaign to get their kids out of jail. And I found all the letters from the mothers that were sent to her while in jail and were sent places like Jacob Javits's office. And then the replies. They had them at home and I always found it so fascinating. And those were some of the things I found in that basement when I was sixteen and I was like, "What is this? This is amazing! You went to jail." And she would be like, "Don't ask me anything." "No, I want to know more!" So, they were all over. She worked for a place for battered women. She was in Annapolis. She was a lawyer. Just that she was in all different places, you know. That, I just loved. When she was really young, she interned at the *Washington Post.* I was like, "What was that like?" It was all of it. She was a member of SNCC. "What was that like?" Just all of it. But, actually, all it is is youth. Because it was in the air. Everywhere. And again, how many members of whatever groups do you know now? Well, if you're living in a time when they're swirling everywhere because everybody's just sorta doing their thing and you're twenty, it's just about living. And I think that's what I love so much.

CB: Recently, women have been a lot more visible, as far as the current movements, but in the '6os, it seems like women were more on the periphery. And I thought that this movie really brings to light some of the experiences that some of the women had during that time period. Patty is very involved, but she is also perhaps viewed as being someone who is there to support the men. Even though she does a lot for them, and who knows where they would be if she wasn't around. Was one of your goals to show what women were going through during that time period and a lot of the work that they did for the movements?

TH: I think that's interesting. I think that I did a lot of research at the time about how women were sort of interacting with the men. I spoke to a bunch of women, like Kathleen Cleaver. I spoke with some of the women in DC who were part of the movement and they were interesting. They really talked about how . . . what's the famous quote? "The only position for women in the movement is prone." So, it was interesting. It was on my mind, but it didn't drive me. And I think that if I were to do it today, I think that, nuance-wise, it would be a little different. I think I've learned a lot more since then.

CB: Is there anything that stands out from any of the conversations that you had while you were doing research for the film?

TH: I talked to Cleaver and these two women in DC who had really been in the thick of the movement. I talked to a woman who was a White Catholic student who sat in in the White House in '65 with my aunt. Sheila Ryan was her name. She just died maybe five or six years ago. And another woman who lives down South. I found them all fascinating. I felt like they all had very interesting and different perspectives and reasons why they were part of the movement. Their stories were different. They had been affected by their various movements and had externalized that affect very differently. Cleaver was tough and intimidating, yet it was fascinating for me to be sitting there with her. The women in DC were so open and it was a mother and daughter so it was wonderful to get the perspective. The perspective of the daughter was of course from her mother's experiences and being a kid of that time, which I thought was great. And the mom as well, I just found super interesting. Again, they were very open. Sheila Ryan was a true believer and I loved her story as a White Catholic who got pulled into the movement versus the woman down South who was really marred by it and was bruised and cynical. They all just had such different experiences. When I was researching it, I stole so much from each of them. Little bits that I could put into the narrative in my head or the narrative that ended up on screen. They all felt very different even though they were all part of the same neighborhood, whether it was civil rights or Black Power. And I think it's not a very well-traveled story but it should be because it's so American. I loved how each of them took different trajectories in life.

CB: You mentioned that the woman you talked to in the South ended up becoming cynical. Why did she express this cynical perspective?

TH: I think there was a brutality that they experienced. It really shaped the way that they now looked at things. And I guess it depends on who you are and where you come from. Sheila Ryan goes into the White House and she's twenty-one or twenty-two, something like that. She's a student at university and she's this White girl who is a Catholic. And she goes in and she ends up going to jail. And she takes this stand. The parents of these girls who end up going to jail for sitting in in the White House, they get them out eventually. Sheila Ryan decides not to go. She finishes a year in jail and she becomes a social worker in New York. And there is a cynicism. But there is this desire, much the same as my aunt until much later in her life, to really participate and to be a part of the way that the world works and to really accept change. I love that Cleaver becomes an intellectual, which she actually always was. And she goes on to educate classes of students to be better than they assume they can be. I did find that the one woman that I spoke with in the South, a big part of her story was a deep dark sense of the emotional violence of the movement and how it affected her.

CB: The emotional violence, was that something that was from the outside/external to the movements?

TH: What I got out of the conversation was not so much of a broad thing in the general sense of the movement. So, in the case of one woman, it was really about the events that had happened. Where she went into the White House to protest and was caught up in being made an example and being sent to jail and what that meant to her. The pain that she felt as a result of it. And the injustice, the racial injustice of it, for her, it was very enormous. And feeling like White kids would come in a few years later and essentially deface the White House. But for them, who had come in with nothing but peace, they would go to jail. And I think about that White House sit-in in '65 because when I crafted the character of Pat, that was something that, just in terms of the history, that I built for her, that was a very big part of her character.

CB: Did you feel that there is a community of support or a community of filmmakers that you're able to go to and receive emotional or professional support?

TH: Yeah. I think there is. It just depends. I definitely feel like I have support in the sense that I know a lot of filmmakers who were in my shoes and trying to make their movies or trying to survive. And we all kind of grew up in the same time frame. So, in that way, yeah, there are plenty of people I know and it's great to see them go from being obscure to being something more. So all of that I think is a really nice reality. I think in some ways that it's different than the relationship that is more meaningful in a deep creative way, if that makes sense. And I think that those relationships are cultivated and they're hard to come by and so I think that I feel very in tune with the fact that I'm a part of this broader community. I feel like there is a very small corner that's reserved creatively for like-minded people who will both support and challenge me. And that feels very small for me . . . that world feels very tiny and something I feel like I'm always trying to find it and hold onto it.

CB: When you were making *Night Catches Us*, during that whole process which you said took nearly ten years from start to finish, how did you find support or where did you find support during that period?

TH: It came from very different sources. Sundance. It was a film that had gone to the lab—to the Sundance writing and directing lab. Sundance was always a creative and a financial source. So that was great and they never left us from the time that I took it to the lab and it was just an idea to the time that we made it and it went to the festival. So, they were a very special force in my life. And I think that they are a beautiful place for young filmmakers. That was great. And then I had the producer of the film who had been my kind of my creative partner and he was very present and that was great. And then my husband who's a fiction writer who's really the best writer I know. Who was very instrumental story-wise in really helping me shape the story and get it right. So, in that way, I was very supported. Again, I think that it's a great synergy, in a way. I've tried to hold on to those relationships in that form. And sometimes they don't stay perfectly that way. Sometimes they morph into other things and sometimes people need me in ways that I might have needed them on a different project. So, it depends, but my web of creative people is quite small. And I have cultivated it for a long time.

CB: To follow up with that, do you feel a sense of responsibility to other film-makers who are making their first film or who are hoping to make their first film?

TH: I do. Very deeply, actually. Very much so. Not just directors, but also writers. I'm a firm believer in that. And I try. I feel like that's such a very important space. I feel like I was helped pretty consistently all along the way and so it always feels to me like a very important thing to take time and have room for other people and their work. To read other people's stuff as much as I can and to just always participate. Just whatever it is I can do. I don't often feel like I have any creative power to help someone but I feel like I should always try because I kind of feel like I'm still being helped by so many people.

CB: Do you feel that there are other filmmakers that identify racially or as far as gender in a similar way that have gone to you because of that sense of a shared identity? And have you ever done the same?

TH: I certainly think that on the female level, a lot of the people I've talked with over the years have been women, which I think is interesting. Certainly, more Black women than women who are not Black or Latina. So, yeah, I think that to me there is something . . . I think it's less about color, but of course it is about color. But, I think there's something for me about the notion of resources. And that what I feel compelled by is when someone doesn't have resources or their resources are small. In that way,

I feel a greater responsibility to share what I have. Because I know exactly what it feels like to not have any resources and to really need even just one tiny thing. Something easy that someone can do but that can really mean a lot. If there's a gauge, I think maybe I'm more receptive and willing to step outside of my work space or my family life for someone who I think is financially disadvantaged. As well as someone who doesn't have a lot of connections. That somehow pulls me in a lot more because again I remember so clearly not having enough money or not feeling like I had enough access to a world that could help me. Both creatively, but also to be more financially able.

FIGURE 2. Kasi Lemmons. Used with permission from Kasi Lemmons.

APPENDIX C

Kasi Lemmons Interview

CB: Since you've been in the situation of writing, directing, and acting, how has each experience been different for you? I'm really interested in your sense of having creative control.

KL: Well, there's a relationship between acting, writing, and directing. I kind of feel like directing is some sort of child of writing and acting. And, there's a relationship between the three, but, they're very, very different. When I was acting—I had a great, great joy in acting. All the jobs I did, I would have done for free. I liked it. It was my first love. I thought it would never grow old. But, I was, kind of, unfulfilled. And, of course, I didn't have any creative control, really. I had a little bit of control over my performance, when I did.

Acting's very elusive, and difficult, and worthy of pursuing, because you never get as great at it as you want to be. But, there's nothing like the feeling of something coming from your imagination, and getting onto screen. That's a completely different exercise, actually, and a very different art form. And, for me, when I'm writing and directing, I get to act, as well. I get to work that muscle out, somehow, through the performances of the actors. And, I'm completely in awe of actors. I love actors, and I love them even more as a director than I did when I was acting.

And somehow, that transmutation, and that alchemy of bringing performances to life in words that you've written, and then, seeing the final product onscreen. And, getting the entire orchestration. Directing is more than directing actors—it's everything. It's everything that you see, and everything that you hear, is orchestrated, and involves a very intense collaboration with many, many people who help bring your vision to fruition. And, it's a very different feeling. It's almost like, playing a really good violin solo, versus conducting an orchestra, with a composition you've written. That's an amazing feeling.

CB: It sounds like it would be a great experience.

KL: Yeah. So, the most artistically fulfilling experiences I've had have been directing. Definitely, directing. Writing/directing is a beautiful thing when you come at a project from zero, and try and capture it. But, honestly, I've had very fulfilling experiences on things that I was involved with—but, I didn't originate the material—I've had very fulfilling experiences on those films, as well. Because there is a lot of creative control, as a director. Of course, it's the collaboration, it's for an audience, and it's financed by other people, and it involves a lot of negotiation. But, at the same time, it's where I felt the most artistically fulfilled.

And, more than that, it's where I feel I have something to give. There are a lot of good actors. And even though, right now, there are a lot of great women directors working. It's still a place where I feel that I'm definitely needed.

CB: You mentioned this collaboration. Do you feel that there have been times when your creative vision as a writer or a director has not been fully realized because of this, perhaps, collaboration or compromise, maybe? Do you feel like you've had to compromise in your work, at times?

KL: Oh, yeah, we all do. I don't know that you would find anyone who says, "I haven't had to compromise." Maybe, if they finance their films themselves. Usually, we have to compromise. And, there've been a couple of times where I felt compromised—I felt that the work was compromised. Not that often, really, not that often, I've gotta say. But, definitely, once; definitely, it's happened. And, in some ways, I think that that's part of it. If you had asked me at the time, it was, kind of, the worst thing. It wasn't great. It hurt. But now, I've become more philosophical, and it's like, "Well, these things happen." If you talk to people that have made a lot of movies, they can, just, cite all kinds of experiences. It's like, "Oh, well that wasn't as good an experience as this was."

If you talk to somebody like Mira Nair, she just worked, and worked, and worked, and worked. I am just completely in awe of her. And, she's somebody that I admire greatly. I've had a chance to interview her, in a very long interview. And, just listening to her talk—it's a storied career. Some experiences are good experiences, some experiences are bad experiences. Sometimes, your artistic vision is fully realized; sometimes, it's compromised. And so, what do you learn from it? And, what do you learn that you're able to bring forward into what you do next? And, honestly, being in show business, I think, so much of the key is, just, not being squashed. Like, getting up. Like, you, just, get up. And, really, it's part of the journey, and part of the trick to it, like, "last man standing wins." You just keep going. If this is what you do, then, just keep going.

CB: Is there a particular experience when you, on the one hand, you felt like you were able to get your vision, or, what you really wanted to come to fruition happen, compared to a time when you did feel like you had to do a little more of the compromising? Are there two experiences that you could, perhaps, compare or contrast?

KL: You know, I could, but, I'd rather keep the weight on myself. Because, in some ways, if there are mistakes that—in some ways, I have to look at my own part in it—and, I think if I start talking about things where I had to compromise, I would start to, perhaps, involve other people. It's unnecessary. Certainly *Eve's Bayou* is a place where, I felt that, very close to 100 percent of what I wanted got on the screen—very, very close.

And, even though there were some big fights, and there were definitely compromises made, it came very close to being the movie that was in my head, and, that was, kind of, a magical experience. And, I've gotta say, *Talk to Me* was the same way. Even though I didn't originate the material, I felt that the movie that I fell in love with, was the movie that I made. And, I loved it after I made it. It's like, "Wow, I love this movie!" Every time I'm watching, I'm like, "Wow, I love this movie!" But, in some ways, *Talk to Me* and *Eve's Bayou* are movies that at this point now, with some distance—it takes me a while to be able to watch my own work—but, at this point now, I really can watch with relish, just enjoy. I can say, "Wow! I really love this sequence! I really love this moment." And so, those are the films where I feel that I've been the most artistically successful, for a number of reasons. And, films where I felt that I've been less artistically successful, I'd rather just, focus on my own part in it. But, those are the films that I feel that, for a number of reasons, I got the support, and had the vision, and had extraordinary collaborators, everybody working towards the same goals. And, yeah, so, those are the ones. But, honestly, in terms of the experience, they're all different.

In terms of the experience of just filming something—*Black Nativity* was a wonderful shoot. It was stressful, but, we liked making the movie. It had a lot of joy in the shooting of it. There was all this art, there were these beautiful dancers. So, it was very, very fun to shoot.

CB: And, I appreciate and I think it's a difficult thing for most people to do, as far as taking responsibility for everything that you do. When you advise students, or when you teach your courses, do you use as examples your experiences from *Eve's Bayou* and *Talk to Me,* and the positive things that you took from those experiences?

KL: Well, I'm very, *very* candid with my students. So, I will definitely tell them what, exactly, I think went wrong, and what, exactly, I think went right, and for what reasons, because I think it's important for them to learn those things. And, I'm philosophical, because it pays to be. So, if I have a difficult relationship, I talk to them about it, because they need to know that there are difficult relationships. So, one thing I try to tell them is, never call anybody a "motherfucker" because life is long, and, you just never know who you're gonna work with again. And so, I tell them, "Try not to curse anybody out," because, even in the most painful situations that I've been in, professionally, I could have dinner with that person, and be perfectly civilized. And so, it's learning when it's appropriate to be explosive, and when—which is, most of the time, I'd say—it's, just to be cool. Roll with the punches. Sleep on important decisions, and, try and treat everybody with respect, while, of course, giving the ultimate respect to your project.

That's the hard thing, how protective are you? And, of course, the big trick of it is, that they hire directors to be protective. So, they want us to prevent them from destroying the work. In some ways, they want you to protect your own work. If you're a pushover, nobody wants to work with you. Or, if you get lost, your compass is not true north, and, you can get thrown off balance easily, nobody wants to work with a director like that. They want you to have backbone, and protect your work. But, it's a fine line, there's many lines, and, you have to keep negotiating them, in terms of how much you protect, and how much you bend, and, that's the tricky thing. And, it, actually requires a certain skill set, and a certain personality, frankly.

CB: Is that something that you feel that you developed, over the years?

KL: Yeah, definitely, as a director, I developed it. And, my entire world view, in terms of directing, did change. I predicted I would be a professor at some point in my life. I'd be a very popular professor. So, that's the part of my life that I can predict. So much has happened, that I could never predict. When I finished *Eve's Bayou,* I was like, "I did not know that I needed to direct again." It's like, "Well, there. I've done it." That was great for me, personally. Just a good experience, and, "Wow!" It was like—I don't know—great sex, or something, it's like, "Okay!" And then, you may get that nagging, like, "Wait a minute, I'm satisfied, but, I'm not done! Because, that felt so good, maybe I can do it again!" You can chase that high. But, that took a minute.

There was a period of time, where, I had finished *Eve's Bayou,* and I was like, "Okay, I don't know what I'm gonna do now, I don't know if I'm gonna write a novel, I don't know if I'm gonna go back to acting. I don't know what I'm gonna do, but I got that off my chest." So, I didn't really predict that I would need to keep going in the way that I have needed to keep going. I knew I was a writer, and by the time I made the movie, I'd become a professional writer, but, I didn't really understand the depth at which writing would be so necessary, and, that I would get to express this many things. Because I write constantly. The odds of what you write going into production, it's very tricky odds. But, I've written many, many, many, many things. And, that has been very sustaining—in a weird way, it's been kind of punishing, too—but, it's been very sustaining, artistically, because I'm always creating.

CB: Do you feel that some sense of community in your field, or that a support system, has been really important for you to keep going, to keep that motivation to keep writing, and directing new projects?

KL: Yeah, absolutely.

CB: Where is that support system for you?

KL: It's kind of where it's always been; it's my friends, my husband. My husband's a big support system. I don't know that I could do what I've done if I wasn't married to somebody who's supportive. So, that's been incredibly important. And then, my friends . . . my friends that are in show business, and my friends that aren't—because, sometimes, you don't want to talk about it—and, that still can be supportive. But, I do have friends in the industry that are a support system to me. And, my editor is a huge support system. Some directors that are friends of mine. And, in a way—this may be an answer to a different question—but, in some ways, even my students are supportive. Because, in talking about their work—I don't know, I can't explain—in ways that are hard to explain, it bolsters me. And, in helping them figure stuff out, and helping them navigate it, and being there for them, it's also supporting me. Everybody that does it, knows it, but, it's hard to articulate how that happens, but, it definitely happens.

CB: I understand.

KL: It definitely happens. Right? You're a teacher.

CB: Yeah, I can understand, what you're saying there. And, would you say that women, or students of color, or African American students, have been the ones who have been more likely to look to you for support? I'm curious if that identification, racially, or as far as gender, has been something that you think has been an important part of that support?

KL: Yeah, I do. Particularly Black students. But, honestly, ethnic, Indian students, gay students—the kids that gravitate to me are not, necessarily, the straight, White men. But, I get them, too. But, I do feel that the students of color, and the women need me. They need me, by example. And, they also need me, specifically. And so, that's been very important to me, and, also incredibly fulfilling for me, in terms of the artists that I'm helping to support. It's gratifying because you feel like you're changing the world, you're changing the landscape.

CB: Okay, yeah, there are so few women, and, certainly, women of color, that have been able to get to the point where you are.

KL: I've had some fabulous women—I'm surrounded by them—that are amazingly talented, women that I mentor. You'll hear from them soon. When I hire an assistant, they're not, necessarily, former students, but, when I hire an assistant, I like them to be inspired filmmakers, because I feel like I can have the most impact, and, it makes it interesting for me. So, if I can help mentor them while they're working with me, that makes it interesting for me. And so, all of the women that I've had assist me, or work with my company, are women that I'm interested in mentoring. They've all done amazing things. They're really starting their careers. It's great.

CB: Have the people that you have worked closely with all been women?

KL: I've had two wonderful men that have worked with me, that I loved. But, recently, yes, they've been women of color. And, there was a woman that I mentored, and she was my assistant. She was my assistant when we made *Talk to Me.* And, she was, in some ways, the first person that I, really, began to have this kind of a relationship with. And, she's somebody that I admired, somebody whose work, I thought, was very strong. And, she's actually the writer/producer of the Madam C. J. Walker thing.[1] So, I'm actually working for her, now. So that, to me, is gratifying.

CB: That's wonderful! I'm sure that's great to see. And, again, as you said, I'm not, exactly, in the same position as you, but, I work with students; it's so fulfilling to see them move on, and to see how they've been successful in various ways. The line isn't as straightforward in the subject that I teach, but, for you, I imagine you get a lot of fulfillment out of seeing your students move on, and write and direct.

KL: I really do, yeah.

CB: I'd like to ask about *Eve's Bayou,* specifically. You did talk about it, a little bit, in general. Can you say a little bit about how your own experiences growing up, or with your family, inspired the characters, and the development of *Eve's Bayou?*

KL: Yeah, I wanted to talk about a few things. How glamorous my parents looked to me. And, in fact, they were. If I look at old pictures of my parents, they look like movie stars. They were very, very beautiful people. And their friends, they were very, very glamorous. And, I wanted to explore a way of speaking that felt very Southern, and felt like my family. And, even the way of talking to children that had a poetry to it, that could be harsh—but it also had a love behind it, and a poetry to it. So, those were issues and themes that I wanted to explore. And then, it developed very organically around a few characters.

I went to an audition, and the casting director, instead of reading me, he said, "Tell me a story about your family." And, I started to talk about my aunt. She was this very extraordinary character. I could do five movies on her. She was very colorful. She was kind of psychic, and she was very dramatic, and she was very beautiful, and, she had five husbands, and she was this character. Really. And I said that one day my

---

1. Lemmons is referring to a TV series about the life of Madam C. J. Walker, in which she is the director.

mother—my mother and my father's sister were very close back in the day, when she was married to my father—and, one day they went to a fair together, and a fortune teller looked at my aunt's hand and said, "Some things are better left unsaid." And then, she told my aunt that all of her husbands would die. And, to my mother, I said, "Well, what did she say to you?" And, she said, "I don't know, something very normal, but, I can't really remember." But, Muriel was very upset—Muriel, that was my aunt's name, was very upset. And so, I told that story. And that, kind of, became Mozelle. Mozelle became an even more fantastical version of my aunt. But, honestly, my aunt was kind of fantastical.

CB: It sounds like it.

KL: When people look for autobiography in *Eve's Bayou*, the craziest character is actually somebody I drew directly from a relative of mine. And then, a lot of the banter, and the closeness between Eve and Cisely was me and my sister, for sure. Even the way that they spoke to each other, and just doing Shakespeare—like my sister and I used to read Shakespeare together. We were very close, and, we were entrusted with each other's secrets in complicated ways. Holding on to a secret can be a very big thing, and, it shaped me. My sister's secrets shaped me, in a way. And so, that's something that ended up in the movie.

But, really, I wrote a series of short stories, and then, I rolled the short stories together; and, that became *Eve's Bayou*. Around the character of Louis Batiste, who, in some ways was my father, but in many ways, wasn't my father. And, he was a character that I liked very much, and was interested in exploring a "sympathetic cad." Basically, somebody who's a very flawed man, who was also heroic to me, in a way. He was my hero in many ways. Of course, Eve is the hero, and the protagonist. But, she's a child trying to navigate an adult world to the best of her ability, at the moment.

CB: How did you decide to incorporate the Gran Mere character?

KL: I was terrified of one of my grandmothers. I had a very interesting relationship with my grandmothers. They were very different from each other. I loved them both, but I was much, much closer to one. The other one, I perceived, as, kind of, eternally cranky. And, Gran Mere is a little bit of both, but, she was my father's cranky mother.

CB: How did you envision Louis's death impacting Roz?

KL: It's just as it was predicted. She will be happy again in three years.

FIGURE 3. Gina Prince-Bythewood.

Gina Prince-Bythewood Interview

CB: One of the first things that I wanted to ask you about is related to the relationship between directing and writing a film. There was one interview that I read where you said that it doesn't feel the same to you directing something that you yourself haven't written, and it almost feels as if it's not yours or not your own. You were referring to directing *Disappearing Acts* in that interview. Do you feel that in your films there is actually a piece of yourself that goes into that—that there's a part of yourself in the film?

GPB: Absolutely. Every film that I write and direct, there is some element of myself or something I'm going through, or something that I aspire to, absolutely. I think that's why when I write and direct it I feel so connected. When I'm writing, it's because I have something to say and something specific to say. And then it's about creating characters in the world around what I want to say. So the thing with *Disappearing Acts*—it was my favorite book, so that's why it's so exciting to direct that. I did work with the writer. But again, when it starts from my brain and from something in my heart or my gut that I feel like I need to say to the world, I just feel more connected to it.

CB: Of the films that you have written and/or directed, is there any one film that you feel that you have a particularly strong attachment or connection to?

GPB: I love all my children, actually. But *Love & Basketball,* a lot of that was autobiographical and I was just really connected to this girl who had a dream to be the first in the NBA. But at its core, it was also about ultimately a woman who wants to have it all; she wants love and she wants a career. Girls are often told you can't do both, so I just wanted to normalize the belief that you can have both. I wanted to normalize girls like Monica who were girls like me who grew up playing sports and were told often that we were a tomboy, or that you're not like other girls and you know, made to feel different. It was important to me to normalize girls who like sports because it's an incredibly important thing for girls to be involved in sports and everything it teaches you. I wanted to put that to the world.

The *Secret Life of Bees,* which I wrote and directed based on Sue Monk Kidd's incredible book, what connected me there was the one line that Lily says where she talks about not feeling that she deserves to be loved. And for me, being adopted and struggling with that at a time—with my self-esteem and why I was given up and was I loved—was really what connected me with that story and that character, and why I wanted to tell that story.

Beyond the Lights, a woman fighting to find her voice and her place in the world absolutely connected to me as an artist and who I want to be as an artist, and being able to speak my mind and speak my truth to the world, and to be authentic. So a little piece of me is in Noni, as well, and Monica, as well as Lily.

CB: You mentioned the word "fight," in describing how Noni was fighting to have her voice heard. That's something I've noticed when I read about your process and some of the challenges that you've faced trying to have your voice heard. You said that it feels like you're fighting to get films made, or to make the kinds of films that you want to make. And so that fight . . . what has that involved for you, or what has that felt like from your perspective within the film industry?

GPB: It can be soul crushing at times, really when you have a story in your head. For me, once I've figured out a story I want to tell, it's with me morning, noon, and night. I think about it all day. I go to sleep thinking about it. I wake up thinking about it and it's so real, and the characters are so real and so it feels almost like there's this thing trapped that needs to get out. It's a visceral thing and so to try to get it set up and be told time and again that that's not a story that we want to tell, or that's not a story we want to put money into, that's not a story we think will do well—you never want to hear that.

So every project is a fight but what I learned very early on with *Love & Basketball* is to overcome "no." Every studio turned it down. And it wasn't until it went to Sundance and they put on a reading of it that Spike Lee's company saw it and from there we took it to New Line and were suddenly in front of the right person, which was Mike De Luca, who saw the value in the story and saw the value in me. You just need one "yes." For me, it's always about that fight to get that "yes." And thankfully again, having that experience with *Love & Basketball* prepared me for the fight of *Beyond the Lights,* where every studio turned it down.

So what do you do after those "no"s? You've got to overcome "no" and find a way to tell the story. But I absolutely attribute my ability to fight and my stamina to growing up playing sports, because that's what you're taught; that you leave everything out on the floor, aggression is good, wanting to be the best is good. And those are absolutely things little girls are not taught outside of sports. So have swagger. When you walk in that court, own that court. Leave your best out there and that is absolutely what helps me in these fights to get the stories that I want to tell made.

CB: Do you feel like the success of *Love & Basketball* has made it easier at all, or do you feel like it's just been a constant fight at the same level; there's always been the same amount of resistance? Or do you feel like it's eased up at all?

GPB: *Love & Basketball* has been great for me. I'm very proud that that was the first film I came out with because it really spoke to who I was as a filmmaker, and really spoke to the kind of stories I've wanted to tell. And it's opened a tremendous amount of doors for me. I'm in the fortunate position where when I write something, still banging on the door, the issue of the folks that are reading it aren't always seeing what I'm seeing immediately. But again, I am in the fortunate position of being able to be in the room with the people who can say "yes."

So every time I do, more opportunities open up and the reality is if I wanted to do a film a year, I could. I do get offered a lot of films and have to turn down a lot of films. What is the hard thing is the ones that I want to write and direct right now focus on women of color, and those are the harder things to get made.

CB: Why do you think that is—that it's harder to make stories about a woman of color? I certainly don't see as many. There are some years where there are maybe a little bit more, but as a whole I don't see as many. Why do you think that is?

GPB: I think it starts with the people in charge of mainline films. There's not a lot of women, and certainly not—there's very few—women of color in positions of power in Hollywood. People make films that they want to see, and if you're a White guy—not every White guy is attracted to a film about a Black woman. Now, my hope is that people see past that and see, "Oh, this is a good love story," or "This is a good sports story," or "This is a good period piece" or a good horror film, as opposed to this is a Black horror film, a Black period piece.

Because that's the issue that I have and many of us have with Hollywood. It's the boxes that we're put in, and as soon as there are people of color in a film, it loses its genre and just becomes a Black film. So the hope is that the more success we have—and this is a really good year with *Hidden Figures* and *Moonlight* and *Get Out*. These films are so totally different, but they all had success. Success begets success and the hope is that clearly there's an audience out there and it's time for us to contribute and make different types of films because an audience is there.

CB: Do you think or do you feel that there's been a group of other women or women of color within your field that have been helpful as far as being supportive of the kinds of films that you want to make? Being a source of emotional support or social support?

GPB: Kasi Lemmons has been a huge support, and I talked to her before I started *Love & Basketball*. *Eve's Bayou* I loved so much sitting in the theater watching that film. It just filled me. It was just such a beautiful film and I was just so enamored with the film and with her. I had the opportunity to talk with her right before I was going to shoot *Love & Basketball* and she was incredibly supportive, and that was really a gift. I'm very fortunate that I'm married to a very good filmmaker, Reggie Bythewood, who is incredibly supportive and supportive of the stories I want to tell. I absolutely could not be doing this without that support.

So having that, I'm absolutely lucky. But there's different women. The way that Kasi was supportive of me is how I've tried to be for filmmakers that I identify that have talent. Tina Mabry—I saw her film *Mississippi Damned*, and was really struck—"How did you do that? You had no money. You got an incredible cast. You told this beautiful story." And I just reached out and offered up my support. Lena Waithe, who is a young filmmaker on the rise, she was my assistant and she's such an incredible hustler and a good writer, and wanted to be great.

As a filmmaker you're inspired by that so it's been fun to really help her and see the success that she's been getting. Again, when you see talent in other women, you absolutely want to support that because people like Kasi Lemmons supported me.

CB: Switching subjects a little bit, can you say a little bit about some of the research that you did for *Beyond the Lights* and *Love & Basketball?* Because both are narratives about these two very specific fields, sports or entertainment/music, and so from what I understand, it does seem that you did quite a bit of research to make the films not just interesting but reflect what women actually experience trying to break into or be successful in those fields. So can you say a little bit about the research?

GPB: With *Love & Basketball*, I played ball my whole life. So much of it was familiar to me. But I had the opportunity to interview a number of professional basketball players, and women that were heroes of mine—Lisa Leslie and Dawn Staley, to be able to hear their experiences, what they went through growing up, what it was like playing overseas and the loneliness. That was right before the WNBA. Talking with coaches. One of my favorite documentaries was a documentary on Pat Summitt and the Tennessee Vols in their championship run; that was a big source of research. And there are just a couple really great books about the female dream team. And then also, there was a group of women that I was still playing ball with, so talking with them as well.

CB: When you were working on *Love & Basketball*, you were still an athlete yourself?

GPB: Yes, absolutely. So that was great. And what was also exciting was being able to put these women I played ball with, put them into the film as well, which was a great kick for them. For *Beyond the Lights*, that was much more intensive because I'm not a singer, but I love R&B and hip-hop—a lot of familiarity with the world and just had the opportunity to talk to some really great singers, some very, very big, some up and coming. They were just such an incredible resource and opened up to me about what goes on behind the scenes.

We see all the beautiful things on Instagram, and we see the videos and we see the awards shows and everything seems so great. But underneath that is a lot, and so I really wanted to really dive into the underbelly of what happens to someone who has found love but because she's being inauthentic. And the fear people have of if you show your true self, are you going to lose that love? So just incredible to be able to talk to singers and then really go to concerts and see Beyoncé and Rihanna and go to awards shows and go behind the scenes at the Grammys.

And then really it was about surrounding Gugu, my lead actress, with people in the industry. Our choreographer was Laurieann Gibson, who worked with Nicki Minaj and Lady Gaga. Her hair person, Kim Kimble, does Beyoncé's hair and Shakira's hair so just having that kind of vibe around her and being able to hear from them the things that they see. I loved the research because I love the world. But research is what makes things authentic and real, and that's what was really important for both of those films—was to be authentic and real.

CB: That definitely comes through. When we see Black women or women of color, a lot of times the characters don't feel authentic; what they're going through doesn't feel . . . there's not enough depth to it. But, I definitely feel that in your films. As far as *Beyond the Lights,* the song "Blackbird," Nina Simone's "Blackbird," plays a central role. How did that come to be?

GPB: I create playlists for every script I write because I write to music, and Nina Simone usually ends up on every playlist that I do. For the character Noni, I just felt that she would listen to Nina Simone and Nina Simone would be a singer that she would aspire to be. Nina was so authentic and so raw and so real, and spoke about real things, which was such the antithesis to what Noni was being forced to sing. And Nina celebrated her authentic self. And so again, I just felt that was somebody that Noni would absolutely aspire to, so I knew that I would want her to sing a Nina Simone song at some point.

I just went through all of my Nina Simone CDs and I came across "Blackbird" and it was like a lightning bolt. It just felt like it was written for the movie and for the character, and it actually changed the trajectory of the script. Then it was the fear of "Oh my God, please let me get the rights to this song" because it is so deeply embedded into the story now that I don't know what I would do if I didn't. But we got it, thankfully. *Beyond the Lights* was originally called *Blackbird.* To this day, it drives me nuts that I had to change the title because it was such a perfect title for the film.

CB: I think I knew it was originally *Blackbird* but I didn't know it was something that was not a creative choice as far as changing the title.

GPB: No, it was a "had to," not "want to."

CB: Okay, that's interesting. Why was it that the title had to be changed?

GPB: There were three projects with the "Blackbird" title. One was not shot yet. But one was an independent film based on a book with the same title.

We tried to buy the title from them, but to no avail. The studio was afraid they would release their film at the same time as ours to capitalize on our marketing, so they chose to change my title.

CB: This next question is related to the attempted suicide in *Beyond the Lights*. It brings to mind the play *for colored girls who have considered suicide*. Did you intend for this scene or the movie in general to reflect this racial and gendered oppression faced by Black women that the play is projecting?

GPB: It was more of a personal . . . something that I had dealt with in the family. It was a family issue that I wanted to deal with and writing was great therapy. So what Noni was going through was something I wanted to tackle because I had dealt with it personally.

BIBLIOGRAPHY

"2Pac's 'Dear Mama' Selected for Inclusion in Library of Congress' National Recording Registry." *LA Times Blogs—Pop & Hiss,* June 25, 2010. http://latimesblogs.latimes.com/music_blog/2010/06/2pacs-dear-mama-selected-for-inclusion-in-library-of-congress-national-recording-registry.html.

"A Story about Friendship, Rivalry and Ultimately . . . Love: Epps, Lathan, Woodard Star in Romantic Drama 'Love and Basketball.'" *New Pittsburgh Courier,* April 12, 2000. Ethnic NewsWatch.

Adams, Sam. "Simmering in the City." *The Philadelphia Inquirer,* February 4, 2010.

Alexander, Elizabeth. "Forward: In Search of Kathleen Collins." In *Whatever Happened to Interracial Love?: Stories by Kathleen Collins,* xi–xv. New York: Ecco, 2016.

Alexander, George. *Why We Make Movies: Black Filmmakers Talk about the Magic of Cinema.* New York: Harlem Moon, 2003.

Alexander, Michelle. *The New Jim Crow: Mass Incarceration in the Age of Colorblindness.* New York: The New Press, 2012.

"All's Fair in Love & Basketball: Childhood Adversaries Turned Sweethearts Are the Subjects of Romantic Love Story." *Sacramento Observer,* April 26, 2000. Ethnic NewsWatch.

Anderson, Melissa. "Night Catches Us Takes a Brutally Honest Look at Black Power." *The Village Voice,* December 1, 2010. http://www.villagevoice.com/film/night-catches-us-takes-a-brutally-honest-look-at-black-power-6429376.

Anderson, Tre'vell. "25 Years Later, Writer-Director Julie Dash Looks Back on the Seminal 'Daughters of the Dust.'" *Los Angeles Times,* November 24, 2016. http://www.latimes.com/entertainment/movies/la-et-mn-daughters-of-the-dust-julie-dash-20161114-story.html.

———. "Director Cheryl Dunye on Her Groundbreaking LGBTQ Film 'The Watermelon Woman,' 20 Years Later." *Los Angeles Times,* November 29, 2016. http://www.latimes.com/entertainment/movies/la-et-mn-cheryl-dunye-watermelon-woman-20161127-story.html.

Ascher-Walsh, Rebecca. "Lemmons and Lines." *Entertainment Weekly,* no. 405 (November 14, 1997): 60.

"Ava DuVernay: A New Director, After Changing Course." *NPR.Org,* October 22, 2012. http://www.npr.org/2012/10/22/163406259/ava-duvernay-a-new-director-after-changing-course.

Bale, Miriam. "Beyoncé's 'Lemonade' Is a Revolutionary Work of Black Feminism: Critic's Notebook." *Billboard,* April 25, 2016. http://www.billboard.com/articles/news/7341839/beyonce-lemonade-black-feminism.

Bambara, Toni Cade. *The Black Woman: An Anthology.* Edited by Eleanor W. Traylor. Reprint edition. New York: Washington Square Press, 2005.

———. *Deep Sightings & Rescue Missions: Fiction, Essays, and Conversations.* 1st Vintage Contemporaries edition. New York: Vintage, 1999.

Banks, Ingrid. *Hair Matters: Beauty, Power, and Black Women's Consciousness.* New York: NYU Press, 2000.

Baron, Cynthia. "Not Just Indie: A Look at Films by Dee Rees, Ava DuVernay and Kasi Lemmons." In *Indie Reframed: Women's Filmmaking and Contemporary American Independent Cinema,* edited by Linda Badley, Claire Perkins, and Michele Schreiberm, 204–20. Edinburgh: Edinburgh University Press, 2016.

Beverly, Michele Prettyman. "No Medicine for Melancholy: Cinema of Loss and Mourning in the Era of #BlackLivesMatter." *Black Camera: The New Series* 8, no. 2 (April 1, 2017): 81–103.

———. "Phenomenal Bodies: The Metaphysical Possibilities of Post-Black Film and Visual Culture." Diss., Georgia State University, 2012. http://scholarworks.gsu.edu/cgi/viewcontent.cgi?article=1037&context=communication_diss.

Biccum, April. "Third Cinema in the 'First' World: 'Eve's Bayou' and 'Daughters of the Dust.'" *Cineaction,* April 1999, 60–65.

Black Film Center/Archive. "Into the Archive: Exploring the Jessie Maple Collection." *Black Film Center/Archive,* April 12, 2012. https://blackfilmcenterarchive.wordpress.com/2012/04/12/exploring-the-jessie-maple-collection/.

Black, Rachel, and Aleta Sprague. "The 'Welfare Queen' Is a Lie." *The Atlantic,* September 28, 2016. https://www.theatlantic.com/business/archive/2016/09/welfare-queen-myth/501470/.

Bobo, Jacqueline. *Black Women as Cultural Readers.* New York: Columbia University Press, 1995.

———, ed. *Black Women Film and Video Artists.* New York: Routledge, 1998.

Bogle, Donald. *Toms, Coons, Mulattoes, Mammies, and Bucks: An Interpretive History of Blacks in American Films.* 4th ed. New York: Continuum, 2001.

Bonilla-Silva, Eduardo. *Racism without Racists: Color-Blind Racism and the Persistence of Racial Inequality in America.* 3rd ed. Lanham: Rowman & Littlefield Publishers, 2009.

Braxton, Greg, and Anne Valdespino. "Dust-Up Over an Oscar Role." *Los Angeles Times,* July 1, 2002. http://articles.latimes.com/2002/jul/01/entertainment/et-braxton1.

Brody, Richard. "The Front Row: 'Losing Ground.'" *The New Yorker,* March 28, 2016. http://www.newyorker.com/culture/richard-brody/the-front-row-losing-ground.

———. "Lost and Found: Kathleen Collins's Feature Gets Its First Release at Film Society of Lincoln Center." *The New Yorker,* February 9, 2015. http://www.newyorker.com/magazine/2015/02/09/lost-found.

Brooks, Libby. "'Now I'm Really at the Party.'" *The Guardian,* June 3, 2002, sec. Film. https://www.theguardian.com/culture/2002/jun/03/artsfeatures.

Brown, DeNeen L. "Movie Director Tanya Hamilton Talks about Debut Film 'Night Catches Us.'" *The Washington Post,* December 26, 2010, sec. Arts & Living. http://www.washingtonpost .com/wp-dyn/content/article/2010/12/25/AR2010122502538.html.

Butler, Bethonie. "Why Ava DuVernay Hired Only Female Directors for Her New TV Show 'Queen Sugar.'" *The Washington Post,* September 15, 2016. https://www.washingtonpost .com/news/arts-and-entertainment/wp/2016/09/15/why-ava-duvernay-hired-only-female -directors-for-her-new-tv-show-queen-sugar/?utm_term=.d695c6e8b374.

Butler, Judith. *Gender Trouble: Feminism and the Subversion of Identity.* New York: Routledge, 2006.

Byrd, Ayana, and Lori Tharps. *Hair Story: Untangling the Roots of Black Hair in America.* 2nd ed. New York: St. Martin's Griffin, 2014.

Cahn, Susan K. *Coming on Strong: Gender and Sexuality in Women's Sport.* 2nd ed. Urbana: University of Illinois Press, 2015.

Campbell, Loretta. "Reinventing Our Image: Eleven Black Women Filmmakers." *Heresies* 4, no. 4 (1983): 58–62.

Carter, Kelley L. "Reel Mama Drama." *Ebony* 70, no. 1 (November 2014): 21.

Cepeda, Raquel. "Courting Destiny." In *Women and Sports in the United States: A Documentary Reader,* edited by Jean O'Reilly and Susan K. Cahn, 186–92. Boston: Northeastern, 2007.

Clarke, Cheryl. "The Failure to Transform: Homophobia in the Black Community." In *Home Girls: A Black Feminist Anthology,* edited by Barbara Smith, 190–201. New Brunswick, NJ: Rutgers University Press, 2000.

———. "Lesbianism: An Act of Resistance." In *Words of Fire: An Anthology of African-American Feminist Thought,* edited by Beverly Guy-Sheftall, 242–51. New York: The New Press, 1995.

"Collins, Kathleen, 1941–1988." *Literature Online Biography,* n.d. Accessed January 25, 2017.

Collins, Lisa Gail, Margo Natalie Crawford, and Alondra Nelson, eds. *New Thoughts on the Black Arts Movement.* New Brunswick, NJ: Rutgers University Press, 2006.

Collins, Patricia Hill. *Black Feminist Thought: Knowledge, Consciousness, and the Politics of Empowerment.* 2nd ed. New York: Routledge, 2000.

———. *Black Sexual Politics: African Americans, Gender, and the New Racism.* New Ed edition. New York: Routledge, 2004.

———. *Fighting Words: Black Women and the Search for Justice.* Minneapolis: University of Minnesota Press, 1998.

———. "What's in a Name? Womanism, Black Feminism, and Beyond." *The Black Scholar* 26, no. 1 (1996): 9–17.

Cooper, Brittney C. *Beyond Respectability: The Intellectual Thought of Race Women.* Urbana: University of Illinois Press, 2017.

Cooper, Nekisa. "Love on the Outside." *Filmmaker Magazine,* November 1, 2012. http:// filmmakermagazine.com/57145-love-on-the-outside/#.V4QH1DWPWkJ.

Craig, Maxine Leeds. *Ain't I a Beauty Queen?: Black Women, Beauty, and the Politics of Race.* Oxford/New York: Oxford University Press, 2002.

Crenshaw, Kimberlé. "Demarginalizing the Intersection of Race and Sex: A Black Feminist Critique of Antidiscrimination Doctrine, Feminist Theory and Antiracist Politics." *University of Chicago Legal Forum,* no. 1 (1989): Article 8.

———. "Why Intersectionality Can't Wait." *The Washington Post,* September 24, 2015. https://www .washingtonpost.com/news/in-theory/wp/2015/09/24/why-intersectionality-cant-wait/?utm _term=.6a5c07aa23c3.

Dash, Julie. *Daughters of the Dust: The Making of an African American Woman's Film.* New York: The New Press, 1992.

David, Marlo D. *Mama's Gun: Black Maternal Figures and the Politics of Transgression.* Columbus: The Ohio State University Press, 2016.

———. "More Than Baby Mamas: Black Mothers and Hip-Hop Feminism." In *Home Girls Make Some Noise: Hip Hop Feminism Anthology,* edited by G. D. Plough, E. Richardson, A. Durham, and R. Raimist, 345–67. Mira Loma, CA: Parker, 2007.

Davis, Angela Y. *Angela Davis: An Autobiography.* New York: International Publishers Co, 2013.

———. *Are Prisons Obsolete?* New York: Seven Stories Press, 2003.

———. *Freedom Is a Constant Struggle: Ferguson, Palestine, and the Foundations of a Movement.* Chicago: Haymarket Books, 2016.

———. *Women, Race, & Class.* New York: Random House, 1981.

de Lauretis, Teresa. *Technologies of Gender: Essays on Theory, Film, and Fiction.* Bloomington: Indiana University Press, 1987.

DeFrantz, Anita. "Overcoming Obstacles." In *The Unlevel Playing Field: A Documentary History of the African American Experience in Sport,* edited by David K. Wiggins and Patrick B. Miller, 383–86. Urbana: University of Illinois Press, 2003.

Demby, Gene. "The Truth behind the Lies of the Original 'Welfare Queen.'" *NPR.Org,* December 20, 2013. http://www.npr.org/sections/codeswitch/2013/12/20/255819681/the-truth-behind -the-lies-of-the-original-welfare-queen.

Diawara, Manthia, ed. *Black American Cinema.* New York: Routledge, 1993.

Donalson, Melvin. *Black Directors in Hollywood.* Austin: University of Texas Press, 2003.

DuMonthier, Asha, Chandra Childers, and Jessica Milli. *The Status of Black Women in the United States.* Washington, DC: Institute for Women's Policy Research. Accessed June 13, 2017. https://www.domesticworkers.org/status-black-women-united-states?mc_cid=e3138548b9& mc_eid=56ba9b44b4.

DuVernay, Ava. "Watch the Throne: A Militant Masterpiece." *Huffington Post,* August 8, 2011. http://www.huffingtonpost.com/ava-duvernay/watch-the-throne_b_920907.html.

Ebert, Roger. "'Eve's Bayou' a Remarkable Directing Debut." *Roger Ebert: Festival and Awards Archives,* September 11, 1997. http://www.rogerebert.com/festivals-and-awards/eves-bayou-a -remarkable-directing-debut.

———. "Eve's Bayou Movie Review & Film Summary (1997)." *RogerEbert.com,* November 7, 1997. http://www.rogerebert.com/reviews/eves-bayou-1997.

———. "Monster's Ball Movie Review & Film Summary." *RogerEbert.com,* February 1, 2002. http://www.rogerebert.com/reviews/monsters-ball-2002.

———. "Night Catches Us Movie Review (2010)." *RogerEbert.com,* December 8, 2010. http://www .rogerebert.com/reviews/night-catches-us-2010.

Edwards, Shelby. "Relaxer Hair Sales Continue Decline as Black Hair Industry Aimed to Be Worth Over $774 Million." *Atlanta Black Star,* July 29, 2015. http://atlantablackstar.com/2015/ 07/29/relaxer-hair-sales-continue-decline-as-black-hair-industry-aimed-to-be-worth-over -774-million/.

Ehrenfreund, Max. "The Major Flaw in President Clinton's Welfare Reform That Almost No One Noticed." *Washington Post,* August 30, 2016. https://www.washingtonpost.com/news/wonk/wp/2016/08/30/how-president-clintons-welfare-reform-failed-millennials/.

Elliott, Sinikka, and Megan Reid. "The Superstrong Black Mother." *Contexts (Berkeley, Calif.)* 15 (2016): 48–53. doi:10.1177/1536504216628840.

Farmer, Ashley D. *Remaking Black Power: How Black Women Transformed an Era.* Chapel Hill: The University of North Carolina Press, 2017.

Feldstein, Ruth. "'I Don't Trust You Anymore': Nina Simone, Culture, and Black Activism in the 1960s." *The Journal of American History* 91, no. 4 (2005): 1349–79. doi:10.2307/3660176.

Field, Allyson. "Rebellious Unlearning: UCLA Project One Films (1967–1978)." In *L.A. Rebellion: Creating a New Black Cinema,* edited by Allyson Field, Jan-Christopher Horak, and Jacqueline Najuma Stewart, 83–118. Oakland: University of California Press, 2015.

Field, Allyson, Jan-Christopher Horak, and Jacqueline Najuma Stewart, eds. *L.A. Rebellion: Creating a New Black Cinema.* Oakland: University of California Press, 2015.

Fleetwood, Nicole R. *Troubling Vision: Performance, Visuality, and Blackness.* Chicago: University of Chicago Press, 2011.

Ford, Rebecca. "Gina Prince-Bythewood." *Hollywood Reporter* 420, no. 40 (November 21, 2014): 126.

Foster, Gwendolyn Audrey. *Women Filmmakers of the African & Asian Diaspora: Decolonizing the Gaze, Locating Subjectivity.* Carbondale: Southern Illinois University Press, 1997.

Frankenberg, Ruth. *White Women, Race Matters: The Social Construction of Whiteness.* Minneapolis: University of Minnesota Press, 1993.

Galloway, Stephen. "Capitalizing on Success." *Hollywood Reporter—International Edition* 372, no. 10 (February 19, 2002): 44.

Gibson, Gloria J. "Cinematic Foremothers: Zora Neale Hurston and Eloyce King Patrick Gist." In *Oscar Micheaux and His Circle: African-American Filmmaking and Race Cinema of the Silent Era,* edited by Pearl Bowser, Jane Marie Gaines, and Charles Musser, 195–209. Bloomington: Indiana University Press, 2001.

———. "The Ties That Bind: Cinematic Representations by Black Women Filmmakers." *Quarterly Review of Film and Video* 15, no. 2 (July 1, 1994): 25–44.

Giddings, Paula J. *When and Where I Enter: The Impact of Black Women on Race and Sex in America.* New York: W. Morrow, 1984.

Gill, Tiffany M. *Beauty Shop Politics: African American Women's Activism in the Beauty Industry.* Urbana: University of Illinois Press, 2010.

Gillespie, Michael Boyce. *Film Blackness: American Cinema and the Idea of Black Film.* Reprint edition. Durham: Duke University Press Books, 2016.

Gilmore, Ruth Wilson. *Golden Gulag: Prisons, Surplus, Crisis, and Opposition in Globalizing California.* Berkeley: University of California Press, 2007.

Glenn, Evelyn Nakano, ed. *Shades of Difference: Why Skin Color Matters.* Stanford, CA: Stanford University Press, 2009.

Goldberg, David Theo. *The Threat of Race: Reflections on Racial Neoliberalism.* Malden, MA: Wiley-Blackwell, 2008.

Grant, Kimberly. "'Beyond' Director Ponders Perception of Black Love." *South Florida Times,* November 13, 2014. Ethnic NewsWatch.

Grayson, Sandra M. *Symbolizing the Past: Reading Sankofa, Daughters of the Dust, & Eve's Bayou as Histories.* Lanham, MD: University Press of America, 2000.

Greenstein, Colette. "Black Love." *The Boston Banner; Boston, Mass,* November 20, 2014, sec. Arts and Entertainment.

Grierson, Tim. "'Daughters of the Dust': Why the Movie That Inspired 'Lemonade' Is Back." *Rolling Stone,* November 18, 2016. http://www.rollingstone.com/movies/features/why-we-need-indie-movie-daughters-of-the-dust-right-now-w450955.

Griffin, Pat. "Changing the Game: Homophobia, Sexism, and Lesbians in Sport." In *Women and Sports in the United States: A Documentary Reader,* edited by Jean O'Reilly and Susan K. Cahn, 217–34. Boston: Northeastern, 2007.

Grundy, Pamela, and Susan Shackelford. *Shattering the Glass: The Remarkable History of Women's Basketball.* Chapel Hill: The University of North Carolina Press, 2007.

Guerrero, Ed. *Framing Blackness: The African American Image in Film.* Philadelphia: Temple University Press, 1993.

Guy-Sheftall, Beverly, ed. *Words of Fire: An Anthology of African-American Feminist Thought.* New York: The New Press, 1995.

Hall, Stuart. "The Whites of Their Eyes: Racist Ideologies in the Media." In *Gender, Race, and Class in Media: A Critical Reader,* 3rd ed., edited by Gail Dines and Jean Humez, 81–84. Thousand Oaks, CA: Sage, 2011.

Hall, Stuart, Jessica Evans, and Sean Nixon, eds. *Representation: Cultural Representations and Signifying Practices.* 2nd ed. Los Angeles/Milton Keynes, UK: Sage Publications Ltd, 2013.

Hancock, Ange-Marie. *The Politics of Disgust: The Public Identity of the Welfare Queen.* New York: NYU Press, 2004.

Hannon, Lance, Robert DeFina, and Sarah Bruch. "The Relationship between Skin Tone and School Suspension for African Americans." *Race and Social Problems* 5, no. 4 (December 1, 2013): 281–95. doi:10.1007/s12552-013-9104-z.

Hansberry, Lorraine. *To Be Young, Gifted and Black: Lorraine Hansberry in Her Own Words.* Edited by Robert Nemiroff. New Jersey: Prentice-Hall, 1969.

Hardy, Ernest. "Interview with Dee Rees, Director of Pariah." *Village Voice,* December 28, 2011. http://www.villagevoice.com/film/interview-with-dee-rees-director-of-pariah-6433766.

Harris-Perry, Melissa. "Beyoncé: Her Creative Opus Turned the Pop Star into a Political Force." *TIME.Com.* Accessed February 16, 2017. http://time.com/time-person-of-the-year-2016-beyonce-runner-up/.

———. "A Call and Response with Melissa Harris-Perry: The Pain and the Power of 'Lemonade.'" *ELLE,* April 26, 2016. http://www.elle.com/culture/music/a35903/lemonade-call-and-response/.

———. *Sister Citizen: Shame, Stereotypes, and Black Women in America.* Reprint edition. New Haven: Yale University Press, 2013.

Henderson, Odie. "Beyond the Lights Movie Review." *RogerEbert.com,* November 14, 2014. http://www.rogerebert.com/reviews/beyond-the-lights-2014.

Herring, Cedric, Verna M. Keith, and Hayward Derrick Horton, eds. *Skin Deep: How Race and Complexion Matter in the "Color-Blind" Era.* Chicago: Institute for Research on Race and Public Policy, 2003.

Hester Williams, Kim D. "'Fix My Life': Oprah, Post-Racial Economic Dispossession, and the Precious Transfiguration of PUSH." *Cultural Dynamics* 26, no. 1 (2014): 53–71.

Heywood, Leslie, and Shari L. Dworkin. *Built to Win: The Female Athlete as Cultural Icon*. Minneapolis: University of Minnesota Press, 2003.

Higginbotham, Evelyn Brooks. *Righteous Discontent: The Women's Movement in the Black Baptist Church, 1880–1920*. Revised edition. Cambridge, MA: Harvard University Press, 1994.

hooks, bell. *Ain't I a Woman: Black Women and Feminism*. Boston: South End Press, 1981.

———. *All about Love: New Visions*. New York: William Morrow Paperbacks, 2001.

———. "Beyoncé's Lemonade Is Capitalist Money-Making at Its Best." *The Guardian*, May 11, 2016, sec. Music. https://www.theguardian.com/music/2016/may/11/capitalism-of-beyonce -lemonade-album.

———. *Feminist Theory: From Margin to Center*. 2nd ed. Cambridge, MA: South End Press, 2000.

———. "Neo-Colonial Fantasies of Conquest: Hoop Dreams." In *Reel to Real: Race, Sex and Class at the Movies*, 96–103. New York: Routledge, 2008.

———. *Reel to Real: Race, Sex and Class at the Movies*. New York: Routledge, 2008.

———. *Salvation: Black People and Love*. Reprint edition. New York: Harper Collins, 2001.

———. "Straightening Our Hair." *Z Magazine*, September 1988. https://zcomm.org/zmagazine/ straightening-our-hair-by-bell-hooks/.

———. *Talking Back: Thinking Feminist, Thinking Black*. Cambridge, MA: South End Press, 1989.

Hull, Akasha, Patricia Bell-Scott, and Barbara Smith, eds. *All the Women Are White, All the Blacks Are Men, But Some of Us Are Brave: Black Women's Studies*. Old Westbury, NY: The Feminist Press at CUNY, 1993.

Hunter, Margaret L. *Race, Gender, and the Politics of Skin Tone*. New York: Routledge, 2005.

Hurston, Zora Neale. *I Love Myself When I Am Laughing and Then Again When I Am Looking Mean and Impressive*. Edited by Alice Walker. New York: The Feminist Press at CUNY, 1979.

"Indie Appeal and Black Experience Meet In 'Middle.'" *NPR.Org*, October 12, 2012. http://www .npr.org/2012/10/12/162819731/publicist-turned-filmmaker-part-of-a-new-wave.

Jewell, K. Sue. *From Mammy to Miss America and Beyond: Cultural Images and the Shaping of US Social Policy*. London: Routledge, 1993.

Johnson, E. Patrick. *Appropriating Blackness: Performance and the Politics of Authenticity*. Durham, NC: Duke University Press Books, 2003.

———. *Sweet Tea: Black Gay Men of the South*. 2nd ed. Chapel Hill: The University of North Carolina Press, 2011.

Jolivette, Andrew. *Louisiana Creoles: Cultural Recovery and Mixed-Race Native American Identity*. Lanham, MD: Lexington Books, 2007.

Jordan, June. "The Creative Spirit." In *Revolutionary Mothering: Love on the Front Lines*, edited by Alexis Pauline Gumbs, China Martens, Mai'a Williams, and Loretta J. Ross, 11–18. Oakland, CA: PM Press, 2016.

———. *Some of Us Did Not Die: New and Selected Essays*. New York: Civitas Books, 2003.

Joseph, Ralina L. "Strategically Ambiguous Shonda Rhimes: Respectability Politics of a Black Woman Showrunner." *Souls* 18, no. 2–4 (October 1, 2016): 302–20. doi:10.1080/10999949 .2016.1230825.

Julious, Britt. "Julie Dash's Work Is More Important Than Ever." *ELLE.Com*, November 23, 2016. http://www.elle.com/culture/movies-tv/interviews/a40983/daughters-dust-julie-dash -interview/.

Kahn, Mattie. "Ava DuVernay Thinks Little Brown Girls Should Be Space Travelers, Too." *ELLE*, September 19, 2016. http://www.elle.com/culture/movies-tv/a39103/ava-duvernay-interview -a-wrinkle-in-time/.

Kang, Biba. "Beyoncé's Lemonade Didn't Win That Grammy Because It Wasn't Made for Every-one—and Adele Knows That." *The Independent*, February 13, 2017. http://www.independent .co.uk/voices/beyonce-adele-grammy-lemonade-25-didnt-win-african-american-black -racism-knows-a7577451.html.

Kathleen Collins Interview, 1984. Milestone Film & Video, 2017. https://vimeo.com/203379245.

Katz, Jackson. *The Macho Paradox: Why Some Men Hurt Women and How All Men Can Help*. Naperville, IL: Sourcebooks, 2006.

Katz, Susan Bullington. *Conversations with Screenwriters*. Portsmouth, NH: Heinemann Drama, 2000.

Katznelson, Ira. *When Affirmative Action Was White: An Untold History of Racial Inequality in Twentieth-Century America*. Reprint edition. New York: W. W. Norton & Company, 2006.

Keeling, Kara. "'Joining the Lesbians': Cinematic Regimes of Black Lesbian Visibility." In *Black Queer Studies: A Critical Anthology*, edited by E. Patrick Johnson and Mae G. Henderson, 213–27. Durham, NC: Duke University Press Books, 2005.

Kein, Sybil, ed. *Creole: The History and Legacy of Louisiana's Free People of Color*. Baton Rouge: LSU Press, 2000.

Khaleeli, Homa. "#SayHerName: Why Kimberlé Crenshaw Is Fighting for Forgotten Women." *The Guardian*, May 30, 2016. https://www.theguardian.com/lifeandstyle/2016/may/30/ sayhername-why-kimberle-crenshaw-is-fighting-for-forgotten-women.

"Killer of Sheep—A Film by Charles Burnett." Accessed February 8, 2017. http://www .killerofsheep.com/about.html.

King, Jamilah. "Beyoncé's 'Lemonade' Is What Happens When Black Women Control Their Art." *Mic.Com*, April 25, 2016. https://mic.com/articles/141680/beyonc-s-lemonade-is-what -happens-when-black-women-control-their-art.

King, Susan. "For Ava DuVernay, Making 'I Will Follow' Is Personal." *Los Angeles Times*, March 11, 2011. http://articles.latimes.com/2011/mar/11/entertainment/la-et-ava-20110311.

Kovan, Brianna. "Interview with Ava DuVernay on 'Selma' and Telling the Stories of Black Women." *Bitch Media*, January 5, 2015. https://bitchmedia.org/post/interview-with-ava -duvernay-on-selma-hollywood-and-telling-the-stories-of-black-women.

Kuhn, Sarah. "Distaff and Distinguished." *Back Stage West* 14, no. 29 (July 19, 2007): 13–14.

Landis, Lerone. "GBF Looking for Love." *The Gay & Lesbian Review Worldwide* 19, no. 3 (June 2012): 49.

Lee, Trymaine. "Director Ava DuVernay Talks Race, Hollywood and Doing It Her Way." *NBC News*, October 6, 2015. http://www.nbcnews.com/news/nbcblk/director-ava-DuVernay-talks -race-hollywood-doing-it-her-way-n439676.

Levine, Josh. "The Welfare Queen." *Slate Magazine*, December 19, 2013. http://www.slate.com/ articles/news_and_politics/history/2013/12/linda_taylor_welfare_queen_ronald_reagan _made_her_a_notorious_american_villain.html.

Littleton, Cynthia. "'Bessie' Director Dee Rees on Bessie Smith's Ferocity and Facing Prejudice." *Variety*, May 6, 2015. http://variety.com/2015/tv/features/dee-rees-bessie-smith-queen-latifah -hbo-1201488009/.

López, Ian Haney. *Dog Whistle Politics: How Coded Racial Appeals Have Reinvented Racism and Wrecked the Middle Class*. Reprint edition. Oxford: Oxford University Press, 2015.

Lorde, Audre. *Sister Outsider: Essays and Speeches*. Reprint edition. Berkeley, CA: Crossing Press, 2007.

Loudermilk, A. "Nina Simone & the Civil Rights Movement: Protest at Her Piano, Audience at Her Feet." *Journal of International Women's Studies* 14, no. 3 (July 2013): 121–36.

Lubiano, Wahneema. "Black Ladies, Welfare Queens, and State Minstrels: Ideological War by Narrative Means." In *Race-Ing Justice, En-Gendering Power: Essays on Anita Hill, Clarence Thomas, and the Construction of Social Reality*, edited by Toni Morrison, 323–63. New York: Pantheon, 1992.

Lull, James. "Hegemony." In *Gender, Race, and Class in Media*, 2nd ed., edited by Gail Dines and Jean Humez, 61–66. Thousand Oaks, CA: Sage Publications, 2003.

Marchevsky, Alejandra, and Jeanne Theoharis. "Why It Matters That Hillary Clinton Championed Welfare Reform." *The Nation*, March 1, 2016. https://www.thenation.com/article/why-it-matters-that-hillary-clinton-championed-welfare-reform/.

Martin, Michael T. "Conversations with Ava DuVernay—'A Call to Action': Organizing Principles of an Activist Cinematic Practice." *Black Camera* 6, no. 1 (2014): 57–91. doi:10.2979/blackcamera.6.1.57.

———. "Madeline Anderson in Conversation: Pioneering an African American Documentary Tradition." *Black Camera* 5, no. 1 (2013): 72–93.

Masilela, Ntongela. "Women Directors of the Los Angeles School." In *Black Women Film and Video Artists*, edited by Jacqueline Bobo, 21–42. New York: Routledge, 1998.

Mask, Mia. "Eve's Bayou: Too Good to Be a 'Black' Film?" *Cineaste* 23, no. 4 (December 1998): 26.

———. "Monster's Ball." *Film Quarterly* 58, no. 1 (2004): 44–55. doi:10.1525/fq.2004.58.1.44.

McDonald, Soraya Nadia. "Effie Brown Challenged Matt Damon. Now She's Ready to Challenge an Entire Industry." *The Washington Post*, October 14, 2015. https://www.washingtonpost.com/news/arts-and-entertainment/wp/2015/10/14/effie-brown-challenged-matt-damon-now-shes-ready-to-challenge-an-entire-industry/?utm_term=.e35ea49e5b5d.

McElya, Micki. *Clinging to Mammy: The Faithful Slave in Twentieth-Century America*. Cambridge, MA: Harvard University Press, 2007.

McKay, James, and Helen Johnson. "Pornographic Eroticism and Sexual Grotesquerie in Representations of African American Sportswomen." In *Gender, Race, and Class in Media*, 3rd ed., edited by Gail Dines and Jean Humez, 85–94. Los Angeles: Sage, 2011.

Messner, Michael A. *Taking the Field: Women, Men, and Sports*. Minneapolis: University of Minnesota Press, 2002.

Missouri, Montré Aza. *Black Magic Woman and Narrative Film: Race, Sex and Afro-Religiosity*. New York: Palgrave Macmillan, 2015.

Mondello, Bob. "Movies: When Life Is This Hard, Stubbornness Is a Virtue." *NPR.Org*, November 9, 2009. http://www.npr.org/templates/story/story.php?storyId=120058151.

Moore, Mignon. *Invisible Families: Gay Identities, Relationships, and Motherhood among Black Women*. Berkeley: University of California Press, 2011.

Moraga, Cherríe, and Gloria Anzaldúa, eds. *This Bridge Called My Back: Writings by Radical Women of Color*. 4th ed. Albany: State University of New York Press, 2015.

Morgan, Joan. *When Chickenheads Come Home to Roost: A Hip-Hop Feminist Breaks It Down*. New York: Simon & Schuster, 1999.

"National Film Preservation Board." Library of Congress, Washington, DC. Accessed February 1, 2017. https://www.loc.gov/programs/national-film-preservation-board/about-this-program/.

Nelson, Mariah Burton. *The Stronger Women Get, the More Men Love Football.* New York: PerfectBound, 2001.

Nocenti, Annie. "Writing and Directing Eve's Bayou: A Talk with Kasi Lemmons." *Scenario: The Magazine of Screenwriting Art* 4, no. 2 (1998): 192–99.

Norwood, Kimberly Jade, ed. *Color Matters: Skin Tone Bias and the Myth of a Postracial America.* New York: Routledge, 2013.

———. "'If You Is White, You's Alright . . .' Stories about Colorism in America." *Washington University Global Studies Law Review* 14, no. 4 (2015): 585–607.

NPR Staff. "A Gay Black Teen Learns How to Be in 'Pariah.'" *NPR.Org,* December 27, 2011. http://www.npr.org/2011/12/28/144328186/in-pariah-high-stakes-of-embracing-gay-identity.

Omi, Michael, and Howard Winant. *Racial Formation in the United States.* 3rd ed. New York: Routledge, 2014.

O'Reilly, Jean. "The Women's Sports Film as the New Melodrama." In *Women and Sports in the United States: A Documentary Reader,* edited by Jean O'Reilly and Susan K. Cahn, 283–98. Boston: Northeastern, 2007.

Oxendine, Alece. "Remembering Jessie Maple and Her Landmark 1981 Feature-Length Film, 'Will.'" *IndieWire,* July 31, 2013. http://www.indiewire.com/2013/07/remembering-jessie -maple-and-her-landmark-1981-feature-length-film-will-166316/.

Page, Yolanda Williams, ed. *Encyclopedia of African American Women Writers.* Westport, CT: Greenwood, 2007.

Perry, Imani. *More Beautiful and More Terrible: The Embrace and Transcendence of Racial Inequality in the United States.* New York University Press, 2011.

———. *Prophets of the Hood: Politics and Poetics in Hip Hop.* Durham, NC: Duke University Press Books, 2004.

Pough, Gwendolyn D. *Check It While I Wreck It: Black Womanhood, Hip-Hop Culture, and the Public Sphere.* Boston: Northeastern University Press, 2004.

"Preservation." *Cinema Journal* 45, no. 3 (2006): 142–44.

Quadagno, Jill. *The Color of Welfare: How Racism Undermined the War on Poverty.* New York: Oxford University Press, 1994.

Ransby, Barbara. *Ella Baker and the Black Freedom Movement: A Radical Democratic Vision.* New edition. Chapel Hill: The University of North Carolina Press, 2005.

Rastegar, Roya. "Evolving Narrative Structures Forge New Cine-Love at the 2012 Sundance Film Festival." *Camera Obscura* 27, no. 3 (2012): 149–57.

Regester, Charlene B. "Monstrous Mother, Incestuous Father, and Terrorized Teen: Reading Precious as a Horror Film." *Journal of Film & Video* 67, no. 1 (2015): 30–45.

Richie, Beth E. *Arrested Justice: Black Women, Violence, and America's Prison Nation.* New York: New York University Press, 2012.

Rickey, Carrie. "She's a Graduate of an Unusual Film School: Ava DuVernay and 'Middle of Nowhere.'" *The New York Times,* October 5, 2012, sec. Movies. https://www.nytimes.com/2012/10/07/movies/ava-duvernay-and-middle-of-nowhere.html.

Roberts, Dorothy. *Killing the Black Body: Race, Reproduction, and the Meaning of Liberty.* New York: Vintage, 1998.

———. *Shattered Bonds: The Color of Child Welfare.* Reprint edition. New York: Civitas Books, 2002.

Roberts, Kimberly C. "Playing the Game of 'Love and Basketball.'" *Philadelphia Tribune*, April 21, 2000.

Robertson, Regina R. "Behind 'Beyond the Lights.'" *Essence*, November 2014.

Robinson, Zandria F. "How Beyoncé's 'Lemonade' Exposes Inner Lives of Black Women." *Rolling Stone*, April 28, 2016. http://www.rollingstone.com/music/news/how-beyonces-lemonade -exposes-inner-lives-of-black-women-20160428.

Robnett, Belinda. *How Long? How Long?: African American Women in the Struggle for Civil Rights*. New York: Oxford University Press, 1997.

Rondilla, Joanne L., and Paul Spickard. *Is Lighter Better?: Skin-Tone Discrimination among Asian Americans*. Lanham, MD: Rowman & Littlefield Publishers, 2007.

Rooks, Noliwe M. *Hair Raising: Beauty, Culture, and African American Women*. New Brunswick, NJ: Rutgers University Press, 1996.

Rose, Tricia. *Black Noise: Rap Music and Black Culture in Contemporary America*. Hanover, NH: Wesleyan, 1994.

———. *The Hip Hop Wars: What We Talk About When We Talk About Hip Hop—and Why It Matters*. New York: Civitas Books, 2008.

"Rutgers Players Describe How Imus' Remarks Hurt." *CNN.Com*, April 10, 2007. http://www.cnn .com/2007/SHOWBIZ/TV/04/10/imus.rutgers/.

Ryan, Judylyn S. "Outing the Black Feminist Filmmaker in Julie Dash's Illusions." *Signs: Journal of Women in Culture & Society* 30, no. 1 (September 2004): 1319–44.

Scott, A. O. "The Glamorous Life, With All Its Woes: 'Beyond the Lights,' a Diva's Romance." *The New York Times*, November 13, 2014, sec. Movies. https://www.nytimes.com/2014/11/14/ movies/beyond-the-lights-a-divas-romance.html.

"Seattle International Film Festival Winners Announced." *FilmmakerMagazine.com*, June 14, 2010. http://filmmakermagazine.com/9607-seattle-international-film-festival-winners -announced/#.WizMgjdrzIU.

Semuels, Alana. "The End of Welfare as We Know It." *The Atlantic*, April 1, 2016. https://www .theatlantic.com/business/archive/2016/04/the-end-of-welfare-as-we-know-it/476322/.

Sentinel News Service. "Gina Prince-Bythewood Selected Woman of the Year." *Los Angeles Sentinel*, March 19, 2015, sec. NEWS.

Shakur, Assata. *Assata: An Autobiography*. Chicago: Lawrence Hill Books, 2001.

Shange, Ntozake. *for colored girls who have considered suicide / when the rainbow is enuf*. Reprint edition. New York: Scribner, 1997.

Sharkey, Betsy. "Tanya Hamilton's 'Night Catches Us' Captures a Point in Time." *Latimes. com*, January 26, 2010. http://articles.latimes.com/2010/jan/26/entertainment/la-etw -hamilton26-2010jan26.

Smith, Judith. "Bessie." *Journal of American History* 102, no. 3 (December 2015): 963–65.

Smith, Stacy, Katherine Pieper, and Marc Choueiti. "Inclusion in the Director's Chair? Gender, Race, & Age of Film Directors Across 1,000 Films from 2007–2016," February 2017. http:// annenberg.usc.edu/pages/~/media/MDSCI/Inclusion%20in%20the%20Directors%20Chair %202117%20Final.ashx.

Spencer, Robyn C. *The Revolution Has Come: Black Power, Gender, and the Black Panther Party in Oakland*. Reprint edition. Durham, NC: Duke University Press Books, 2016.

"Sport Sponsorship, Participation, and Demographics Search." *National Collegiate Athletic Association,* 2016. http://web1.ncaa.org/rgdSearch/exec/main.

Stack, Carol B. *All Our Kin: Strategies for Survival in a Black Community.* New York: Basic Books, 2008.

Suggs, Welch. "'Left Behind:' Title IX and Black Women Athletes." In *The Unlevel Playing Field: A Documentary History of the African American Experience in Sport,* edited by David K. Wiggins and Patrick B. Miller, 387–93. Urbana: University of Illinois Press, 2003.

Swadhin, Amita. "GLAAD Interviews 'Pariah' Director Dee Rees." *GLAAD,* December 16, 2011. http://www.glaad.org/blog/glaad-interviews-pariah-director-dee-rees.

"Tanya Hamilton Joins the 'Queen Sugar' All-Female Directorial Team." *Hollywood's Black Renaissance,* April 26, 2016. http://hollywoodsblackrenaissance.com/tanya-hamilton-queen -sugar/.

Tapley, Kristopher. "Naomie Harris Had to Overcome Her Own Judgment to Play 'Moonlight' Role." *Variety,* October 3, 2016. http://variety.com/2016/film/awards/naomie-harris -moonlight-1201875695/.

Tharps, Lori. "The Difference Between Racism and Colorism." *Time,* October 6, 2016. http://time .com/4512430/colorism-in-america/.

"Third Act: The Journey of a Hollywood Director." *TheAtlantic.com.* Accessed February 19, 2017. http://www.theatlantic.com/sponsored/forevermark-2016/article-2/816/.

Thompson, Lisa B. *Beyond the Black Lady: Sexuality and the New African American Middle Class.* Reprint edition. Urbana: University of Illinois Press, 2012.

Tillet, Salamishah. "Nina Simone's Time Is Now, Again." *The New York Times,* June 19, 2015, sec. Movies. https://www.nytimes.com/2015/06/21/movies/nina-simones-time-is-now-again .html.

Travers, Peter. "Precious." *Rolling Stone,* November 5, 2009. http://www.rollingstone.com/movies/ reviews/precious-20091105.

Ventura, Elbert. "Night Catches Us: A Criminally Overlooked Film about the Legacy of the Black Power Movement." *Slate.Com,* February 1, 2011. http://www.slate.com/articles/arts/ dvdextras/2011/02/night_catches_us.html.

Viglione, Jill, Lance Hannon, and Robert DeFina. "The Impact of Light Skin on Prison Time for Black Female Offenders." *The Social Science Journal* 48 (2011): 250–58.

Walker, Alice. *Anything We Love Can Be Saved: A Writer's Activism.* Reprint edition. New York: Ballantine Books, 1998.

———. *In Search of Our Mothers' Gardens: Womanist Prose.* Reprint edition. Orlando, FL: Mariner Books, 2003.

Wallace, Michele. *Black Macho and the Myth of the Superwoman.* Reprint edition. London: Verso, 2015.

———. "Spike Lee and Black Women." In *The Spike Lee Reader,* edited by Paula Massood, 23–29. Philadelphia: Temple University Press, 2008.

Ward, Jervette R., ed. *Real Sister: Stereotypes, Respectability, and Black Women in Reality TV.* New Brunswick, NJ: Rutgers University Press, 2015.

Washington, Marian E. "Black Women in Sports: Can We Get off the Track?" In *The Unlevel Playing Field: A Documentary History of the African American Experience in Sport,* edited by David K. Wiggins and Patrick B. Miller, 336–39. Urbana: University of Illinois Press, 2003.

"Water Ritual #1: An Urban Rite of Purification." UCLA Film & Television Archive. Accessed November 18, 2017. https://www.cinema.ucla.edu/la-rebellion/films/water-ritual-1-urban-rite -purification.

West, Cornel. Forward to *Freedom Is a Constant Struggle,* by Angela Y. Davis, vii–viii. Chicago: Haymarket Books, 2016.

Wiggins, David K., and Patrick B. Miller. *The Unlevel Playing Field: A Documentary History of the African American Experience in Sport.* Urbana: University of Illinois Press, 2005.

Williams, John. "Re-Creating Their Media Image: Two Generations of Black Women Filmmakers." *Black Scholar* 25, no. 2 (1995): 47–53.

Wilson-Combs, Lana K. "'Beyond the Lights' Is a Box Office Hit." *Sacramento Observer,* November 27, 2014.

Wiltz, Teresa. "'Love and Basketball's' Champion Director Gina Prince-Bythewood Takes a (Successful) Shot at the Hollywood Game." *The Washington Post,* April 20, 2000.

Workneh, Lilly, and Taryn Finley. "27 Important Facts Everyone Should Know about the Black Panthers." *Huffington Post,* February 18, 2016, sec. Black Voices. http://www.huffingtonpost .com/entry/27-important-facts-everyone-should-know-about-the-black-panthers_us _56c4d853e4b08ffac1276462.

Yearwood, Gladstone L. *Black Film as a Signifying Practice: Cinema, Narration and the African American Aesthetic Tradition.* Trenton, NJ: Africa World Press, 1999.

Young, Josh, and Albert Kim. "'Eve's' Plum." *Entertainment Weekly,* no. 422 (March 13, 1998): 22.

Zacharack, Stephanie. "Love & Basketball." *Sight & Sound* 10, no. 8 (August 2, 2000): 52.

Zack, Jessica. "'Pariah' Director Dee Rees Confronts Disapproval." *SFGate,* December 25, 2011. http://www.sfgate.com/movies/article/Pariah-director-Dee-Rees-confronts-disapproval -2420456.php.

INDEX

BLACK PERFORMANCE AND CULTURAL CRITICISM

VALERIE LEE AND E. PATRICK JOHNSON, SERIES EDITORS

The Black Performance and Cultural Criticism series includes monographs that draw on interdisciplinary methods to analyze, critique, and theorize black cultural production. Books in the series take as their object of intellectual inquiry the performances produced on the stage and on the page, stretching the boundaries of both black performance and literary criticism.

Contemporary Black Women Filmmakers and the Art of Resistance
CHRISTINA N. BAKER

Reimagining the Middle Passage: Black Resistance in Literature, Television, and Song
TARA T. GREEN

Conjuring Freedom: Music and Masculinity in the Civil War's "Gospel Army"
JOHARI JABIR

Mama's Gun: Black Maternal Figures and the Politics of Transgression
MARLO D. DAVID

Theatrical Jazz: Performance, Àṣẹ, and the Power of the Present Moment
OMI OSUN JONI L. JONES

When the Devil Knocks: The Congo Tradition and the Politics of Blackness in Twentieth-Century Panama
RENÉE ALEXANDER CRAFT

The Queer Limit of Black Memory: Black Lesbian Literature and Irresolution
MATT RICHARDSON

Fathers, Preachers, Rebels, Men: Black Masculinity in U. S. History and Literature, 1820–1945
EDITED BY TIMOTHY R. BUCKNER AND PETER CASTER

Secrecy, Magic, and the One-Act Plays of Harlem Renaissance Women Writers
TAYLOR HAGOOD

Beyond Lift Every Voice and Sing: The Culture of Uplift, Identity, and Politics in Black Musical Theater
PAULA MARIE SENIORS

Prisons, Race, and Masculinity in Twentieth-Century U. S. Literature and Film
PETER CASTER

Mutha' Is Half a Word: Intersections of Folklore, Vernacular, Myth, and Queerness in Black Female Culture
L. H. STALLINGS

CPSIA information can be obtained
at www.ICGtesting.com
Printed in the USA
LVHW041815170820
663417LV00004B/606

9 780814 254998